Unit 3: 8,9,12

21st Century Ethics
An Introduction to Moral Philosophy
Glenn Rogers

Table of Contents

Introduction

The title of this book is *21st Century Ethics: An Introduction to Moral Philosophy*. What is ethics and what is moral philosophy? Our modern word "ethics" is from the Greek *ethos*, meaning character, one's habitual way of living. Ethics involves rational reflection (serious thoughtful analysis) about concepts such as ought, obligation, duty, responsibility, moral right and wrong and so forth. Our modern word "moral" or "morality" is derived from the Latin word *moralis*, which has to do with human behavior as it is considered to be right or wrong, good or bad, moral or immoral. Technically, morals or morality has to do with behavior and ethics has to do with thinking about (trying to decide) what is or is not acceptable or moral behavior. For most ethicists today, however, the technical difference between the words is put aside and they are used interchangeably. In that case, questions such as "What is the ethical thing to do?" and "What is the moral thing to do?" have the same meaning. Ethics, then, as a philosophical discipline, and Moral Philosophy as a philosophical discipline are the same activity: *rational reflection about concepts such as right and wrong, good and bad, obligations, duties, responsibilities, and how those concepts impact (or should impact) human behavior.*

Moral philosophers, or ethicists, ask questions such as: Is there such a thing as good? Is there such a thing as evil? What makes an act good or evil? What, exactly is morality? If an animal kills another animal and eats it, is that act moral, immoral, or amoral? If a human kills and eats an animal, is that act moral, immoral or amoral? If a human kills and eats another human is that act moral, immoral or amoral? Most people would say that for a human to kill and eat another human would be immoral. Why? What is the difference between an animal killing and eating another animal and a human killing and eating another human? Could it be that humans are moral creatures who make moral choices and animals are not? Is there a fundamental difference between *creatures* that do not make moral choices and *beings* who do make moral choices? If there is a difference, does it need to be factored into an answer to the question, *what is morality*? Certainly it does. Moral philosophy is about trying to identify and clarify the concepts associated with and involved in moral behavior. Is there a right thing to do? What is it? Am I *obligated* to do it? Of course there are many additional questions that must be asked and answered but these are sufficient to illustrate what moral philosophy (ethics) is about.

What is necessary for us to be able to do moral philosophy well in our complex contemporary society? There are, I believe, four things: 1) an understanding of our moral and ethical past; 2) an understanding of the moral and ethical climate of our contemporary society; 3) the construction of a paradigm (the building of a framework) for effective moral thinking, deciding, and acting; and 4) testing one's ethical paradigm on real-life moral dilemmas to see if it works, if it provides meaningful guidance for the ethical dilemmas we face. To this end I have divided this material into three sections: 1) Ethical Systems: A Historical Overview; 2) Moral Challenges, Moral Solutions; and 3) Contemporary Ethical Dilemmas.

The first major section, *Ethical Systems: A Historical Overview*, includes an overview of ten ethical systems, beginning with ancient Hebrew moral philosophy and ending with contemporary feminist ethics – the ethics of care. The second major section, *Moral Challenges, Moral Solutions*, includes a discussion of the unreflective embracing of absolute cultural relativism, that is, embracing it without analyzing the implications and consequences. The section also includes an explanation and presentation of a working model for moral thinking and acting, a functional moral paradigm that I refer to as *Critical Ethical Eclecticism*. The third section, *Contemporary Ethical Dilemmas*, includes discussions of nine significant moral dilemmas that trouble contemporary Western society, issues that will allow us to determine whether or not Critical Ethical Eclecticism is, in fact, a functional paradigm for effective moral thinking, deciding and acting.

A quick scan of the Table of Contents will reveal sections on ancient Hebrew moral philosophy, the moral philosophy of Jesus, and early Christian moral philosophy. Why include this kind of material when it is not normally considered in philosophically oriented ethics presentations? My reason for including it has to do with the significant impact Hebrew and Christian moral philosophy have had on the development of Western culture in general and specifically on values and morality of American society. In my book, *Understanding American Culture: The Theological and Philosophical Shaping of the American Worldview*,[1] I have explained how Judeo-Christian theology and Classical Greek philosophy blended over time in the West[2] to generate the general worldview that characterizes Western society. It's not that one can look at the rules for conduct in the Old or New Testament and find exact equivalents in State or Federal law codes. I doubt there is anything in any of our State legal codes that says, "Thou shalt not commit adultery," or "Thou shalt not steal." However, adultery, generally speaking, is considered unacceptable in our society, as is stealing. When one understands the basic

[1] Rogers, 2006.
[2] The process can be seen, for example, in the works of Augustine, as he blended Judeo-Christian theology with Neo-Platonism, and of Thomas Aquinas, as he blended Judeo-Christian theology with Aristotelian philosophy.

tenants of ancient Judeo-Christian codes of conduct, one can see very striking parallels between those ancient ethical norms and our contemporary ethical norms. This is not surprising when one understands Western history. When the Roman Empire (that had been Christianized by the 4th century) collapsed in the 5th century, the Christian church stepped in to provide (replace) the social structure lost when the Empire collapsed. The code of conduct the church taught and sought to enforce was the traditional Judeo-Christian ethical code it had been teaching since the middle of the 1st century. That Judeo-Christian ethical code became the foundation for the civil laws that were subsequently established in European countries and that served as the foundation for many of our American laws and social norms.

Given the significant impact of Judeo-Christian moral thinking on the development of Western society, it is useful, I think, to include it here so students will understand that ancient Hebrew and Christian moral philosophy have a legitimate place in contemporary moral philosophy, even if it is methodologically different[3] from the moral philosophy that grew up out of the Classical Greek context.

Even though there are sections that cover Hebrew and Christian moral philosophy, the bulk of the material in this book is what one would find in a standard presentation of Western moral philosophy. It is set out in a historical framework so that students may see how thinking about morality developed from one time to another and from one social context to another.

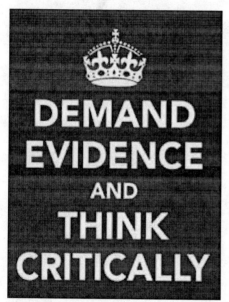

Before beginning our study, it might be helpful to discuss the nature of philosophizing about morality and ethical behavior. The process of moral philosophy is first and foremost one of ongoing discussion. Because it is an ongoing discussion, lots of questions are asked. Few, however, are answered, at least in any definitive manner. That means that the student who assumes moral philosophy will provide definitive and authoritative answers to complex contemporary questions or solutions to the ethical dilemmas prominent in our modern society is likely to be disappointed. If the student is not going to get much in the way of definitive answers or solutions, what is to be gained from reading this material? My intention (my hope) is that the student will: 1) develop an appreciation of the complexity of moral philosophy; 2) will develop his or her own functional moral paradigm (or adopt the one I have suggested), enabling him or her to think, decide and act morally; and 3) work through the examples of contemporary ethical dilemmas in this text, developing informed opinions on those issues.

---

[3]   The methodological difference between Judeo-Christian moral philosophy and Greek and subsequent Western moral philosophy will be discussed in Chapter 1.

Chapter 1
Ancient Hebrew Moral Philosophy

Introduction

The word *philosophy* can be defined as the love of wisdom. If this is the case, the ancient Hebrews were philosophers of the highest caliber for they had an enduring love of wisdom. A sizable section of the Hebrew Scriptures is referred to as *Wisdom Literature*. It includes the books of Job, Psalms, Proverbs, Ecclesiastes, and Song of Solomon. If philosophy is the love of wisdom in general, then moral philosophy must involve an appreciation of the quest for insight into morality and ethics, into the right and good way to live. Even a cursory reading of Hebrew Wisdom Literature reveals the keen interest the Hebrews had for the subject. While their Wisdom Literature deals with a wide range of subjects – the problem of evil, the meaning of life, the appropriateness and importance of physical love, the importance of faith and devotion to God – much of it (especially the book of Proverbs) is rooted in reflection concerning how to live a good life, a life characterized by wisdom. And this, in the broadest sense, is the subject of moral philosophy.

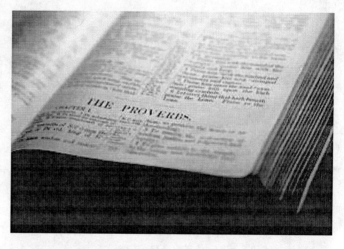

The ancient Hebrews had produced a good portion of their moral philosophy, at least 600 years before Plato and Aristotle wrote theirs.[1] While the methodological differences between the Hebrew and Greek moral philosophy causes some philosophers to question whether or not the Hebrew material is, in fact, moral philosophy, I believe it is. The methodological differences do not produce ethical conclusions on the part of the Hebrews that are so different from those of the Greeks that the Hebrew material cannot be considered moral philosophy. What are the methodological differences? They are rooted in the differing assumptions of the two peoples. The Hebrew methodology was *theocentric,* that is, God-centered, rooted in divine revelation and relationship, while the Greek methodology was clearly *anthropocentric*, that is, human-centered or humanistic. The Greeks engaged in moral philosophy on the basis of rational reflection alone, while the Hebrews approached the

---

[1] Much of the Hebrew Wisdom Literature, specifically the collection of material known as the book of Proverbs, was written in the time of King Solomon in the 8th century BCE. While it was probably edited in post-exilic times much of it was written considerably earlier, sections of it following one of the forms of ancient Egyptian wisdom literature (Kidner, 25). Since Plato and Aristotle probably produced their moral philosophy between 380 and 330 BCE, the older sections of Hebrew moral philosophy predate their work by at least 600 years if not a little more.

process using rational reflection in collaboration with *Yahweh* (the personal name God selected to identify himself to Moses and the Israelites). Yahweh had revealed himself to the Hebrews and had explained how he wished them to live. Since he was a holy God, and since they had agreed to be his special people, they needed to be holy people (Leviticus 19:2). The basis of Hebrew moral philosophy was not simple obedience to divine commands, but was rooted in an imitation of Yahweh's character. The kind of God he was served as an example of the kind of people they were to be.[2] But this imitation of the divine character was not simply following a list of rules. It involved a thoughtful process of rational reflection that was not dissimilar to the process used by the Greeks. It is certainly true that Yahweh did give the ancient Hebrews many specific laws to follow. The Ten Commandments (Exodus 20) serves as the foundation or preamble for a detailed covenant (agreement) that involved over 600 additional rules and regulations that covered both religious and civil life in ancient Israel. However, there was a considerable difference between obedience to the Law of Moses and the acquisition of the kind of wisdom that allowed one to live well, that is, to live in harmony with Yahweh, with oneself, and with others. Acquiring that kind of wisdom involved a process of learning, of contemplation, of rational reflection.

"The Ten Commandments"

For instance, note carefully the opening of the book of Proverbs:

> *The proverbs of Solomon son of David, king of Israel: for attaining wisdom and discipline; for understanding words of insight; for acquiring a disciplined and prudent life, doing what is right and just and fair; for giving prudence to the simple, knowledge and discretion to the young – let the wise listen and add to their learning, and let the discerning get guidance – for understanding proverbs and parables, the sayings and riddles of the wise.[3]*

[2]   While it is beyond the scope of this chapter to discuss the laws of the Mosaic Covenant that appear to be at odds with ethical conduct, the practice of slavery for instance, along with some of the commands of God, such as the wholesale extermination of groups of people, it is necessary to acknowledge the ethical concerns that have been raised. I would also add that I believe that the questions raised can be satisfactorily answered.

[3]   Proverbs. 1:1-6, NIV. References to the book of Proverbs in the balance of this chapter will be cited with chapter and verse notation taken from the New International Version (NIV) translation unless otherwise noted.

Look at Solomon's phraseology: attaining wisdom, understanding words of insight, acquiring a disciplined and prudent life, doing what is right and just and fair, giving prudence to the simple, giving knowledge and discretion to the young, the wise listening and learning, the discerning receiving guidance, the understanding of proverbs, parables and riddles. The process Solomon has in mind is clearly not one of simple compliance to a list of rules but one that involves thoughtful contemplation and rational reflection. Even though the basis of this contemplation and reflection was the knowledge of Yahweh, who revealed himself to the Hebrews in the Mosaic Covenant and in his ongoing relationship (interaction) with them, without the thoughtful contemplation and rational reflection of individuals who valued wisdom, there would be no acquisition of wisdom. For the ancient Hebrews as for the ancient Greeks, wisdom was the product of contemplation. To be sure, for the Hebrews the contemplation grew out of a theocentric perspective while for the Greeks it grew out of an anthropocentric perspective. But that difference does not mean that the Hebrew process does not qualify as moral philosophy, as some philosophers might suggest. The Hebrews contemplated what is right and just and fair and how one ought to live just as the Greeks did. Hebrew moral philosophy deserves a place in the study of moral philosophy.[4] *END*

The Content of Ancient Hebrew Moral Philosophy

What kind of ethical questions and moral concerns did the ancient Hebrews include in their moral philosophy? The book of Proverbs discusses a number of considerations the Hebrews believed were of crucial importance to living a life of wisdom. Some are discussed from a positive point of view as things that ought to be embraced, others from a negative point of view as things that must be avoided if wisdom is to characterize the life one lives. The material is

[4]   One reason Hebrew moral philosophy is overlooked much of the time may be that those who write about biblical or Christian ethics often deal with the Hebrew Scriptures from a Divine Command, law orientation. They focus on the Law of Moses or on the decrees of God issued by the prophets when the people of Israel fell into disobedience and were being chastised by God. Kaiser, for instance, in his book, *Toward Old Testament Ethics*, focuses his attention on God's expectation for holiness in different aspects of daily life. His is a fine study and offers many excellent insights into God's expectations for his chosen people. Yet it all but ignores the moral philosophy of the Wisdom Literature. So, too, in Barton's study entitled, *Understanding Old Testament Ethics: Approaches and Explorations*. Barton also offers a number of excellent insights into the ethical framework God provided for his ancient people, focusing especially on the moral content of the prophetic messages. But again, the moral philosophy of the Wisdom literature is not included in any substantial way. The material they cover and how they do so is firmly rooted in a theological approach that is, I suspect, foreign to most philosophers and ethicists. Thus the prevailing attitude among philosophers and ethicists appears to be that if it is in the Bible it must be theology not philosophy. Therefore the material that is, in fact, moral philosophy is overlooked. This is unfortunate.

presented as if a father is giving advice to his son (1:8-10), which results in a different tone than one finds in Plato's dialogs, for instance, as in the discussion between Socrates and Glaucon in *Republic* concerning moral behavior, or Aristotle's discussion of the virtues in *Nicomachean Ethics*. The Hebrew method of presentation (advice from a father rather than a dialog or a thoughtful presentation) is part of the methodological difference between Hebrew and Greek moral philosophy.

Fear of God

A major feature of Hebrew moral philosophy had to do with a person's relationship with God, specifically, that they needed to "fear" him. Ancient peoples in general practiced some form of religion, either monotheism or polytheism. To them, that God (or gods) existed was simply a given that only a few people questioned. The Hebrews believed that they had overwhelming evidence that the one true God, who referred to himself as Yahweh (which means *the existing One*), had selected them to be his people and interacted with them on the basis of a special agreement, the Mosaic Covenant,

that he and they had entered into after he had delivered them from slavery in Egypt (see Exodus 19-20). In numerous places scattered throughout the Wisdom Literature the idea of *fearing* God is reiterated in the following examples. "*The fear of the LORD is the beginning of knowledge, but fools despise wisdom and instruction*" (1:7). "*The fear of the LORD is the beginning of wisdom; all who follow his precepts have good understanding*" (Psalm 111:10). "*Now all has been heard; here is the conclusion of the matter: Fear God and keep his commandments for this is the duty of all mankind*" (Ecclesiastes 12:13). Why would fear of Yahweh be crucial to a life of wisdom? In what way did they mean fear? There are a number of factors that must be considered in trying to determine (in the ancient Hebrew language) how the word fear is used in a given context. One is the lexical definition of the word. The Hebrew word used in each of these texts means fear or dread. But why would God want his people to fear him? In what sense were they to fear? If one considers the overall context of the God's interaction with the Hebrew people, the patience, forgiveness, grace, and mercy that characterize his dealings with them, and the close relationship that a number of the people developed with him (Samuel and David for instance, just to mention two) one can see that what was meant was not outright fear as if God was a monster who might, without provocation, destroy them. That was not the point. God loved his people and wanted them to return his love. But he was serious about their responsibility to be a holy people – they were to mirror his character in their personal and national lives. It is quite clear in reading the Hebrew Scriptures that if they were trying to be the people God asked them to be that they had nothing to fear. But if they broke the agreement they had made with God, if they accepted his blessings but ignored his expectations for how they ought to live, then there would be consequences. That is where the fear came into play. The idea was that if they understood the seriousness of the covenant (agreement) with God, if they understood that God was serious about his expectation for how to live, they would "fear" him, that is, they would fear the consequences of ignoring him.

So exhortations to "fear the LORD" were another way of saying, "*Pay attention to what God has asked of you; remember the agreement you entered into with him; listen to what he has said; learn the lessons he has presented; pay attention to your relationship with God – otherwise, there will be consequences.*" For the ancient Hebrews, a life of wisdom began by looking to God for guidance in how to live.

Wisdom vs. Foolishness

Throughout the Hebrew version of moral philosophy, especially in Proverbs, there is a contrast between wisdom and foolishness:

> *The fear of the LORD is the beginning of knowledge, but fools despise wisdom and instruction* (1:7). *Walk with the wise and become wise, for a companion of fools suffers harm* (13:20). *The discerning [wise] heart seeks knowledge, but the mouth of a fool feeds on folly* (15:14). *Prudence* [wisdom] *is a fountain of life to the prudent, but folly brings punishment to fools* (16:22). *It is better to hear the rebuke of a wise person than to listen to the song of fools* (Ecclesiastes 7:5).

The broad general term *the fool* refers to three different kinds of people. Three different Hebrew words describe what we might refer to as: *the simple, the foolish* and *the boorish*. The simple are those who are naïve, gullible, easily led, and who are, therefore, silly. The foolish are those who are dull and obstinate. The boorish are those who may be simple or foolish but who are also crude, insensitive and closed off to the influence of sound reasoning.

The interesting thing is that none of these descriptions refers to a person's mental abilities (or lack thereof). The fool, regardless of the specific Hebrew word used to describe him, is not a person who is mentally impaired and cannot think well, but is a person who chooses a given path or lifestyle, one that is not the path of wisdom.

Another kind of person who is often linked with the foolish person is one who can be described as a scoffer, a mocker, an instigator and troublemaker who dislikes correction. His path is not the path of wisdom. He lives in the company of fools and suffers the same consequences.

For the Hebrews, moral philosophy involved making a choice about what kind of life one would live, wise or foolish. The wise began their quest for wisdom by paying attention to their relationship with God and by intentionally choosing the path of wisdom.

Industry vs. Laziness

Living a life of wisdom meant avoiding idleness and laziness, which lead to ruin. Instead, the wise would be industrious. Proverbs 6:6-11 alludes to the industrious ant as an example.

> *Go to the ant, you sluggard; consider its ways and be wise! It has no commander, no overseer or ruler, yet it stores its provisions in summer and gathers its food at harvest. How long will you lie there, you sluggard? When will you get up from your sleep? A little sleep, a little slumber, a little folding of the hands to rest, and poverty will come on you like a thief and scarcity like an armed man.*

Like foolishness, laziness is not compatible with a life of wisdom. The wise person makes a choice to be mindful of the future and prepare for it through active industry. A wise life is an industrious life.

"The Grasshopper and the Ants"

Friendship

The Hebrew word translated "friend" can also be translated "neighbor." It may refer to another person, to an acquaintance, or to someone who is a close friend. Thus, the word does not necessarily include the idea of closeness. But God had instructed the Hebrews that they were to love their neighbor (Leviticus 19:18), not merely think of them simply as another person without any connection or relationship. Beyond simple obedience to the requirements of the covenant, the wise are to understand the value of neighborliness and true friendship.

The wise are good neighbors. The good neighbor is one who prefers peace and does nothing to stir up strife or start trouble (3:29). If a problem does arise he prefers to resolve the problem with the neighbor directly rather than go to court (25:8-9). The good (wise) neighbor does not rejoice at the misfortune of neighbors, even those who have (unfortunately) become enemies. Loving others, even enemies, precludes such ugly behavior. But the wise good neighbor also realizes that there are some people he must avoid lest he be unduly influenced by them (22:24-25). He remains circumspect in that regard.

Beyond neighborliness there is the true good friend. "*One who has unreliable friends soon comes to ruin, but there is a friend who sticks closer than a brother*" (18:24). How can one be this kind of a friend? One way, according to Hebrew wisdom, was to be candid. Do not engage in empty flattery (29:5), and be willing to tell your friend what he or she needs to hear, even if it hurts (27:6). Another feature of true friendship is the practice and presence of what might be described as counsel. In the course of time spent together talking and sharing ideas and perspectives good friends advise and stimulate thought and encourage each other (27:6, 10, 19). Finally, there is what might be classified as ethical tactfulness – a respect for the feelings of others and an unwillingness to use a friend's affection as a means to one's own end. Instead of examples of how to be a friend in this regard, Proverbs provides examples of how to behave badly in such matters: overstaying one's welcome, being an unwanted presence (25:17); being cheerful in contexts that require soberness (27:14; 25:20); carrying celebration and humor too far, and allowing things to get out of hand (26:18-19). The wise person will also protect and nurture friendship. Jealousy and malice can destroy friendships. So can believing everything one hears (16:28). Forgiveness in friendship is essential (17:9).

For the ancient Hebrews being a good neighbor and a good friend were marks of wisdom. The wise person valued a good neighbor and wanted to be a good neighbor. So, too, with friendship: to cultivate friendship, to have good friends and to be a good friend, was part of living a life of wisdom.

Communication

It does not take an Aristotle-level genius to recognize that how one uses words affects all of one's relationships and, therefore, all of one's life. The Hebrews understood this and their Wisdom Literature contains a good deal of material related to the use of words: what words can and cannot do and what is involved in the wise use of words.

The wise person realizes that, "*The words of the mouth are deep waters*" (18:4) and that, "*Death and life are in the power of the tongue*" (18:21). Words are powerful and one must exercise caution and discipline (wisdom) when speaking. Proverbs 10:11 contrasts how good and bad (wise and unwise) people use words, "*The mouth of the righteous is a fountain of life, but the mouth of the wicked conceals*

violence." Another contrast notes that, *"The words of the reckless pierce like swords, but the tongue of the wise brings healing"* (12:18). Proverbs 16:27-28 (NRSV) comments on how unscrupulous people use words to hurt and harm: *"Scoundrels concoct evil, and their speech is like a scorching fire. A perverse person spreads strife, and a whisperer separates close friends."*

In the context of a father advising his son as to how to live a life of wisdom, the point for the young person to take away from the lesson is to understand the power of words and to use them well – wisely – to help and to heal rather than to hurt and harm.

But one must also realize that words have their limitations. Words, while powerful, cannot take the place of action; *"All hard work brings profit, but mere talk leads only to*

poverty" (14:23). Also, affirmations or denials, no matter how forcefully or eloquently spoken, cannot alter reality. Truth is truth and fact is fact regardless of affirmations or denials (26:23-28; 28:24), and even the strongest words cannot guarantee an appropriate response. *"Servants cannot be corrected by mere words, though they understand, they will not respond"* (29:19). The point is that the wise person will not only use words wisely, but will also recognize that words by themselves are not always sufficient. Sometimes action is required.

What else must the wise person understand about words to use them well? The wise know that words must be truthful, honest; *"An honest answer is like a kiss on the lips"* (24:26). The wise also know that words ought to be few rather than many: *"When words are many transgression is not lacking, but the prudent are restrained in speech,"* (10:19 NRSV). Wisdom also dictates that words be used in a context of temperance; *"The one who has knowledge uses words with restraint, and whoever has understanding is even-tempered"* (17:27). Finally, the wise also understand that words must be appropriate or apt for the occasion; *"A person finds joy in giving an apt reply – and how good is a timely word"* (15:23).

What is the source of the wisdom to use words wisely? The wisdom to speak wisely can be traced to a good character. In 4:23-24 the young man is encouraged, *"Above all else, guard your heart, for everything you do flows from it. Keep your mouth free of perversity, keep corrupt talk far from your lips."* But a good character alone is not enough. The wise will also engage in introspective reflection, thinking, studying, and learning to speak in a way that reflects wisdom. *"The mind of the righteous ponders how to answer"* (15:28). The mind that *ponders* is engaged in rational reflection regarding what is right.

Family

The family was the foundation of ancient Hebrew society. Marriage and children were the expectation for everyone. Fidelity between spouses was expected and children were to honor and obey their parents. The Law of Moses included serious consequences for those who did not conform to these expectations. However, beyond the laws of the covenant, wisdom dictated that family relationships be given the most serious consideration and thoughtful reflection. The husband's sexual interest and activity were to be focused on his own wife (5:18-19). Wives were not to be considered property, but partners, friends. To break one's marriage vows, to forsake one's partner and friend, was considered despicable (2:11-19). The wise understood that finding a good wife was a blessing from God (19:14; 18:22). They also realized that both the

husband and wife needed to be involved in teaching children – and it was taken for granted that they would be (1:8; 6:20). They were to take the job of training their children seriously, providing positive and corrective discipline so children could become wise, responsible adults (13:24; 22:6). The wise man would recognize what a treasure he had in a good and honorable wife. The kind of virtue the wise woman displays is discussed and praised at length in 31:10-31, revealing the significant value and importance given her in Hebrew society.

Hebrew moral philosophy had much to say about love and relationships, including the joys of a healthy sexual relationship (the Song of Solomon is dedicated entirely to the topic), because family was the foundation of their social structure. Strong families meant a strong nation. Thus, wise men and women would pay careful attention to family relationships and think deeply about how to enhance each aspect of family life.

Life

For the ancient Hebrews life is not only lived between birth and death, but can only be lived well when one contemplates what life is and how it ought to be lived. Contemplation about life – its meaning, purpose, and how it ought to be lived – is the essence of moral philosophy in general, not just Hebrew moral philosophy. Life in the book of Proverbs involves features of one's material, social and psychological life as well as one's relationship with God. In 16:15, for instance, *life* seems to refer to *flourishing*, to things going well and the individual being happy. In 15:27 the idea is that a life of wisdom generates the opposite of greed, which results in ruin. Thus, a life of wisdom generates satisfaction and contentment.

Note the contribution of wisdom and understanding to the young man's life; "*My son, do not let wisdom and understanding out of your sight, preserve sound judgment and discretion; they will be life for you, an ornament to grace your neck. Then you will go on your way in safety, and your foot will not stumble*" (3:21-23). In 14:30 the inner life, *a heart at peace*, (which is the product of a life of wisdom) impacts the quality of one's physical life. This holistic view of the person reflects the Hebrew view that the person is a dualistic blend of the material and the immaterial. For the Hebrews, the concept of the soul referred to the whole person. Thus, wisdom impacts the whole of one's life, the material aspect and the immaterial aspect.

But the most significant references to life in Hebrew Wisdom Literature are those that focus on one's relationship with God. "*He who finds wisdom finds life*" (8:35). Of course, for the Hebrews, since Yahweh was the source of wisdom, to find wisdom was to find Yahweh. And to live a life of wisdom was to live the kind of life Yahweh wanted his people to live. To live a life of wisdom was to live a life in harmony with the will of God. Wisdom of this kind could only come from a relationship with Yahweh, through two mediums: 1) the content of the Mosaic Covenant, and 2) rational reflection on God's nature, the nature of life, and on human nature.

The Goal of Ancient Hebrew Moral Philosophy

The goal of ancient Hebrew Wisdom Literature was two-fold. First, to understand what a life of wisdom was through the use of rational reflection, and second, to pass on to successive generations the results of that reflective process, to pass on the wisdom acquired by long and thoughtful contemplation on the dictates of wisdom. Those familiar with Hebrew Wisdom Literature understand that it is much more than a poetic or proverbial restating of the laws of the Mosaic Covenant. It is the collective advice of generations of (mostly) unnamed moral philosophers who sought to understand and to advise based on their insights about how to live a life that was meaningful, happy, content, and purposeful. Hebrew moral philosophy was not so much about figuring out what was right and wrong, as more recent ethical theories have been. The covenant the Hebrews had made with Yahweh provided them with guidelines of right and wrong (in their historical timeframe and cultural context). It was simply a given that they would obey the Law of Moses (though often they did not obey). Instead of attempting to determine right and wrong, Hebrew moral philosophy was focused on how to live the best kind of life, which required much more than simply obeying a list of rules.

Summary

Just because Hebrew moral philosophy does not, on the surface, sound like Greek moral philosophy or does not appear to involve a similar process (Socratic dialectic or Aristotelian logical reflection) does not mean that it is not moral philosophy. It is. And yet it is often left out of discussions of ancient moral philosophy. Why is that? Perhaps many philosophers, untrained in ancient Hebrew literature, are uncomfortable with their cultural expressions, many of which are rooted in theological assumptions. However, it is a mistake to think that because their holistic worldview did not dichotomize the sacred and the secular that rational reflection was absent or unduly influenced by religious assumptions. The ancient Hebrews were quite capable of observing, analyzing, and reaching conclusions about the nature of life and what constituted a good and wise life apart from their covenant with Yahweh. What they concluded (and perhaps this is what bothers many contemporary philosophers) was that one cannot live a good and wise life apart from a relationship with Yahweh. In other words, God is integral to a good life, that is, to a life rooted in and guided by wisdom.

In the final analysis, when one considers the content of Hebrew moral philosophy one sees that the Hebrews arrived at conclusions regarding wisdom that were not very different from those of Socrates, Plato, and Aristotle. For instance, as Parry observes, in *Apology* (29d-e), Socrates "chides [the citizens of Athens] for being absorbed in the acquisition of wealth, reputation, and honor while they do take care for nor think about wisdom, truth, and how to make their souls better."[5] The Hebrews were also concerned with the acquisition of wisdom and the benefit it provided for the soul. Some of the Hebrew assumptions may have been different and some of their methods may have been different, but their conclusions were remarkably similar. Hebrew moral philosophy appears to be a viable framework for considering the kind of person one ought to be.

Thought and Discussion Questions

1. Explain the difference between Hebrew Wisdom Literature and Covenantal Literature (for example between the book of Proverbs and Exodus 20:1-17).

2. Discuss your insights into the purpose of Hebrew wisdom Literature.

3. Explain and discuss how the Hebrews saw a connection between a life of wisdom and a relationship with Yahweh.

---

5   Parry, Richard, "Ancient Ethical Theory", *The Stanford Encyclopedia of Philosophy.*

4. Explain the Hebrew view of the soul and how that idea manifests itself in the book of Proverbs.

5. Discuss possible reasons why Hebrew Wisdom Literature is often left out of discussions of ancient moral philosophy.

Chapter 2
Greek Moral Philosophy

Introduction

Two forces shaped Western culture into what it is today: Judeo-Christian theology and Classical Greek Philosophy. These two separate streams of thought merged to become one powerful force, broadly identified as the Western worldview, and as a single force impacted humanity more than any other way of thinking ever has. A good deal of the material in both systems, Judeo-Christian theology and Greek philosophy, has to do with moral philosophy. Each system has had a lot to say about how people ought to live and what constitutes the good life. We have looked briefly at Hebrew moral philosophy. Now we turn our attention to Greek moral philosophy, beginning our overview with a consideration of Socrates and Plato.

Socrates and Plato

Socrates (469-399 BCE) is regarded as the father of moral philosophy. He had studied the material of the philosophers who preceded him, known today as pre-Socratic philosophers, signifying that they lived and philosophized before Socrates. The pre-Socratic philosophers focused their energies on attempting to understand and describe the physical cosmos. But Socrates preferred to think about other concerns. He felt that issues related to how one lived life, what constituted the good life, and what it meant to be a good person were more important concerns than the nature of the physical cosmos. Instead of natural philosophy, Socrates was interested in moral philosophy (though neither of those terms existed in his day).

"Socrates Biography"

Though Socrates is one of the most influential philosophers in history, he wrote nothing. We only know of his philosophy through the writings of others who tell us about him; mostly through the work of Xenophon and Plato. Of these two, the writings of Plato provide us with the most extensive, and probably the most accurate, information we have of Socrates and his thinking. The challenge related to the thinking and teaching of Socrates is that Plato (424-347 BCE) uses Socrates as a character in his dialogs (Plato's vehicle for presenting his philosophy), and it is difficult to determine whether we are reading the ideas of the real historical Socrates or those of

Plato, the author of the dialogs. This challenge is known as the Socratic Problem. However, most scholars believe that in the dialogs Plato wrote earlier in his long career tend to represent, for the most part, the actual views of his teacher, Socrates. We may proceed then to discuss the moral philosophy of Socrates, but must also be aware that some of what Socrates says may be what Plato thought as much as what Socrates thought.[1] Thus, this section is entitled *Socrates and Plato*.

"Plato Biography"

Socrates (along with Plato and Aristotle) believed that all human endeavor was rooted in the quest for happiness.[2] People do what they believe will make them happy. This was accepted in Greek society as entirely appropriate. However, they also had some very specific ideas of what constitutes happiness, ideas that are considerably different from what we think of as "happiness" today. For us happiness is an emotional state. I feel happy today because I just got a raise or a promotion, or because our vacation begins today and we're going to Hawaii for two weeks. But this kind of happiness is impacted by many things in many ways. Suppose my wife and I are at the airport getting ready to board our plane for our vacation to Hawaii and we learn that the flight has been delayed for 24 hours due to bad

weather. Suddenly, we may not be so happy. For us, happiness can change not only from one day to the next, but from one moment to the next depending on immediate circumstances. This is not the way the Greeks thought of happiness.

The Greek word often translated happiness is *eudaimonia* and has more to do with living well or doing well than with one's happy emotional state.[3] It had to do with how well one lived one's life, with whether or not one was flourishing or thriving. A life well-lived was a *eudaimonia* kind of a life. But what constituted a well-lived life of thriving and flourishing? A well-lived life was one in which the person was the best person he could be, a person who was in the process of achieving his potential for excellence. Related to this was the idea expressed in the word *arête*, often translated as *virtue*. Our contemporary idea of virtue doesn't really match up to what the word *arête* meant for the Greeks. The word *excellence* might be a better translation than virtue. One could

---

1   Penner has an excellent discussion of the problem is his article, "Socrates and the Early Dialogs," in *The Cambridge Companion to Plato*, 121.

2   Penner, "Socratic Ethics and the Socratic Psychology of Action: A Philosophical Framework," in *The Cambridge Companion to Socrates*, 260.

3   *Stanford Encyclopedia of Philosophy*.

live a *eudaimonia* kind of life, a well-lived life, when one was engaged in the pursuit of *arête*, that is, of excellence. But what constituted the pursuit of excellence? A life of excellence was one in which one accomplished his purpose, achieved his full potential. The purpose of a knife is to cut. A sharp knife that cut well was *arête*; it was an excellent knife. A horse that ran well or pulled well was an excellent, or an *arête,* horse. So what was it for a person to be an excellent person, an *arête* person? Answering that question required discovering what the purpose or potential of personhood was. Greek moral philosophy was about discovering the purpose of life (or of a given kind of a life), figuring out how people could achieve their purpose or reach their potential. To the degree they fulfilled their purpose in life, achieving their potential, they were considered to be living a *eudiamonia* kind of life, that is, a flourishing, thriving and, therefore, a happy life.[4]

"A Guide to Happiness: Socrates on Self-Confidence"

To this end, Plato has his character Socrates, in some of the dialogs, engaged in conversations with different people trying to determine what qualities the person must have to fulfill his purpose and achieve his potential in order to be an *arête* (excellent) person who will then be a *eudiamonia* (thriving, flourishing, happy) person. Rowe suggests that the question Socrates is asking is: "how should a man live in order that we may reasonably say of him that he has lived successfully,"[5] Several of the Socratic dialogs discuss five "virtues" (qualities or character traits) that were considered essential among the ancient Greeks if one was to be an excellent person enjoying a well-lived life. Those traits were: bravery, temperance, piety, wisdom, and justice.[6] Socrates and Plato believed that having these (and perhaps a few other crucial) virtues was essential to a happy life.[7] How so? The virtues themselves did not bring happiness, but were the tools, so to speak, that a person used to achieve excellence in life. And living an excellent life is what constituted a well-lived or happy life.[8]

Another part of the challenge to live well had to do with discovering how to understand the concept of good. What is good? What does it mean to be good? What is

4   Kraut, "Aristotle's Ethics," *Stanford Encyclopedia of Philosophy*.
5   Rowe, "Ethics in Ancient Greece," *A Companion to Ethics*, 123.
6   Irwin, *Plato's Ethics*, 31.
7   Annas, *Plato, A Very Short Introduction*, 54-55.
8   Kraut, "Aristotle's Ethics," *Stanford Encyclopedia of Philosophy*.

involved in living a good life? A conversation Socrates had with a young man named Euthyphro (in the Platonic dialog of the same name) sheds some light on how complex the question can be. Socrates, on his way into the Athenian court to schedule his appearance for the charges brought against him, runs into Euthyphro coming out of the court. Euthyphro explains that he is prosecuting his father for killing a slave. In the friendly exchange between Socrates and Euthyphro the conversation comes around to the meaning of piety (that is, reverent or appropriate or good behavior). Socrates has been charged with impiety so he wants to know what this is. If Euthyphro can help him understand what pious and impious behavior is, then Socrates will understand more clearly what he has been charged with. I believe Socrates knew exactly what he had been charged with and why. His goal, on this occasion, was to help Euthyphro understand that he, in fact, did not understand what constituted pious behavior. If he did, he would not be prosecuting his father. As the conversation unfolds, Euthyphro offers a number of definitions (or what he thinks are definitions) of piety. Socrates, in his customary manner, demonstrates that each of Euthyphro's attempts to define piety fails. Finally Euthyphro says that piety is what all the gods agree is good. Now Socrates thinks that Euthyphro is on to something. If all the gods agree that a thing is good then perhaps it is. Maybe this is the beginning of understanding what is, in fact, good. But still, Socrates sees a problem. To help Euthyphro see the problem Socrates asks one of his most penetrating questions: *Is a thing good because the gods say it is good or do the gods says a thing is good because it is good?* To put this question in our contemporary monotheistic framework, it might be asked this way: *Is an act good or bad (moral or immoral) simply because God says it is, or does God say an act is either good or bad (moral or immoral) because it is either moral or immoral?* This question remains as perplexing today as it was when Socrates first asked it. The implications of how one answers it are considerable.[9] This is a highly significant question when considering the

[9] Note that Socrates asks his question in an either/or format. If one replies that a thing is good because God says it is good, then anything God says is good is good just because he says so. Theoretically, if God said lying was good, then lying would be good. If he said sadism was good than it would be good. Can this be right? The typical response is, but God would never say lying or sadism are good. Why not? Because God is good and would not say bad things were good things. But if the concept of good arises from God's decree, then if God says a thing (lying or sadism) is good, then it is good and would not be considered bad. So the answer that God would not declare a bad thing to be good does not work. It involves circular reasoning. The other alternative is that the concept of good coexists along with God and is recognized by God for what it is. If so, then it appears that something other than God, even if it is only a concept, has always existed. And if that is so, how many other concepts have always existed? Some people might be comfortable with this alternative, others might not be. Is there a third alternative I believe there is.

A third alternative involves understanding that Socrates' question does not have to involve an either/or dichotomy. The third alternative is to understand God as the eternal self-existing REALITY, the total REALITY from which all else emanates. God is the infinite mind in which all concepts exist. Human rationality exists because God is a rational mind. Logic and mathematical realities exist as part of the ultimate REALITY because God is the rational mind from which all realities, physical or conceptual, flow. Concepts such as truth, justice, good, evil and so forth exist because God is the rational mind in which all such aspects of REALITY are generated. Without a rational mind, conceptual reality would not

validity of the Divine Command Theory, discussed in Chapter Four: Early Christian Moral Philosophy.

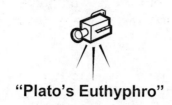

"Plato's Euthyphro"

While Socrates did not get a satisfactory answer to the question he posed to Euthyphro – indeed, he rarely got satisfactory answers to most of his questions – at least he asked. He searched; he struggled. Socrates and Plato struggled with the idea of what it meant to live a *good life*. Their conclusion was that certain character traits need to be present in one's life in order for one to live a good life, an *arête* kind of life, an excellent life, that allowed one to live a *eudaimonai* kind of life, a successful, meaningful and, therefore, happy life.

Aristotle

Aristotle (384-322 BCE), Plato's most brilliant and famous student, embraced similar assumptions as Socrates and Plato regarding *eudaimonia* (flourishing) as the goal of life. Aristotle wrote two books on ethics, *Eudemian Ethics* and *Nicomachean Ethics*. Most scholars agree that *Eudemian Ethics* was written first and that *Nicomachean Ethics* is probably a revised version of it. The differences between the two works are minor. In each, the focus is how to live a *eudaimonia* kind of life and how *arête* enables one to do so. In this way, Aristotle's thinking on the subject is similar to that of Socrates and Plato. However, one of the differences in Aristotle's work is his focus on human reasoning in the process of achieving the excellence involved in a life well-lived.[10]

Aristotle defined man as the *rational* animal, meaning that it was man's ability to rationalize, to engage in high-level *abstract conceptualization*, that lifts him above the

exist. So concepts flow from God; concepts exist because God exists. It is not a matter of God recognizing the existence of concepts that exist apart from him (for they cannot exist apart from him), or of God arbitrarily selecting things (concepts or behaviors) and labeling them as good or evil. Such concepts emanate from God because he is the ultimate rational REALITY. Good is good because of who God is, because of his nature and character. God does not decide what is good, he is the measure of what is good (and evil) and the very concept of good only exists in the context of the REALITY of God and who and what he is. (These possible answers to Socrates' question are borrowed from: Rogers, *Becoming: A Philosophical Treatise on Human Potential* (146-148).

[10] *Nicomachean Ethics* 1098a 1-15.

lower animals. Aristotle, in fact, believed that rationality was that which connected humans with the divine, for the only other beings who were capable of higher abstract conceptualization were the gods. Rationality, then, as that which not only separates us from lower animals but links us with the divine, is the basis for an *arête* (excellent) and thus a *eudaimonia* (flourishing) kind of a life.[11]

An essential component of a thriving, flourishing life for Aristotle was the pursuit of that which was of value in and of itself. Some things are of value because they assist us in achieving or accomplishing some greater goal or fulfilling some desire. But that which is most valuable, the greatest good, is that which is not a means to some other end, but that which is itself an end, that which is sought for its own sake. For Aristotle, this was a *eudaimonia* kind of a life, a life where the individual was clearly flourishing and would, therefore, be happy and satisfied. Discovering what this kind of a life was and what kind of things would lead to it was Aristotle's goal.

One of the features that distinguished Aristotle's moral philosophy from that of Socrates or Plato was his lengthy study and discussion of the role of *arête* (achieving excellence in life through the presence of virtuous character traits) in the achieving of *eudaimonia*. What are these traits and how do they help one live a life that can be described as thriving or flourishing, a successful and therefore a happy life? Not everyone reads Aristotle's list of virtues the same way and the number he discusses appears, for some, to be in question, ranging from 9 to 12 virtues. MacIntyre, for instance, lists 9, including: "courage, temperance, liberality, magnificence, greatness of soul, good temper or gentleness, being agreeable in company, wittiness, and lastly, modesty."[12] The longer list (of 12), however, seems to represent more exactly what Aristotle discussed in Books 3 and 4 of *Nicomachean Ethics*: *courage*, *temperance* (i.e., moderation or self-restraint), *liberality* (or generosity), *magnificence* (or being magnanimous), *pride* (i.e., accurate self-evaluation and appropriate self-respect), *appropriately ambitious*, *good tempered* (as in amiable, good natured), *friendliness*, *truthfulness*, *wittiness*, *modesty*, and *just*.

"Aristotle's Ethics 1/3"
"Aristotle's Ethics 2/3"
"Aristotle's Ethics 3/3"

In addition to Aristotle's list is his interesting way of defining each virtue as a mean (or middle ground) between two extremes. For instance, Aristotle considered courage to be the mean between cowardice and rashness or foolhardiness. The following chart will set out the vices, the deficit in one direction and the excess in the other, of each virtue identified by Aristotle.

[11]   utchinson, "Ethics," in *The Cambridge Companion to Aristotle*, 202-205.
[12]   MacIntyre, *A Short History of Ethics*, 68.

The Deficiency	The Virtuous Mean	The Excess
Cowardice	Courage	Foolhardiness
Lack of restraint	Temperate	Ascetic self-denial
Stinginess	Liberality	Wasteful extravagance
Pettiness	Magnanimous	Ostentatious exhibitionism
Overly humble	Proud	Vainglorious arrogance
Indolent	Ambitious	Overreaching
Disagreeable	Good Tempered	Overly affable
Unfriendly surliness	Friendliness	Overly accommodating
Deceitfulness	Truthfulness	Exaggeration
Humorless	Wittiness	Buffoonery
Shamelessness	Modesty	Bashfulness
Callousness	Just	Vengeful

Aristotle's belief was that the presence of these virtues, along with the exercise of one's rationality (*phronesis*, practical wisdom), allowed one to be the best person he could be, an *arête* (excellent) kind of a person, which in turn allowed one to enjoy a *eudaimonia* kind of life, a life well-lived.

It is important to notice that the Greeks (like the Hebrews) were not asking, "What is the right thing to do?" but were instead asking, "What kind of a person ought I to be?" This, of course, is a different question than is often asked in modern moral philosophy. Our contemporary Western orientation is more focused on *doing* (activity) than on *being* (*intra* and *inter*personal being). And so the modern question, "What is the right thing to do?" is asked more often than the ancient question, "What kind of a person should I be?" But the ancient Greeks may have been aware of an important idea – that *being* that is done well leads to *doing* that is done well. *Is it possible that when one is the kind of person one ought to be, an excellent person, that one will very likely do the right thing in whatever circumstance may arise?* The answer must certainly be that excellent people are inclined (and likely) to do excellent things. Keep in mind also that for Aristotle, being an excellent person involved the use of one's rationality, rational reflection of life's perplexities, which would include, one must presume, contemplation of questions about the right thing to do.[13]

Because he wrote extensively about moral philosophy and discussed the "virtues" associated with it so thoroughly, Aristotle's *Virtue Ethics* (as it has come to be known) continues to hold an important place in contemporary moral philosophy. This brief overview serves only as an introduction to his ideas as they existed as part of a larger historical context in ancient Greece. In Chapter Eleven we will encounter his ideas again in the context of contemporary virtue ethics. *END*

Epicureanism

Epicurus (341-270 BCE) was born seven years after Plato's death and was another of the important Greek philosophers. Around 306 BCE he moved from his home on the island of Samos to Athens where he founded a philosophical community and school known as The Garden.[14] Epicurus' philosophy was rooted in what would be described today as *egoistic hedonism*, the idea that the only thing intrinsically valuable or good is one's own pleasure. However, a closer look at how Epicurus defined pleasure is necessary if we are to understand exactly what he advocated – a philosophical framework known as Epicureanism.

EPICURUS

Epicureanism (and Stoicism, which we will consider in the next section) was rooted in the same assumptions at work in the thinking of Socrates, Plato, and Aristotle; assumptions that led to the question, "What kind of a person ought one to be?" rather than, "What is the right thing to do?"[15] Epicurus' answer to the question, "What kind of a person ought one to be?" was that one ought to be a happy person. For Epicurus, the happy life was one where there was more pleasure than pain. The goal was to eliminate, or at least minimize, pain as far as possible and to maximize pleasure as far as possible.

[13]   Technically, it is important to keep in mind that Aristotle's students were young men from wealthy families who were not going to have to engage in a trade in order to make a living. They would have considerable time to think philosophically. Aristotle's conclusion as to what is the best kind of a life, a life that is a *eudaimonia* kind of a life, is one spent in philosophical contemplation. The average person, of course (then or now) is not afforded such a luxury. However, Aristotle's framework, usually referred to as Virtue Ethics, remains viable if one approaches it from the perspective of a *eudaimonia* kind of life as one in which a person is working at achieving his or her potential to be the best person he or she can be, using virtuous character traits to become an *arête* kind of a person, that is, an excellent person. This idea will be discussed in more detail in the chapter on Contemporary Virtue Ethics.

[14]   O'Keefe, "Epicurus," in *Internet Encyclopedia of Philosophy*.

[15]   Sharples, *Stoics, Epicureans and Sceptics*, 82.

Epicurus distinguished between two different kinds of pleasure: *moving* and *static* pleasures. Moving pleasures are those that involve satisfying a desire, such as eating to satisfy hunger or drinking to satisfy thirst. Moving pleasures involve physical sensation and are what most people identify with the idea of pleasure. But Epicurus identified another feature of the pleasure matrix. After one's physical needs have been satisfied (when the drive for food or sex or whatever has been satiated), the state of satisfaction where no need or drive is present is also a pleasurable state. Epicurus called this kind of pleasure *static* and insisted that it was the best kind of pleasure.[16] Satisfying needs is pleasurable, but being in a state of satisfaction so that no needs are felt (at least for the time being) is more pleasurable. The goal, then, is to create for oneself the kind of life where pain is eliminated and one's needs are met (recurring needs such as hunger are met as they occur) so that one lives in a state of ongoing satisfaction. This is the best form of pleasure – the absence of pain and the state of satisfaction and contentment.

Epicurus does not think only in terms of physical pleasures, but of mental pleasures as well. While physical pleasures involve only the immediate present, mental pleasures (or pains) involve the past and the future. On the pain side there is guilt over past failures and mistakes and anxiety over the future. On the pleasure side there are fond memories of past significant pleasures (loved one's, achievements, etc.) and confidence and optimism about the future. Because these mental pains and pleasures involve more than just the present moment, they are more significant. Epicurus believed that the most significant impediment to happiness was worry about the future. If one could banish worry and anxiety from one's life one could achieve a state of tranquility that would be a pleasurable state and thus result in happiness. O'Keefe observes that given Epicurus' ideas about pleasure and what tends to generate the best kind or highest form of happiness, perhaps he should be thought of as a tranquillist rather than a hedonist.[17]

Even though Epicurus believed that the kinds of virtues Aristotle had discussed were necessary in order to attain happiness, because his ultimate goal included physical satisfaction, his philosophy was considered (perhaps wrongly so) hedonistic and a threat to traditional Greek morality. There was, in fact, another school of thought or group of philosophers, known as Cyrenaics, who deserve the reputation of sensualists and hedonists. The Cyrenaics insisted (in opposition to Epicurus) that physical pleasures were superior to mental or intellectual pleasures, suggesting that people ought to seek physical pleasure now rather than delaying gratification in order to secure better results (more secure circumstances) in the future.[18] Clearly, the Cyrenaics deserved the label of hedonists much more than the Epicureans did. Still, the judgment of philosophers and ethicists in general is that Epicureanism is fundamentally hedonistic in nature and therefore of questionable value as a viable moral theory.

---

[16] O'Keefe, "Epicurus," *Internet Encyclopedia of Philosophy.*
[17] O'Keefe, "Epicurus," *Internet Encyclopedia of Philosophy.*
[18] O'Keefe, "Cyrenaics," *Internet Encyclopedia of Philosophy.*

Stoicism

The founder of the Stoic school of philosophy was Zeno of Citium (in Cyprus) who was born in 344 and lived until 262 BCE. Zeno had studied under the Cynic, *Crates*. Relocating to Athens from Cypress, he began his school around 300 BCE, lecturing in one of the *stoa* (a columned portico or porch) in Athens. Because he taught in a *stoa,* his school became known as Stoicism.[19]

As Socrates, Plato and Aristotle before them, the Stoics did not ask, "What is the right thing to do?" but "What kind of a person ought one to be?" They also understood that living a *eudaimonia* kind of life was the goal of life, though they defined it somewhat differently than Aristotle had. For the Stoics, virtue and wisdom were the same things in the sense that if one had wisdom one also had and exhibited the virtues. To not exhibit the virtues indicated that one was not wise. Also, the virtues were not a means to an end, they were the end. Being virtuous was not the means to ultimately having a *eudaimonia* kind of a life, being virtuous *was* a *eudaimonia* kind of life. Only virtue was intrinsically good. To be virtuous was to flourish.[20] The difference may be subtle, but it is significant.

Along with Aristotle, the Stoics believed that the human capacity for reason (higher level abstract conceptualization) was uniquely human and that utilizing it was what allowed humans to live (wisely/virtuously) in *agreement with nature*. The Stoics believed that the cosmos was a rationally ordered reality that ran according to Zeus' will. Living in agreement with it (i.e., nature) meant aligning one's personal will with cosmic events; that is, being wise enough to go with the flow of cosmic events, to accept what happens as inevitable.[21] But as a wise person living in agreement with nature, one exhibited the character traits associated with *arête*: courage, justice, prudence, moderation and so forth. Living this kind of a life was to flourish, to thrive, the enjoy *eudaimonia*.

Summary

While there was some disagreement and variation between ancient Greek philosophers and schools of ethical thought, there is a remarkable similarity between them as well. The major philosophers and schools of thought believed that people (rightly) sought to achieve *eudaimonia*. They

---

[19] Baltzly, "Stoicism," *Stanford Encyclopedia of Philosophy*.
[20] Sharples, *Stoics, Epicureans and Scpetics*, 100.
[21] Stephens, "Stoic Ethics," Internet Encyclopedia of Philosophy.

wanted to thrive, to flourish, to be happy, to live a "successful" life. And they believed that living this *eudaimonia* kind of life involved or required that a person live a certain kind of a life, an *arête* or an excellent kind of life that was characterized by traits such as: courage, temperance, pride, liberality, moderation, justice, and so forth. They believed that as rational beings, humans must live by the dictates of rationality and wisdom. And I believe that though they did not appear to be very concerned to ask, "What is the right thing to do?" they believed that the person who was the right kind of a person, an *arête* kind of a person, was the kind of person who would do the right (or excellent) thing when faced with a moral or ethical dilemma. Ancient Greek moral philosophy appears to provide a viable framework for considering the kind of person one ought to be.

Thought and Discussion Questions

1. Discuss the differences between our contemporary Western concept of happiness and the Greek concept of *eudaimonia*.

2. Explain how being an *arête* kind of a person leads (in Aristotle's view) to *eudaimonia*.

3. Explain the differences between Aristotle, Epicurus, and the Stoics.

4. Discuss Rogers' contention that an *arête* kind of a person is one that is likely to do the right thing when faced with a moral dilemma.

5. Discuss the strengths and weaknesses as you see them of the Greek focus on being the right kind of a person rather than on doing the right thing. Why do you think they focused on being rather than doing?

Chapter 3
Jesus' Moral Philosophy

Introduction

Jesus had a moral philosophy? But wasn't Jesus a religious teacher? Isn't there a difference between religion and philosophy? Yes and no. In today's world, religion and philosophy are two separate disciplines or realms of activity. But it was not always so. In fact, Cambridge philosopher F. M. Cornford, argued that the earliest speculations of the pre-Socratic philosophers emerged directly from the religious thought of the preceding era.[1] Many issues and concerns that are important in religion are also important in philosophy. There is more overlap between religion and philosophy than many people realize. But philosophers, including moral philosophers, are hesitant to discuss what might be considered religious. In an essay on Jesus and philosophy, Paul Moser suggests that this might be due to a general uneasiness on the part of philosophers with stepping onto *theological ground.*[2] Perhaps Moser is right. I believe, however, that discussions of moral philosophy would be greatly enhanced by including Jesus' thinking on moral philosophy. Why? For two basic reasons: 1) Much of Jesus' teaching fits into the ancient Hebrew Wisdom Literature tradition, which as we have already seen is a branch of moral philosophy; and 2) he developed an effective framework for ethical thinking and moral behavior.

Jesus in the Hebrew Wisdom Literature Tradition

The ancient Hebrews, in their view, knew God (Yahweh) existed. He had spoken to them and had done amazing things in establishing them as a nation of people. Since they were fully aware of his existence, there was no need to spend time discussing the existence of God or whether or not they should conform to the terms of the agreement (covenant) into which he and they had entered. God's existence and their covenant relationship were assumptions they accepted and did not need to discuss. God had provided rules that they were to obey. The need for obedience was also a given – at least for the philosophers among them. The prophets felt compelled to warn the people that disobedience would result in serious negative consequences. But the philosophers among the ancient Hebrews assumed this to be the case and did not spend a lot of time on such issues. They were more concerned with reflecting on how to live the best kind of life, a life of wisdom.

---

[1] Cornford, *From Religion to Philosophy.*
[2] Moser, "Introduction: Jesus and Philosophy," in *Jesus and Philosophy,* 1.

Jesus shared these same assumptions. He did not spend time discussing the existence of God because the people he dealt with on a day-to-day basis knew that God existed. He also knew that they understood the expectation of obedience. And though Jesus did occasionally stress the need to obey, mostly what he was concerned with was how people (beyond simple obedience to a list of rules) ought to live. Neither did Jesus spend time repeating the same kind of advice available in the book of Proverbs or other sections of the Wisdom Literature. The people Jesus worked among were familiar with that material, and going over it again would not have been very helpful. Instead, Jesus offered new insights rooted in the traditional Hebrew wisdom approach. It is in this sense that Jesus carried on the long tradition of a Hebrew moral philosophy, a philosophy rooted in wisdom focused on how one ought to live. In his article about Jesus and philosophy, entitled *Sipping From the Cup of Wisdom*, Crenshaw observes that the underlying question that drove Jesus' ministry was about how to live in light of God's existence.[3] Explaining this from a slightly different point of view, Preston notes that the framework for Jesus' ministry and message was the establishment of the (spiritual) kingdom of God. The question that arose out of this spiritual reality was "What is conduct appropriate to a citizen of the kingdom of God?"[4]

"Jesus the Teacher"

Much of the moral philosophy Jesus did was rooted in *reinterpreting accepted social norms* for daily life and social interaction. Jesus' approach to moral philosophy in the Hebrew Wisdom tradition often involved saying something like, "You have heard it said, 'Love your neighbor and hate your enemy,' but I'm telling you that you ought to love your enemy" (Matthew 5:43-44 NRSV). This kind of reinterpreting was designed (to a degree) to shock people into thinking about their assumptions, to get them to

reevaluate thinking and change their behavior. For Jesus, the best kind of life, a life of wisdom, was one where one's standards for how to live successfully were not taken from existing social norms, but were rooted in God's character and behavior. God loves not only those who love him, but also those who do not love him, and even those who hate him. The person reflecting on the best way to live life will look to God as the model for how to live successfully. This was the foundation idea behind Jesus' moral philosophy – the best life, the wise life was lived in relationship with God, reflecting on,

---

[3]   Crenshaw, "Sipping From the Cup of Wisdom," in *Jesus and Philosophy*, 42.
[4]   Preston, "Christian Ethics," in *A Companion to Ethics*, 95.

identifying, and emulating his character. For those who found it too challenging to identify and emulate the character of an immaterial thinking substance, Jesus' own life served as a model for wise and successful living. And even though Jesus' moral philosophy surpassed the wisdom of the typical Hebrew sage who came before him, Jesus still fits within that basic framework of focusing on how to live the best kind of a life, a life that is meaningful and therefore successful. Understanding Jesus' focus on wisdom and living the best life possible, if he had spoken Greek instead of Arabic, one would not be surprised to hear him discussing a *eudaimonia* kind of life. Instead, Jesus says, "Be complete as your Father in heaven is complete" (Matthew 5:48).[5]

Jesus' Framework for Ethical Thinking and Behavior

Beyond this broad and general wisdom tradition, what did Jesus advocate regarding how to live? Did he offer a basic ethical or moral framework for thinking and acting? Yes, he did.

The Ethics of Love

On one occasion a teacher of the Law of Moses asked Jesus a question. "Teacher, which is the greatest commandment in the law?" If we translate this question and Jesus' answer out of that 1st century Jewish culture into 21st century American culture, the question is, "Teacher, what is the most important thing there is?" Jesus' answer was, "Love the Lord your God with all your heart and with all your soul and with all your mind.

This is the most important thing there is. And the second most important thing is like it: Love your neighbor as yourself" (Matthew 22:36-40). What did Jesus mean and how does it impact one's morality?

Loving God

There are several things that must be clarified if we are to understand what Jesus said here. The word in the text for love is the Greek word *agape*, which refers to the highest form of love, a love rooted not in an emotional feeling, but in the right kind of action. To *agape* someone is to behave appropriately toward them for who they are. In this sense of the word, you can behave appropriately toward someone regardless of how you might feel toward them. This is the word Jesus used when he said, "Love your enemies." But in this text, Jesus said that one ought to *agape* God with all his heart,

---

[5] Although the Greek word in Matthew 5:48 is often translated perfect, *"Be perfect as your Father in heaven is perfect"* the Greek word (*teleioi,* from *teleios*) would be better translated complete or mature, as in lacking nothing. The idea is that the wise person who seeks to live a life of wisdom seeks to be complete, to lack nothing, as God lacks nothing.

which presumably includes an emotional element. How does an *agape* kind of love manifest itself toward God in Jesus ethical framework? When Jesus said that the most important thing in the world is to love God with all of one's heart, soul, and mind, he meant that one is to act toward or to respond to God appropriately both emotively and cognitively. Thus, an *agape* kind of love for God will (emotively and cognitively) acknowledge him, respect him, obey him, and emulate him as far as possible.

"Agape Love"

The primary foundational principle in Jesus' ethical framework is love for God. And that love prompts us to respond to God in a certain manner, in a loving, obedient, respectful, humble manner.

Loving Oneself and Loving Others

When the teacher that approached Jesus asked him what the most important thing was, Jesus not only answered that question but followed up with the second most important thing: loving others as much as one loves oneself. The idea of loving oneself is significant. Many people are under the impression that Jesus' system of living involves an ascetic kind of self-denial where one's own interests and desires must be ignored. That is simply not the case. Self-love, or self-interest, is a normal and important aspect of human nature, a human nature created by God. While we must be careful not to let self-interest degenerate into selfishness caring for oneself is normal and healthy. Jesus understood this.

How do we love ourselves appropriately, that is, without self-love degenerating into selfishness? We love ourselves appropriately by taking care of ourselves. When we are hungry we eat, when thirsty we drink. When we are tried we rest. We enjoy relationships with other people and take time to relax and rejuvenate. When we are cold we find a way to get warm. When we are too warm we find a way to get cool. When we are sick we take medicine and rest until we get better. Occasionally we treat ourselves to an indulgence. We take a vacation to unwind and refocus. We do things that we enjoy. But we also engage in meaningful activities, things that matter to us, to others, and to life in general. We

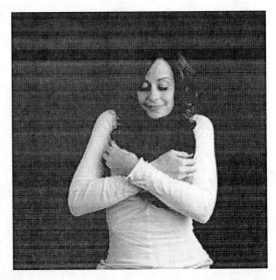

work hard, sometimes even to the point of exhaustion, because working hard and accomplishing something important is a very satisfying and crucial form of self-interest.

There are all sorts of ways that we love ourselves. Jesus' point in saying that it is important to love others as much as we love ourselves is to remind his audience that not only is self-interest appropriate, but that it serves as a guide as to how we ought to interact and respond to others. If we know how to love ourselves we know how to love others. Loving others is no different than loving ourselves. Unless our appropriate self-interest has degenerated into selfishness, we know how to love others. And if the question of how much we are to love others should arise, the answer is – as much as you love yourself.

Why would Jesus say the second most important thing in the world (after loving God) is to love others as much as you love yourself? How is loving others an appropriate feature of a moral philosophy rooted in living a life guided by wisdom? It is appropriate because life is lived in relationship with others. We are relational beings. We do not live in isolation. We are interdependent. It is essential, then, that appropriate attention be given to interpersonal relations. In fact, any system of ethics that does not address the matter of interpersonal relationships is incomplete and, therefore, flawed.

How does Jesus' focus on routine interpersonal relationships impact ethical issues where doing the right thing (or knowing the right thing to do) is the crucial concern? Most ethical concerns or dilemmas occur in the context of interpersonal relationships. How are they to be resolved? How is one to know what is the right thing to do? Regardless of other considerations, paradigms, or methodologies utilized in determining the right thing to do, the foundational concern, according to Jesus, must include loving the other people involved in the issue. When you love them as much as you love yourself, your response to whatever the ethical issue is will include an appropriate level of loving concern for the people that will or might be impacted by your decision or action.

Golden Rule Ethics

In Matthew 7:12 Jesus said, "*So in everything, do to others what you would have them do to you, for this sums up the Law and the Prophets.*" Let us consider the last phrase of the quotation before looking at the first part of it. "*… for this sums up the Law and the Prophets.*" What did Jesus mean? He meant that what he had just said summed up the intent of the rest of the Hebrew Scriptures regarding how one ought to live in relation to others. In that 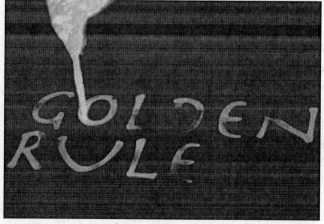 one brief statement, Jesus was presenting a summary of the main concern of the Old Testament Scriptures. Jesus was saying that the focus of God's law to the ancient Israelites and the comments of the Prophets regarding that law had to do with how they interacted with each other. He was saying that the point of the Hebrew Scriptures was to instruct people about living well, living in a harmonious way with other people. He was saying that if one is going to emulate God, one will focus his attention on living well with other people.

How did Jesus suggest people live well with other people? He said that you should treat other people the way you want them to treat you. I think there is considerable confusion regarding exactly what Jesus was suggesting in this brief comment. To understand it thoroughly it is important that we see what Jesus was saying and what he was not saying. What he was not saying is that you should treat people the way you want to be treated *so that* they will treat you that way. In other words, Jesus was not advocating ethical egoism or any kind of reciprocal ethics.[6] Many people often assume, and therefore read into Jesus' comment, a form of reciprocal egoism. But it is important to note that Jesus does not say, *so that people will treat you the way you want to be treated*. Neither does he imply such. In fact, in light of his overall teaching on the foundations of moral behavior (love for God and love for others, including one's enemies) one cannot conclude that Jesus is working out of an egoist paradigm. In Jesus' ethical system one is to love *whether or not* the love is returned, not *so* the love will be returned. To the question, "How should I treat other people?" Jesus answers, "Treat them the way you want to be treated," – whether they reciprocate or not. That is his point. Jesus was not an ethical egoist. Such an idea is not at all compatible with Jesus' teachings or his own personal actions.

"The Golden Rule: True Ethics"

How does this bit of moral philosophy help in considering what is the right thing to do when faced with an ethical dilemma? It provides a foundation to build on. When faced with an ethical dilemma, especially those that involve interpersonal relations, one ought to behave (decide or act) the way he would want others to act if their decision or action would impact him. A young woman considering getting an abortion ought to ask, "If I were the baby, what would I want me to do?" Someone struggling with whether or not to disconnect life support from grandma who is comatose ought to ask, "If I were grandma, what would I want me to do?" Treating people the way you want to be treated, giving them the same consideration you would like to receive is the place Jesus says we

[6] Preston makes this same point in his material on the ethics of Jesus, "Christian Ethics," in *A Companion to Ethics,* 95-96.

should begin. There may be other paradigmatic factors that might need to be considered or utilized (Kant's categorical imperative, for instance), but the Golden Rule, as part of Jesus' ethical framework, provides a place to begin one's ethical reasoning.

The Wisdom of Jesus

Having considered Jesus' basic framework for ethical thinking and acting, it is time to look at some of the specific wisdom he had to offer. Instead of compiling a list of virtues as Aristotle did, Jesus preferred to offer wisdom that was more relationship or situation oriented. One's audience determines one's methodology. But the goals of each (Aristotle and Jesus) were not that different. The following passages taken from the Gospels of Matthew and Luke are representative samples of the kinds of wisdom Jesus offered in an attempt to help people live life wisely.

A crucial factor that must be considered in understanding Jesus' advice is the historical context in which his wisdom is dispensed. This advice was offered 2,000 years ago to Palestinian Jews who lived in a State occupied by Roman Legions. Some of the advice Jesus gave, some of the wisdom he dispensed, for that time and place may seem very out of place in our contemporary society. Applying ancient wisdom in modern contexts requires careful consideration. What parts ought to remain and which need to be set aside are issues that require serious deliberation. With that in mind, consider some of the wisdom of Jesus.

But to you who are listening I say: Love your enemies, do good to those who hate you, bless those who curse you, pray for those who mistreat you. If someone slaps you on one cheek, turn to them the other also. If someone takes your coat, do not withhold your shirt from them. Give to everyone who asks you, and if anyone takes what belongs to you, do not demand it back. Do to others as you would have them do to you. "If you love those who love you, what credit is that to you? Even sinners love those who love them. And if you do good to those who are good to you, what credit is that to you? Even sinners do that. And if you lend to those from whom you expect repayment, what credit is that to you? Even sinners lend to sinners, expecting to be repaid in full. But love your enemies, do good to them, and lend to them without expecting to get anything back (Luke 6:27-35a).

The wisdom in this passage grows out of Jesus' basic ethic of love. Love everyone, not just those who love you, but even those who do not. It must be remembered, however, that the kind of love Jesus is advising is *agape* love, focusing on behavior rather than feeling. Loving people is behaving appropriately toward them, helping them when they need help. For Jesus, being a person of love is living wisely.

Why do you look at the speck of sawdust in your brother's eye and pay no attention to the plank in your own eye? How can you say to your brother, 'Brother, let me take the speck out of your eye,' when you yourself fail to see the plank in your own eye? You hypocrite, first take the plank out of your eye, and then you will see clearly to remove the speck from your brother's eye (Luke 6:41-42).

The wisdom is this passage involves a commonsense approach of personal introspection and responsibility. Instead of criticizing the flaws and shortcomings of other people, pay attention to your own. Only when you have addressed your own flaws are you in a position to address the flaws in people's lives.

On one occasion an expert in the law stood up to test Jesus. "Teacher," he asked, "what must I do to inherit eternal life?"
"What is written in the Law?" he replied. "How do you read it?"
He answered, "'Love the Lord your God with all your heart and with all your soul and with all your strength and with all your mind'; and, 'Love your neighbor as yourself.'"
"You have answered correctly," Jesus replied. "Do this and you will live."
But he wanted to justify himself, so he asked Jesus, "And who is my neighbor?"
In reply Jesus said: "A man was going down from Jerusalem to Jericho, when he was attacked by robbers. They stripped him of his clothes, beat him and went away, leaving him half dead. A priest happened to be going down the same road, and when he saw the man, he passed by on the other side. So, too, a Levite, when he came to the place and  *saw him, passed by on the other side. But a Samaritan, as he traveled, came where the man was; and when he saw him, he took pity on him. He went to him and bandaged his wounds, pouring on oil and wine. Then he put the man on his own donkey, brought him to an inn and took care of him. The next day he took out two denarii and gave them to the innkeeper. 'Look after him,' he said, 'and when I return, I will reimburse you for any extra expense you may have.'*

"Which of these three do you think was a neighbor to the man who fell into the hands of robbers?"
The expert in the law replied, "The one who had mercy on him."
Jesus told him, "Go and do likewise" (Luke 10:25-37).

"Parable of the Good Samaritan"

The wisdom here is that if you love God appropriately and love others as much as you love yourself, you will behave appropriately toward them. What makes Jesus' example so compelling is the story he told to illustrate what he was talking about. In his story, the Samaritan was part of an ethnic group despised by the Jews. In some cases the word *hated* would not be too strong a word. As the Samaritan travelled he encountered an injured Jewish man, a man who felt nothing but contempt for all Samaritans. But even though the Samaritan man knew this about the injured man who lay on the ground, bruised and bleeding, he felt compassion and stopped to help the injured man, a man who despised him. The injured man needed help, so the Samaritan man helped him. He loved him in that he behaved appropriately toward him.

"Daniel Goleman on Compassion"

Jesus' point is that a loving person is the best kind of a person. If he had been speaking Greek, Jesus could have said that a loving person is an *arête* kind of a person who will live a *eudaimonia* kind of a life. But Jesus wasn't Greek, and he was not speaking to Greek people. He was Jewish speaking to Jewish people. So he offered his advice, his wisdom, in ways that made sense to the Jewish people.

> *"Again, you have heard that it was said to the people long ago, 'Do not break your oath, but fulfill to the Lord the vows you have made.' But I tell you, do not swear an oath at all: either by heaven, for it is God's throne; or by the earth, for it is his footstool; or by Jerusalem, for it is the city of the Great King. And do not swear by your head, for you cannot make even one hair white or black. All you need to say is simply 'Yes' or 'No'; anything beyond this comes from the evil one (Matthew 5:33-37).*

In this bit of wisdom Jesus is saying that one ought to be a person of his or her word, a person of integrity that is trustworthy. One should not need to promise or take an oath so others will believe what he or she says. A trustworthy person is dependable and responsible in every way. If they say they will do something, they will. If they say they will not, they will not. If they promise to be at a certain place at a certain time, unless something completely beyond their control keeps them from it, they will be there. The wise person is a trustworthy person that people know can be depended on to keep his or her word.

"Be careful not to practice your righteousness in front of others to be seen by them. If you do, you will have no reward from your Father in heaven.

"So when you give to the needy, do not announce it with trumpets, as the hypocrites do in the synagogues and on the streets, to be honored by others. Truly I tell you, they have received their reward in full. But when you give to the needy, do not let your left hand know what your right hand is doing, so that your giving may be in secret … (Matthew 6:1-4).

The wisdom Jesus offers here is based on the assumption that people will be engaged in charitable giving. The Law of Moses required it, so Jesus assumes it will occur. But how should it be done? That is Jesus' concern. His advice is that it ought not to be done in a way that draws attention to oneself. It should be done humbly and privately. It ought to be done to benefit the needy person, not the donor by the notoriety or publicity received from the help being offered in a public manner. The one who goes about doing good (loving his neighbor) quietly and humbly is helping for the right reason and is living wisely.

"Do not judge [others]*, or you too will be judged* [by God]*. For in the same way you judge others, you will be judged, and with the measure you use, it will be measured to you* (Matthew 7:1-2).

The wisdom Jesus is offering here is to avoid being judgmental and condemning people. Being judgmental and condemning does not generate happy and healthy interpersonal relations. Since Jesus' wisdom is geared toward generating healthy interpersonal relations by being a loving person there is no room for being a judgmental person.

These six examples of the kind of wisdom Jesus offered provide only a brief glimpse into a very thorough and complex system of how to live well, in relation to God and to others. While it is undoubtedly true that Jesus was a religious teacher it is also true that he was a significant moral philosopher who offered people a wisdom regarding how to live well that has impacted more people than any other philosophical vision for how people ought to live moral lives. If we were going to name the system Jesus advocated we might call it: Golden Rule Ethics of Love.

Summary

Jesus was a moral philosopher in the long tradition of the Hebrew moral philosophers who emphasized living a life of wisdom. And though Jesus' methodology was different from, say, Aristotle's, they both focused on a very similar goal – how to live well. Without a doubt, Jesus also had concerns for salvation from sin and an eternal reality that was not part of Aristotle's philosophical framework. That, however, does not diminish Jesus' standing as a moral philosopher.

The foundational idea or framework for Jesus' moral philosophy was what I have described as an ethic of love – *agape* love for God and for others. One's love for others was to be gauged by one's love for oneself. As a practical way to enact the ethic of love, Jesus used what is now referred to as the Golden Rule, "Do to others as you have them do to you." Treat others the way you want to be treated. But Jesus was not an Ethical Egoist. His point was not to treat others well so they will treat you well. Jesus' ethical

system was not reciprocal. Jesus' point was to treat others the way you want to be treated … *regardless of how they treat you*. If they reciprocate and treat you well, that is good for you. But if they do not, you should still treat them the way you want to be treated. Motive or intention (rather than results or consequences) is the point of what Jesus advocates as it concerns the Golden Rule. Could this be where Kant got the idea that intention rather than consequences is what generates moral behavior?

Finally, Jesus offers advice rooted in a wisdom that is designed to lead one to a life of healthy interpersonal relationships, with God and with other people. Sometimes his advice is intuitive; sometimes it is counterintuitive. But it is advice rooted in the wisdom of ancient Hebrew moral philosophy. The moral philosophy of Jesus appears to offer a viable framework for considering how to live morally.

Thought and Discussion Questions

1. Explain how Jesus stands in the tradition of ancient Hebrew moral philosophy.

2. Explain how Jesus' moral philosophy is rooted in love for God and love for others.

3. Discuss why the specific Greek word for love in texts such as, "Love you enemies," is crucial.

4. Discuss the significance of self-love in Jesus' ethical system.

5. Explain why Jesus' ethical system is not Ethical Egoism.

Chapter 4
Early Christian Moral Philosophy

Introduction

Why focus on early Christian moral philosophy rather than Christian ethics in general? Because what early Christianity was and what it has become today are two very different things. And what early Christian moral philosophy was and what today passes for "Christian Ethics" are two different things. An example of how contemporary Christian Ethics often proceeds can be found in Stephen Long's *Christian Ethics: A Very Short Introduction*. Chapter Four, for instance, The History of Christian Ethics, is simply a tracing out of theological history.[1] There is very little in it, or in the rest of the book for that matter, that a philosophically trained ethicist would recognize as ethics. It is theology. Another example is Joe Trull's *Walking in the Way: An Introduction to Christian Ethics.*

One of the reasons Christian Ethics is normally ignored in most ethics texts is because often it is, for all intents and purposes, nothing more than conservative Christian theological moralizing. Most books on Christian Ethics utilize the approach known as the Divine Command Theory,[2] which focuses on identifying the rules God gave in the Bible, roughly between 3,500 and 2,000 years ago. The Divine Command Theory says simply that the right thing to do is what God says is the right thing to do – a system that might work if everyone believed in God, if everyone believed the Bible to be the authoritative word of God, and if all of the ethical dilemmas we face today (or ever will face) were addressed in the Bible. But everyone does not believe in God and not all who believe in God believe that the Bible is God's inspired word and, therefore, authoritative in matters of morality.[3] And even if the Bible is God's communication to human beings, it does not address all the ethical dilemmas we face in the world today. Even if the Bible provides guidance in some matters of morality, it does not do so in all of them.

---

[1]   Long, *Christian Ethics*, 51-79.

[2]   For an excellent overview of the Divine Command Theory see Austin, "Divine Command Theory," in *Internet Encyclopedia of Philosophy*.

[3]   Garth Jones discusses the authority of Scripture in Christian ethics in an article of that name in *The Cambridge Companion to Christian Ethics*, 16-28.

"Matthew Flannagan on Divine Command Theory"

One of the most serious shortcomings of the Divine Command Theory (as it is normally presented) is that it suggests that God's rules be obeyed simply because they are God's rules. God says murder is wrong so murder is wrong. End of discussion. There is no room for rational reflection as to why murder is wrong, or why stealing is wrong, or why adultery is wrong. God says they are wrong, so they are wrong. I believe that sort of an approach is intellectually crippling. God expects his human children to use their rational faculties to figure out *why* he would say that murder is wrong, why stealing is wrong, and why adultery is wrong. If we can discover why those things are wrong, perhaps we can discover what actions are appropriate and inappropriate when considering ethical dilemmas God has not commented on.

For these reasons the Divine Command Theory that usually characterizes Christian Ethics comes up short. As an ethical theory that would aid humans in discovering right and wrong and knowing what God would have them do when faced with situations they are unsure about, especially those where God has not provided guidance, the Divine Command theory is inadequate. Additionally, it is worth noting that Christianity is not a rule-oriented religion. The New Covenant is not based on a list of rules as was the Mosaic Covenant. Given this reality, the Divine Command Theory is again seen to be inappropriate as a methodology for Christian Ethics.

Instead of the Divine Command Theory, the approach in this chapter will be to discover how the first and second generations of Jesus' followers approached the task of moral philosophy in their ancient Hellenistic context. END

Christian Moral Philosophy
as a Continuation of Hebrew Moral Philosophy

The New Testament as we know it today was not recognized until the late 4th century. Discussions of what writings should be considered authoritative had been carried on for nearly two hundred years. Finally, in 367 CE, Athanasius, Bishop of Alexandra, wrote a letter that included a list of the writings considered to be inspired. The list included the twenty-seven books recognized

then and now as inspired by God. This collection of writings became the New Testament as we know it today. Before it began to be circulated, the Christian community utilized mostly the Hebrew Scriptures, the Old Testament, as their "Bible."

"How did the New Testament Canon Develop?"

There were two ways to read the Old Testament. For those who lacked spiritual insight, it was read as a list of rules, with the shallow, superficial idea that all God wanted was compliance. Obey the rules and you were acceptable to God. However, for those who were spiritually mature and had the insight to know better, the Hebrew Scriptures were more than just a list of rules to be obeyed, they were a reservoir of divine wisdom that could enlighten the heart and mind, opening one's eyes so he could see what constituted a life of wisdom.[4] For those who read the Hebrew Scriptures with this insight, the search for wisdom included reflection on the nature and purpose of life. Those who sought to live a life of wisdom knew that it began with living a holy life. Being in a covenant relationship with God meant emulating the qualities and characteristics of God – as much as humanly possible. One whose goal was to be like God was not satisfied with a list of rules. Instead, he sought the wisdom of God, the kind of wisdom contained in the book of Proverbs, wisdom that would aid him in living the best kind of life. Jesus had been identified as the wisdom of God (personified) and had focused his own teaching on how to live the best kind of life. Those who had faith in Jesus, therefore, sought to live a life of wisdom, a wisdom that was anchored in faith and godly living, but that also reflected rationally on what it meant to live a life of wisdom. In this since, the first and second generations of Jesus' followers lived lives of wisdom, as had many of the ancient Hebrews. Ethically speaking, early Christianity was, at least in part, a continuation of the Hebrew ethical tradition. Why only *in part*? Because early Christian moral philosophy was also influenced by Greek moral philosophy.

---

[4] As John Rogerson points out in his article, "The Old Testament and Christian Ethics," in *The Cambridge Companion to Christian Ethics,* 29-41, one of the earliest controversies in the Christian community had to do with whether or not non-Jewish followers of Jesus had to obey the Mosaic Covenant. The Apostles Peter and Paul along with James, Jesus' brother and Jerusalem church leader, argued that they did not (Acts 15:1-30). The non-Jewish Christians did not need to obey the Law of Moses. This, of course, impacted the way they read the Hebrew Scriptures. There is little in the New Testament that would make it clear that an ethic based on Hebrew wisdom was being followed. Yet when one sees the kind of ethical advice being given in the New Testament, beginning with the teachings of Jesus and continuing with the teaching of the Apostles, it coincides nicely with the kind of Hebrew wisdom represented in the book of Proverbs.

The Influence of Greek Moral Philosophy
on Christian Moral Philosophy

The goal of Alexander the Great was to Hellenize the known world. He accomplished his goal. The Greek culture was so powerful and influential that when the Roman Empire replaced the Greek, it did so only partially. The Roman world was only partially Roman. The common language of the Empire was Greek. Though the names of the gods had been changed to Latin names (Zeus became Jupiter) the religion was basically Greek. The dominant philosophy, Stoicism, was Greek in origin. That the Roman Empire is described as Hellenistic illustrates how powerful the Greek presence was. The philosophical descendants of Socrates, Plato and Aristotle were alive and well throughout the Roman Empire, and Athens remained the center of philosophical speculation in the first century of the Common Era.

"Alexander the Great"

How did this cultural reality impact a religion that began in a Palestinian Jewish context? For the first ten years or so after the establishment of what came to be known as Christianity, the new community of faith was made up entirely of Jewish people who believed Jesus to be the Messiah of God. But as the new faith began to spread beyond the borders of Palestine and beyond Jewish communities, non-Jewish people became part of the new religion. As they did so, their Greek worldview, that is, their assumptions and perspectives, also became part of the community of faith. Additionally, there were Jewish people who lived in the Hellenistic culture of the Empire. Their views were a blend of the Jewish worldview and the Greek. One of those new believers was a man named Saul, from the city of Tarsus. Saul was selected to be an Apostle and changed his name to Paul. Next to Jesus himself, Paul became the most influential person in the Christian church. Paul was a highly educated man well-versed in Judaism as well as having received a traditional Hellenistic education, as evidenced by his ability to converse comfortably with the philosophers of Athens when he visited that city (Acts 17:16-34).

"Apostle Paul 1/4"
"Apostle Paul 2/4"
"Apostle Paul 3/4"
"Apostle Paul 4/4"

The Apostle Paul wrote more of the New Testament than any other individual, having authored fourteen of the letters that are part of it. The Gospel of Luke and the book of Acts, which comprise a large portion of the New Testament were written by a Greek medical doctor named Luke. Reading the portions of the New Testament they wrote is very different than reading those that have a distinctive Jewish feel, such as the books of Hebrews, James, Jude and the letters of Peter. Even the Apostle John, who was a Jewish fisherman before becoming an Apostle of Jesus, was influenced by Greek thinking. John described Jesus in terms of the Greek concept of the *logos* (John 1:1-4).

Within a short time non-Jewish people began embracing Christianity and began to outnumber Jewish believers. The Hellenistic segment of church was much larger than the Jewish segment of the church. The Hellenistic perspective (worldview) soon became the dominant perspective in the Christian community. The rich Jewish heritage and roots of Christianity were not lost, but were blended with Greek perspectives. When it came to thinking about ethical concerns it was inevitable that Greek perspectives would be integrated with ancient Hebrew perspectives. The perspective that is most obvious is Aristotle's virtue ethics. Why? Because as discussed in Chapter One, the ultimate goal for both Hebrew and Greek moral philosophy was living well, that is, living a life guided by wisdom. The Greeks utilized a different methodology, but the goal was very similar. This can be seen in the writing of both Peter and Paul as they discuss the character traits (virtues) Christians need to incorporate into their lives in order to live well as Christians.

The Moral Philosophy of Paul

In discussing Greek moral philosophy we referred often to the word *arête* and the virtues associated with it. *Arête* is used in only four texts in the New Testament, three times by Peter and once by Paul. In none of these texts is it used in the same way the Greeks used it in discussing moral philosophy. However, the idea of character traits (virtues) that aid one in living life well (from a Christian point of view) are clearly present in the New Testament. There are two passages in Paul's writing that illustrate this.

Paul's moral philosophy is built on the idea of love, just as Jesus explained in his teaching. In 1 Corinthians 13:13 Paul said that of the three concepts foundational to Christianity, faith, hope and love, love is the greatest. The kind of love he is has in mind is the *agape* love Jesus spoke about, a love that displays itself in behavior and action. A few verses earlier in his discussion of love Paul described love in a way that clarifies what he has in mind:

> *Love is patient, love is kind. It does not envy, it does not boast, it is not proud. It does not dishonor others, it is not self-seeking, it is not easily angered, it keeps no record of wrongs. Love does not delight in evil but rejoices with the truth. It always protects, always trusts, always hopes, always perseveres. Love never fails*, (1 Corinthians 13 4-8a).

The foundation for morality as far as Jesus was concerned was love. Paul followed Jesus in this regard and proclaimed the same idea. But Paul also knew that the Christian who wanted to live the best kind of life would need additional character traits (virtues) to help him accomplish his goal. What were these? In Galatians 5:22-23 Paul identified several, explaining that they were traits produced by the Holy Spirit who lives in the believer. "*But the fruit of the Spirit is love, joy, peace, forbearance, kindness, goodness, faithfulness, gentleness and self-control ...*"

While it is obvious that Paul's list of *virtues* is different from Aristotle's, the idea is clearly the same. The qualities Paul describes are (some of) the character traits of God himself, and when present in the believer will help him or her live the Christian version of an *arête* kind of life. Clearly, as far as Paul was concerned, how one lived, loving God and loving others, was related to or dependent on (in the sense of being aided by) the character traits that characterize one's life. It seems apparent (to me at least) that the moral philosophy of the early Christians was a kind of virtue ethics. And while it was not the virtue ethics of Aristotle, it was, nonetheless a form of virtue ethics rooted in the same basic idea – the presence of character traits in one's life that aided one in becoming the person he or she wanted to be.

The Moral Philosophy of Peter

As another key leader in the early Christian church, the Apostle Peter can be cited, along with Paul, as one whose writing reflects the thinking of the early Christian movement. Like Paul, Peter wrote to encourage believers in how to live effectively as Christians in an Empire that was, at that time, hostile to the church. In 2 Peter 1:5-7 Peter produces a list of character traits (virtues) that is similar to Paul's and which would serve the same purpose: to aid Christians in living life well. Peter wrote: *"For this very reason, make every effort to add to your faith goodness; and to goodness, knowledge; and to knowledge, self-control; and to self-control, perseverance; and to perseverance, godliness; and to godliness, mutual affection; and to mutual affection, love.*

"The Apostle Peter 1/2"
"The Apostle Peter 2/2"

While Paul began his list with love, Peter ends his list with that foundational concept and trait. It is that same kind of *agape* love that Jesus and Paul wrote about, a love that manifests itself in action. Peter's list is very much like Paul's. And as Paul's list was, Peter's is different from Aristotle's. However, Peter's general idea is the same as Aristotle's. The character traits Peter enumerates are qualities that, in his estimation, will help Christians live well. Again, Peter's approach, like Paul's, can rightly be described as a virtue ethics kind of an approach.

I believe both Peter and Paul wrote as they did because this way of thinking was familiar to the Hellenistic believer. They were familiar with Aristotelian virtue ethics and would recognize the same basic approach when presented from within a Christian framework.

Summary

A lot of what passes for Christian Ethics today is rooted in the Divine Command Theory, a theoretical framework that suggests that moral philosophy is simply a process of discovering what God has commanded and following those commands. Yet this is not the approach used by the first and second generations of Christians. They used an approach that can be identified as Virtue Ethics. Though the Christian lists of virtues, produced by the apostles Paul and Peter, are different from Aristotle's list of virtues, the idea of the approach is the same as Aristotle's: incorporating qualities or character traits in one's life that will help one live a better life – a life rooted in the wisdom of God, a life understood as both godly and successful, in the truest sense of successful. Early Christian moral philosophy appears to remain viable as a framework for considering how to live morally.

Thought and Discussion Questions

1. Explain 1) what the Divine Command Theory is, 2) what its weakness are for serving as a theoretical framework for Christian Ethics as explained by Rogers, and 3) whether or not you agree with Rogers' assessment of it.

2. Explain whether or not you agree with Rogers that early Christian moral philosophy is in part a continuation of Hebrew moral philosophy.

3. Explain how and to what extent Greek moral philosophy may have impacted Christian moral philosophy, especially in the Hellenistic segment of the Christian church.

4. Discuss the similarities and dissimilarities between Peter's and Paul's version of Christian Virtue Ethics and Aristotle's Virtue Ethics.

5. Discuss your opinions regarding the place of Christian Ethics in the larger moral philosophy discussion. Does Christian Ethics have something to offer traditional moral philosophy?

Chapter 5
The Moral Philosophy of Augustine and Aquinas

Introduction

Though the integration of Judeo-Christian and Greek perspectives began, in at least a limited way, with the work of the Apostle Paul and continued to varying degrees thereafter, the two people most responsible for synthesizing the two perspectives to a greater degree were St. Augustine of Hippo (354-430 CE) and Thomas Aquinas (1225-1274). Augustine integrated ideas that were Platonic in origin, while Aquinas integrated ideas that originated with Aristotle. While their integration had to do with Platonic and Aristotelian philosophy in general, each was very interested in how Greek moral philosophy (Plato's and Aristotle's respectively) could be integrated with Judeo-Christian moral philosophy.

Augustine

Mendelson provides an excellent brief overview of Augustine that allows one to put Augustine's work into a historical context, revealing a complex progression of thought that evolved over Augustine's life.[1] The following is an even briefer overview.

Augustine was born in North Africa, in the City of Thagaste (which today is in Algeria) in 354 of the Common Era. His mother, Monica, was a Christian, his father, Patricius was not, although he did become a Christian before his death. Patricius saw to it that his son received a fine education rooted in literature, rhetoric and some law. His early education did not include a lot of philosophy. At age 19, Augustine read Cicero's *Hortensius*, in which Cicero encouraged his readers to study philosophy, which as Mendelson points out was not the same subject as most people think of as philosophy today. In Augustine's time, philosophy was "the paradigmatically Hellenistic pursuit of wisdom that transcended and blurred the boundaries of what are now viewed as the separate spheres of philosophy, religion, and psychology."[2] Augustine followed Cicero's advice and began reading in earnest.

---

[1] Mendelson, "Saint Augustine," in *Stanford Encyclopedia of Philosophy*.
[2] Ibid.

"Augustine of Hippo"

One of Augustine's major concerns was what is referred to today as *the problem of evil*. He needed to make sense of a world created by a good God that is also a place where evil and suffering are pervasive. This concern became one of the issues that shaped, and to a degree even defined, his life and work.

In his early adult years Augustine supported himself by teaching rhetoric. In hope of finding better quality students than he had in North Africa, Augustine moved to Rome in 383, taking his widowed mother Monica with him. Eventually he was offered a professorship, teaching rhetoric in Milan. While there he attended church with his mother, where he heard the preaching of Bishop Ambrose. Ambrose was highly educated, one of the earliest *doctors* of the church, and was a skilled rhetorician. Augustine was impressed as he heard the doctrines of Christianity explained in intellectually respectable terms, noticing how much of what Ambrose said was similar to, and in some case aligned so closely with, Platonic philosophy. Eventually Augustine was convinced of the truth of Christianity and was baptized on Easter Sunday, 387, when he was thirty-three years old. Shortly after his conversion Augustine decided to move back to North Africa. On the journey home his mother died. Not long after, in 389, his son also died. Augustine returned to his place of birth (Thagaste) and in 391 was ordained (reluctantly) as a priest. In 395 he was ordained as Bishop and spent the rest of his life (until his death in 430) teaching, preaching, and writing.

As noted earlier, one of the issues that occupied a great deal of his thinking was the problem of evil. For a period of time he embraced Manichean thinking which postulated two co-equal principles of good and evil that exist in perpetual struggle. Manichaeism taught that one's soul is a particle of light trapped in the darkness of the material cosmos and therefore caught in the eternal struggle between good and evil. Only by gaining sufficient insight and  living an ascetic life can one hope, over several successive lives, to free oneself from the darkness and participate fully in the light. Eventually Augustine saw that Manicheanism was not a viable option, that is, it was not compatible with Judeo-Christian teachings.

Years later, as he reflected on significant events in his life, Augustine realized that one of the most formative had been his encounter with Platonism. He read a number of books that set out Platonic ideas, which he saw as compatible with Judeo-Christian perspectives. Of particular import were the Neo-Platonic perspectives of Plotinus, especially as it related to Plotinus' ideas concerning *The One*, which Augustine understood as similar to God. As Augustine formulated theological theories that made sense to him, Platonic ideas were especially crucial. It is common knowledge that much of Augustine's Christian theology (in general) was heavily influenced by Platonism and Neo-Platonism.[3] But what about his ethical theory? What are the foundational concepts of Augustine's moral philosophy?

Augustine's moral philosophy was, first, *eudaimonistic* in character. Like Socrates and Plato, Augustine believed that happiness (contentment, fulfillment) is and ought to be the goal of life. But unlike Socrates and Plato, Augustine believed that true satisfaction could only be found in God.[4] Augustine was well aware of Epicurean and Stoic philosophy and believed neither system's approach to happiness was acceptable. He considered Epicureanism to be rooted in physical gratification, which he knew could not produce true happiness in life. Stoicism, rooted in the idea that merely having virtuous character traits amounted to a *eudaimonia* kind of life, fared no better in Augustine's estimation. For Augustine, human happiness in the truest sense of the idea could only be attained in a loving relationship with God, who was the eternal and ultimate reality. To know God is to love God, and in that mind-to-mind or spirit-to-spirit communion between creator and created is true happiness to be found.[5] This is the foundational idea in Augustine's moral philosophy.

Second, would be his belief in free will. Humans are moral beings who make moral choices. If humans exist as moral beings then morality also exists. Right and wrong exists and humans are obligated to choose and to choose well. Not that they cannot chose poorly – Augustine was well aware of the human propensity for making poor choices. But as rational beings who must choose a course of action (each decides either implicitly and explicitly who and what he or she will be) humans are obligated to choose morality over immorality, right over wrong, good over evil. What is it that will guide them in the choice and choices they make? If things are as they should be, love for God will provide the guidance they need.

---

[3]   Ibid.
[4]   Copleston, *A History of Philosophy*, Vol. 2, 81-82.
[5]   Ibid.

In this sense, Augustine's moral philosophy is firmly rooted in the teachings of Jesus. "What is the most important thing there is?" Jesus was asked. His answer was, love for God – a pervasive, consuming love for God. Augustine agreed.

Clearly, Augustine's approach remains rooted in the question, "What kind of a person ought one to be?" rather than the question, "What is the right thing to do?" Augustine's answer is that one ought to be a happy person. And to be a happy person one needs to know and love God.

Aquinas

Where Augustine had been influenced by Platonism and incorporated many Platonic and Neo-Platonic ideas into his Christian theology, Aquinas(1225-1274) was influenced by, and incorporated the ideas and methods of Aristotle (referring to him simply as *the philosopher*) into his theology. Augustine's work was so important that he shaped the thinking of virtually all theologians who came after him. In addition to being influenced by Aristotle, Aquinas was also influenced by Augustine, who was one of the sources for the development of Aquinas' *metaethics*,[6] that is, his method of thinking about and discussing moral issues. One's paradigm for moral thinking, including the language used to discuss moral issues, is not ethics *per se*; it is *metaethics*. Aquinas' metaethics was shaped (to a degree) by Augustine.

"St. Thomas Aquinas"

Even though Augustine's influence can be detected in the work of Aquinas, his major philosophical influence was Aristotle. How did Aristotle become such a major influence in the Middle Ages? Over the centuries, after the fall of Rome, the language of the educated changed from Greek to Latin. In the process, many of the Classical Greek texts became unusable – many Latin-speaking scholars could not read Greek. Also, copying manuscripts was time-consuming, labor-intensive work, and there were not many copies of Aristotle's work available. Consequently, Medieval scholars did not have access to the great works of philosophy that had been produced in Athens 1,500 years earlier. Among the material that was not available were the writings of Aristotle. For all intents and purposes his

---

[6]   Floyd, "Thomas Aquinas: Moral Philosophy," in *Internet Encyclopedia of Philosophy*.

work was lost. It was not until the 12th and 13th centuries that scholars, beginning with Islamic scholars who had the necessary linguistic skills, "rediscovered" Aristotle and were able to translate his works into Latin, making them available to scholars such as Aquinas.[7]

Aquinas' moral philosophy is based in part on Aristotle's ethical approach in that it is based on two foundational Aristotelian concepts: that humans are rational beings, and that they seek happiness (a *eudaimonistic* kind of happiness) as their goal in life. Aristotle had incorporated these two fundamental features of humanness (as he recognized them) into his ethical framework. Since humans are rational beings, their happiness (true contentment) must be rooted in and grow out of the rational rather than the sensual. For Aristotle, the virtues one incorporates into his or her life must be, (as Haldane has expressed it) "those habits of action which are conducive to the fulfillment of an agent's rational nature."[8] For Aristotle this meant *theoia*, a contemplation (as in philosophical contemplation) of the highest objects, of metaphysical things, of the Unmoved Mover, that he referred to as God.[9]

So, too, for Aquinas, since human beings are rational beings, the happiness, fulfillment, and contentment they seek must be sought from or be part of the rational process. But where Aristotle had concluded that the presence of the virtues, which allow one to live an *arête* kind of a life and results in *eudaimonia*, Aquinas believes that true, meaningful happiness can only be enjoyed in knowing and having a relationship with God. God is the source of human existence and human happiness. For Aquinas,

knowledge of God that is both rational and relational (though he may not have used that specific terminology) is the key to human happiness and fulfillment.[10]

How do these concepts provide a foundation for building a functional framework for ethics? It is the will, the rational part of the human that desires fulfillment and contentment as the end or goal of life. Human acts are then good or bad, moral or immoral, as they lend themselves to the achievement of that goal.[11] Human behavior that leads to a rational,

[7]   Rubenstein has written an excellent volume, *Aristotle's Children: How Christians, Muslims and Jews Rediscovered Ancient Wisdom and Illuminated the Dark Ages*, that explains the events that led up to the "rediscovery" of Aristotle.

[8]   Haldane, "Medieval and Renaissance Ethics," in *A Companion to Ethics*, 141.

[9]   Copleston, *A History of Philosophy*, Vol. 2, 398.

[10]   Copleston, 399.

[11]   Copleston, 405.

relational ongoing encounter with God is moral. For Aquinas, behavior that does not lead to such an encounter is not moral.

Does Aquinas identify behaviors that he believes lend themselves to the achievement of the human goal? Yes. Aquinas identifies four cardinal virtues: *prudence, justice, temperance* and *courage*.[12] First, by *prudence* Aquinas means an intellectual aptitude (a thoughtful process) that allows one to analyze situations and circumstances and make good choices regarding the kinds of activities or behaviors in any given situation that will bring one closer to the goal of contentment. Prudence does not establish the goal, but helps one attain it.[13]

Second, by *justice* Aquinas means that quality of character that allows one to extend to others that which he or she deserves. But the concept is not only one of personal justice but of legal or communal justice as well. The idea Aquinas has in mind is that the individual, as part of a community, makes choices and acts in ways that affect not only him or herself, but by extension the entire community. And what the community does as a whole impacts each individual of the community. Justice, then, must function at both levels: personal and communal. It must flow in both directions: from one individual to another and from the community as a whole to each individual. As individual interaction must be just, so communal laws (behavior) must be just.[14]

Third, by *temperance* Aquinas means moderated behavior. The word is most often used in relation to the physical pleasures of food, drink, and sex. The temperate person enjoys physical pleasures, but moderates them. The temperate person is a self-controlled, disciplined person who controls his appetites rather than allowing them to control him. Desire itself does not need to be eradicated or even minimized; it simply needs to be controlled. Indulgence needs to be moderated. But the idea of temperance is not limited to physical desires. The temperate person manifests that trait in all areas of his life,  and because he is temperate will also exhibit traits such as meekness, tolerance, forgiveness, and studiousness.[15] The temperate person will also respond proportionately in all situations. When anger is the proper response in a given situation the temperate person is not too angry, giving vent to an angry rant or display, but is

12   Aquinas, *Summa of the Summa*, 462.
13   Floyd, "Thomas Aquinas: Moral Philosophy," *Internet Encyclopedia of Philosophy*.
14   Ibid.
15   Ibid.

appropriately angry – anger held in check, controlled. The same would be true for other emotional responses. The temperate person moderates his or her responses.

Fourth, by *courage* Aquinas means that quality of character that guides us in coping with the challenges involved in avoiding the undesirable and attaining the desirable when doing so (in either case) is unpleasant, difficult, or even dangerous. Courage both motivates and moderates us in how we proceed. It spurs us on in the face of fears, so that we do not give in to fear, but restrains us so that we do not run with reckless abandon into that which could result in hurt or harm. Agreeing with Aristotle, Aquinas sees courage as the mean between cowardice and foolhardiness. Courage does not exist in isolation as a singular[16] but has a number of related (subsidiary) traits that are associated with it: endurance, confidence, patience and perseverance. The courageous person endures what must be endured in the pursuit of his goal. He is confident (though not foolishly overconfident) is his ability to achieve his aim. The courageous person is patient with circumstance and people encountered in the process of his quest. And the courageous person perseveres in the face of obstacles, hardships, setbacks, and challenges.

For Aquinas as for Aristotle, the fundamental question in moral philosophy was "What kind of a person ought one to be?" The unspoken assumption, I believe, was that one who is the person he or she ought to be will do (or will be more likely to do) the right thing in any given circumstance.

Summary

From the time of Socrates and Plato, and probably before, the Greek assumption was that the goal of life is and ought to be *eudaimonia*, that is, happiness – in the sense of fulfillment, contentment. To achieve this kind of happiness one needed to be a certain kind of a person, an *arête* or excellent kind of a person. This required (or was gauged by) the presence of certain character traits in one's life. Because Augustine's moral thinking was shaped not only by Jesus and the larger Judeo-Christian tradition, but also by Platonic and Neo-Platonic thinking, he accepted and worked out of this same basic

[16] Each of the cardinal traits has other traits associated with it that help make it the cardinal trait it is.

premise. The foundation that underlay his moral philosophy was *eudaimonistic*. However, it differed from Socratic and Platonic *eudaimonism* in that Augustine believed that true happiness could only be found in knowing God. This was one of Augustine's foundational premises. Another was the role of free will in the process. Happiness comes as the result of making a choice to seek out God, and to distinguish between and choose good over evil. How can people know what the good is? What will help guide them in the ethical process of deciding and choosing? Love for God. For Augustine, standing firmly on the platform built by Jesus, the love for God is the most important thing there is. If one loves God and enjoys a relationship with him he will have insight into what is right and good. For Augustine, loving God helps one live well.

Aquinas, too, based his moral philosophy on the *eudaimonism* of the ancient Greeks, continuing to focus attention on the kind of person one ought to be. Happiness was the goal. How does one attain it? Aquinas was shaped in his thinking by Augustine and believed that one must know God to be truly happy. But Aquinas also had a deep appreciation for Aristotle (referring to him simply as *the philosopher*) and accepted many of Aristotle's assumptions, perspectives and ideas. Aquinas, like Aristotle, focused on the role of reason in the quest for *eudaimonia*. How does human reason function in Aquinas' ethical framework? It is the will, the rational part of the human that desires fulfillment and contentment as the end or goal of life. Human acts are then good or bad, moral or immoral, as they lend themselves to the achievement of that goal. Human behavior that leads to a rational, relational ongoing encounter with God is moral. Behavior that does not lead to such an encounter is not moral.

Aquinas' approach to ethics was so Aristotelian in nature that he included a list of cardinal virtues (similar to Aristotle's) that aided one in achieving *eudaimonia*. Aquinas' list included: prudence, temperance, justice and courage. Aquinas considered these to be the traits that characterized the life of a person who loved God and approached the living of life from a rational point of view.

It appears that both Augustine and Aquinas offer perspectives that remain viable for contemporary moral philosophy.

Thought and Discussion Questions

1. Explain how Augustine's moral philosophy was similar to, but different from, the moral philosophy of Socrates and Plato.

2. Explain how Aquinas' moral philosophy was similar to, but different from, the moral philosophy of Socrates and Plato.

3. Explain how the moral philosophy of Augustine and Aquinas was specifically rooted in the ethical teachings of Jesus.

4. Discuss the strengths and weaknesses of the integration of Judeo-Christian and Classical Greek moral philosophy.

5. Discuss Aquinas' four cardinal virtues from your own perspective of what virtues are required to live a *eudaimonia* kind of life.

Chapter 6
Social Contract Ethics

Introduction

Social Contract Theory, also known as Contractarianism, is a form of moral and political theorizing rooted in the idea that moral and political obligations exist because people enter into a contract (figuratively speaking), tacitly agreeing that it is in their best interest to relinquish some of their natural rights, cooperating together (which includes embracing morality), in order to gain the benefits (peace, security and so forth) that go along with an interdependent social structure. The concept, though ancient, became popular near the beginning of the modern period in the writing of Thomas Hobbes, with John Locke and Jean-Jacques Rousseau also addressing moral and political issues from the perspective of a Social Contract. Though Social Contract Theory has to do with both political as well as moral philosophy, we will restrict our discussion to morality as it relates to Social Contract Theory.

Social Contract Theory in Antiquity

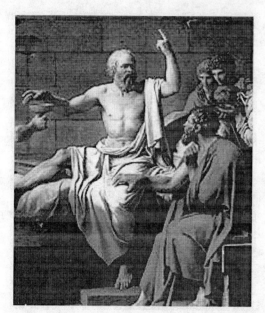

One example of something close to a social contract theory of morality in ancient philosophy is found in the Socratic dialog *Crito*. In that story, Socrates' friends attempt to talk him into escaping from prison and living in exile rather than submit to execution. Socrates responds that he cannot. When his friends ask for an explanation Socrates explains that it is the laws of Athens that have allowed him to live and thrive and be who and what he is. His parents married, gave birth to him, raised and educated him as part of the community of Athens. The laws of Athens guided, protected and made those things possible. When he was grown he was free to take his property and leave if he wanted to. But he chose to stay. Doing so resulted in a tacit agreement to accept and live by the laws of Athens. He had been a willing party to that agreement all his life. He had benefited by being part of the society. Thus, now that the society had convicted him of a crime and determined execution was the appropriate punishment (even though Socrates knew the charges, and thus the conviction, to be without merit), it was not right for him to break the agreement (though it had only been an implicit one) and flee, even if doing so was in his best interest.[1]

---

[1]   Friend notes that there is an apparent conflict between this seeming embracing of a social contract and a rejection of it in book 2 of Republic – "Social Contract Theory," in *Internet Encyclopedia of Philosophy*.

"Socratic Citizenship: Plato's Crito"

While Socrates' explanation is certainly not a formal articulation of Social Contract Theory it captures the spirit of one and provides an example of how one who has entered into a social contract ought to reason and behave.

Perhaps a better example is Protagoras, who according to Guthrie, became the first "promulgator of that theory of the origin of law which we now know as the social contract."[2] In describing Protagoras' view Guthrie explains:

> He said that for their own protection from wild creatures and for the advancement of their standard of living men had at an early stage been obliged to band themselves together into communities. Hitherto they had had neither moral standards nor laws, but life in societies was found to be impossible if the standards of the jungle prevailed, and so, by slow and painful degrees, they learned the necessity of laws and conventions whereby the stronger pledge themselves not to attack and rob the weak simply because they are the stronger.[3]

Thus, the idea of a social agreement that provides benefits while determining one's behavior may be as ancient as philosophy itself. Yet it is in the modern era, in the writing of Thomas Hobbes[4] that the theory is fully articulated and defended.

Thomas Hobbes

Thomas Hobbes (1588-1679) is considered one of the most significant political philosophers of the early modern period. He is also considered an influential moral philosopher. His moral and political theories cannot be separated from his materialist assumptions about the cosmos. For Hobbes, the cosmos is nothing but matter in motion, that is, the only thing that exists is physical matter.[5] There is no immaterial aspect to the cosmos. Humans, as part of the material cosmos are entirely physical in nature. Hobbes' political and moral theories were also impacted by the socio-political

---

2   Guthrie, *The Greek Philosophers from Thales to Aristotle*, 70.
3   Ibid.
4   It may be the case that, as brilliant as Hobbes was, he borrowed "his" social contract theory from ancient sources.
5   It is important to understand that Hobbes' embracing of a materialist or physicalist paradigm was purely arbitrary. There was (and is) no evidence that suggested that only physical matter exists. The embracing of a physicalist paradigm allowed the intellectual elite to ignore metaphysical concerns and focus only on the empirical. Many thinkers after Hobbes followed his lead, embracing a physicalist paradigm, thus removing God from the equation. Physicalism became the accepted paradigm for scientific research.

context in which he lived – a time of intrigue and unrest.[6] The political and moral philosophy he espouses in his book, *Leviathan* (published 1651), represent his attempt to address the challenges of his day and justify the positions he advocates.

"Thomas Hobbes"

Hobbes laid a foundation for describing what society ought to be by describing what, according to him, it had been. His position was that before there were interdependent societies of people who lived in peace, people lived in what he called a *state of nature*, where each was at war with all others, competing ruthlessly for what resources there were. The following are excerpts from *Leviathan*.

Nature hath made men so equal in the faculties of body and mind as that, though there be found one man sometimes manifestly stronger in body or of quicker mind than another, yet when all is reckoned together the difference between man and man is not so considerable as that one man can thereupon claim to himself any benefit to which another may not pretend as well as he. For as to the strength of body, the weakest has strength enough to kill the strongest, either by secret machination or by confederacy with others that are in the same danger with himself…

From this equality of ability ariseth equality of hope in the attaining of our ends. And therefore if any two men desire the same thing, which nevertheless they cannot both enjoy, they become enemies; and in the way to their end (which is principally their own conservation, and sometimes their delectation only) endeavour to destroy or subdue one another. And from hence it comes to pass that where an invader hath no more to fear than another man's single power, if one plant, sow, build, or possess a convenient seat, others may probably be expected to come prepared with forces united to dispossess and deprive him, not only of the fruit of his labour, but also of his life or liberty. And the invader again is in the like danger of another …

So that in the nature of man, we find three principal causes of quarrel. First, competition; secondly, diffidence; thirdly, glory.

The first maketh men invade for gain; the second, for safety; and the third, for reputation. The first use violence, to make themselves masters of other men's persons, wives, children, and cattle; the second, to defend them; the third, for trifles, as a word, a smile, a different opinion,

---

[6]   Friend, "Social Contract Theory," in *Internet Encyclopedia of Philosophy*.

and any other sign of undervalue, either direct in their persons or by reflection in their kindred, their friends, their nation, their profession, or their name.

Hereby it is manifest that during the time men live without a common power to keep them all in awe, they are in that condition which is called war; and such a war as is of every man against every man. For war consisteth not in battle only, or the act of fighting, but in a tract of time, wherein the will to contend by battle is sufficiently known: and therefore the notion of time is to be considered in the nature of war, as it is in the nature of weather. For as the nature of foul weather lieth not in a shower or two of rain, but in an inclination thereto of many days together: so the nature of war consisteth not in actual fighting, but in the known disposition thereto during all the time there is no assurance to the contrary. All other time is peace …

Whatsoever therefore is consequent to a time of war, where every man is enemy to every man, the same consequent to the time wherein men live without other security than what their own strength and their own invention shall furnish them withal. In such condition there is no place for industry, because the fruit thereof is uncertain: and consequently no culture of the earth; no navigation, nor use of the commodities that may be imported by sea; no commodious building; no instruments of moving and removing such things as require much force; no knowledge of the face of the earth; no account of time; no arts; no letters; no society; and which is worst of all, continual fear, and danger of violent death; and the life of man, solitary, poor, nasty, brutish, and short …

Let him therefore consider with himself: when taking a journey, he arms himself and seeks to go well accompanied; when going to sleep, he locks his doors; when even in his house he locks his chests; and this when he knows there be laws and public officers, armed, to revenge all injuries shall be done him; what opinion he has of his fellow subjects, when he rides armed; of his fellow citizens, when he locks his doors; and of his children, and servants, when he locks his chests. Does he not there as much accuse mankind by his actions as I do by my words?...

It may peradventure be thought there was never such a time nor condition of war as this; and I believe it was never generally so, over all the world: but there are many places where they live so now. For the savage people in many places of America, except the government of small families, the concord whereof dependeth on natural lust, have no government at all, and live at this day in that brutish manner, as I said before. Howsoever, it may be perceived what manner of life there would be, where there were no common power to fear, by the manner of life which men that have formerly lived under a peaceful government use to degenerate into a civil war …

To this war of every man against every man, this also is consequent; that nothing can be unjust. The notions of right and wrong, justice and injustice, have there no place. Where there is no common power, there is no law; where no law, no injustice. Force and fraud are in war the two cardinal virtues. Justice and injustice are none of the faculties neither of the body nor mind. If they were, they might be in a man that were alone in the world, as well as his senses and passions. They are qualities that relate to men in society, not in solitude. It is consequent also to the same condition that there be no propriety, no dominion, no mine and thine distinct; but only that to be every man's that he can get, and for so long as he can keep it. And thus much for the ill condition which man by mere nature is actually placed in; though with a possibility to come out of it, consisting partly in the passions, partly in his reason.

The passions that incline men to peace are: fear of death; desire of such things as are necessary to commodious living; and a hope by their industry to obtain them. And reason suggesteth convenient articles of peace upon which men may be drawn to agreement.[7]

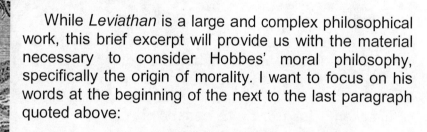

While *Leviathan* is a large and complex philosophical work, this brief excerpt will provide us with the material necessary to consider Hobbes' moral philosophy, specifically the origin of morality. I want to focus on his words at the beginning of the next to the last paragraph quoted above:

To this war of every man against every man, this also is consequent; that nothing can be unjust. The notions of right and wrong, justice and injustice, have there no place. Where there is no common power, there is no law; where no law, no injustice. Force and fraud are in war the two cardinal virtues. Justice and injustice are none of the faculties neither of the body nor mind.

Hobbesian Social Contract Theory

Notice what he says. Nothing can be unjust. There are no notions of right and wrong. There is no law. The concepts of justice and injustice are not in the mind. What does he mean? I believe Hobbes is suggesting that in this state of nature humans are neither moral nor immoral but amoral. They are not moral beings, but are amoral, like animals. No one discusses the morality (or immorality) of a lion killing and eating a gazelle, for such an action on the part of a lion is neither moral nor immoral for a lion is not a moral creature. The lion is amoral and so are its actions. But Hobbes seems to be saying that humans were at one time amoral. He went so far as to suggest that people living in America in the mid 1600s were living in that amoral state of nature!

---

[7] Hobbes, *Leviathan*, Of Man, XIII

How, then, does Hobbes propose that amoral people became moral people? His idea is that people, using their rational capacity, realized that life would be better (safer and more satisfying) if they could live together, get along, trust and help each other. In short, if they could somehow become interdependent moral people life would be better. So enabled by their rational capacities, amoral people became moral people because they realized that being moral was better (more advantageous) than being amoral.

If someone argued that Hobbes is not suggesting that people were amoral, as animals are amoral, but were in fact moral (had a moral core) even if they were not acting morally, I would wonder how one could arrive at that conclusion. Given Hobbes' view of human nature, how could humans be moral? If humans are simply a  mechanistic feature of a mechanistic cosmos, how is it that they are any different, morally speaking, than any other animal? As Hobbes makes his argument, morality was not a part of human nature in the state of nature. Hobbes described a state where nothing can be unjust. There were no notions of right and wrong. There was no law. The concepts of justice and injustice did not exist – not only did they not exist in the human population, Hobbes says they did not exist in the in the human mind. Hobbes is clearly not describing moral beings who are behaving immorally, but is describing amoral beings. Then, after hundreds of thousands of years of amorality it begins to dawn on people that living morally would be more advantageous than continuing with their amoral approach. Morality, as Hobbes describes the process, is a product of rationality. Rationality exists and morality is eventually produced by it.[8]

"Thomas Hobbes Leviathan, Social Contract Theory 1/2"
"Thomas Hobbes Leviathan, Social Contract Theory 2/2"

---

[8]   It is also clear that Hobbes' sees the motivation for the development of morality as psychological egoism (that people do what is in their own best interest) and ethical egoism (that what is morally right is that which is in one's own interest regardless of the interests of others).

Did Humans Invent Morality

For those working out of a materialist (or physicalist) paradigm the answer to the question, "Did humans invent morality?" must be yes. If humans, as Hobbes believed, are simply more highly evolved animals, how would one account for the presence of morality in human animals when it is not present in non-human animals? The only way one can account for it is the way Hobbes has: morality developed in the human population because rational human minds realized that it was to their advantage to be moral rather than amoral. But is this a satisfying answer? I think not.

Morality did not evolve as a product of rationality; morality goes hand-in-hand with rationality[9] and self-determination (freedom of choice). Aristotle identified man (humans) as the rational animal. He believed that rationality is what made humans different from non-rational animals. He could just as easily have said that man is the moral animal.

Because humans are rational, they are also self-determined and responsible for the moral choices they make. Humans make moral choices. They do so because they are rational, self-determined beings. They do so because they are more than very smart animals. Animals make choices but they do not make moral choices. They do not contemplate morality; they do not ask, what is right, what is good, what is just? But humans do. Why? Because we are moral beings. Asking such questions is part of 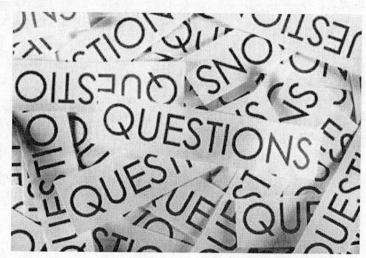 what it is to be human. Unless there has been a malfunction and something has gone very wrong on the inside, humans think about and behave as moral beings. What Hobbes describes as human behavior in the state of nature (no notions of right and wrong, no law, no concepts of justice or injustice in the mind) is not human behavior, but the behavior of non-human animals. Hobbes is mistaken about morality being the product of rationality. Rationality, self-determination and morality are inseparable

[9] When I use the term rationality here I am including in it the idea that humans enjoy what I have referred to as second-level self-awareness (Rogers, *Proof of God*, 165-166). Many animals are self-aware. They are aware of their separate identity. But human second-level awareness is a higher level of awareness that allows us to contemplate our unique individual existence. Not only am I aware that I am me, but I can contemplate what that means; I can consider who and what I am; I can reflect on how I can shape my existence by the choices I make. I can contemplate how my rationality, my second-level awareness and my self-determination make me a moral being not merely a thinking creature. It is this unique nature, this rational self-determination that makes us moral beings, that makes humans human and not merely smarter animals.

(interlocking, interdependent) features of human nature. Morality exists wherever humans exist.

Humans did not invent morality. Humans are moral beings. Sometimes we act in immoral ways, but we are not amoral creatures. We are moral beings. Hobbes is mistaken regarding the origin of morality.

The Hobbesian Basis for Morality

It is clear from Hobbes' writing that the basis for morality as he understood its function in society is what is known as *ethical egoism*.[10] It has long been recognized that people often (perhaps mostly) act in their own interest. We tend to do what we want and what we think will make us happy or what we believe will be best for us. This acting in our own interest is known as *psychological egoism*. This is how we act. Ethical egoism differs from psychological egoism in that ethical egoism suggests that people *ought* to act in their own best interest, that the moral thing to do is to put oneself ahead of all others to secure one's own interests. In Hobbes' view, the basis (motivation) for forming and participating in a social collective is so one can get

what he needs or wants. The idea is that I want to live without having to fear being attacked, robbed, or otherwise deprived of the resources I need to survive and thrive. So I will agree not to attack, rob, or otherwise deprive others of what they want so that they, in turn, will not attack, rob and deprive me. The motive for "moral" behavior in Hobbes' view is entirely one of self-interest. (The reader may need to re-read the excerpts from Hobbes again to see this subtle point.) To get what I want I must give others what they want. There is no concern for what is right or just or good. There is no compassion. There is no altruism. There is only self-interest. In Chapter Nine we will study ethical egoism in more detail. For now, however, the point is simply to establish that Hobbes' moral system is built on the foundation of ethical egoism.

Contemporary Contractarianism

The idea of a social contract remains appealing in political philosophy and in some circles continues to be popular as a framework for moral philosophy. Contemporary contractarianism, as it is called, generally takes two forms, Hobbesian and Kantian contractarianism. The differences between the two approaches are significant.

---

[10] Murphy, "Hobbes's Social Contract Theory," in *Conduct and Character*, 190.

"Hobbesian Contractarianism"

Kymlicka asks, "What are we to make of Hobbesian contractarianism as a moral theory? It does not fit our everyday understanding of morality."[11] Why would he say that? Because of the basis for "morality" as Hobbes proposed it. Kymlicka explains:

> Whenever we try to find objective moral values [in Hobbesian contractarianism] what we find instead are the subjective preferences of individuals. So there is nothing inherently right or wrong about the goals one chooses to pursue, or the means by which one pursues those goals – even if this involves harming others. However, while there is nothing inherently wrong in harming you, I would be better off by refraining from doing so if every person refrains from harming me. Such a convention against injury is mutually advantageous – we do not have to waste resources defending our own person and property, and it enables us to enter into stable co-operation. While injury is not inherently wrong, each person gains by accepting conventions that define it as 'wrong' … Hobbesian contractarianism does not view individuals as having any inherent moral rights or status.[12]

Clearly, for Kymlicka (and for many others, myself included) Hobbesian contractarianism does not provide a satisfactory framework for moral thinking and acting. In his article entitled, *Can Contract Theory Ground Morality*, Pettit lists a number of things that would be involved in either a complete or a partial theory of right – that is, things one would expect to be included in a satisfactory moral theory. If something is going to be called "right," as in the right thing to do, Pettit argues, it ought to be: 1) something desirous (a desired action) in response to failures of will, that is, when someone has not behaved as they would have liked, 2) something we would suggest that others do, not just something we ourselves would do, 3) something we believe will generate additional good results, such as kindness, fairness, or justice, 4) something that a good virtuous person would choose to exercise, and 5) something that we could justify to others if objections were raised.[13]

Pettit's contention is sound: if a moral theory, a framework for moral thinking and acting, is going to be useful, it must at least help us identify what kinds of things are considered right and therefore good. If it does not do that, it is not very helpful. It seems apparent that Hobbes' theory does not provide us with the minimal features of a functional moral theory.

---

[11] Kymlicka, "The Social Contract Tradition," in *A Companion to Ethics*, 190.
[12] Kymlicka, 189.
[13] Pettit, "Can Contract Theory Ground Morality," in *Conduct and Character*, 225-226.

"Kantian Contractarianism"

Kant (1724-1804) did his work in ethics long after Hobbes (1588-1679). And though Kant did not propose a formal social contract theory of morality, his approach to morality has been adapted by proponents of contractarianism to create an ethical framework known as Kantian contractarianism. In Kant's view, human beings have an inherent moral standing. Humans are moral beings with an inherent worth that requires that they be treated appropriately. One articulation of Kant's categorical imperative is that a person ought not be treated as a means to another person's end, but must be treated as an end in himself or herself, valued and treated impartially and equally simply because he or she is a person.

"Kant's Categorical Imperative"

Contemporary contractarians have taken this basic Kantian idea and applied it in a contractarian framework. From this point of view, people in a given social contract context treat each other morally not because it is personally advantageous, as in Hobbesian contractarianism, but because it is the right thing to do (in the sense of the right thing to do being a real objective moral right thing to do). In evaluating Kantian contractarianism, Kymlicka observes that it will be "attractive to those people who endorse the underlying notions of moral equality and justice."[14] Kymlicka may be correct. More to the point perhaps is the idea that Kantian contractarianism is different from Hobbesian contractarianism in that the Kantian version of it is not rooted in psychological or ethical egoism. For Kant, objective right and wrong exist and our interaction with others is based on more than what is best for us.

Because Hobbesian contractarianism operates out of a physicalist paradigm, believing that humans are merely advanced animals who invented morality to serve their own purposes, and because it is rooted in self-serving Ethical Egoism, it appears to have little to offer as a viable paradigm for contemporary moral thinking and acting.

---

[14] Kymlicka, "The Social Contract Tradition," in *A Companion to Ethics*, 192.

Summary

Thomas Hobbes was a brilliant man and made an enormous contribution to political theory. He suggested that humans began living in social groups because it was advantageous for them to do so. Interdependence, though it requires each person to relinquish some of his freedoms, yields rewards and benefits that offset the sacrifices involved. While there is much about Hobbes' contract theory that we did not discuss, we did consider the moral implications of his theory. As a framework for meaningful moral philosophy, for ethical thinking and acting, it leaves a lot to be desired. It assumes that people were at one time rational but not moral, that humans were amoral. It also assumes that morality is the product of rationality. It is rooted in  the idea that people practice psychological egoism (which is true much of the time) and that it is appropriate, therefore, for morality to be based on or rooted in ethical egoism. As a moral theory, Hobbesian contractarianism seems to be insufficient and unsatisfying.

Thought and Discussion Questions

1. Discuss Hobbes' view of humans living in what he calls the *state of nature* and discuss the likelihood of this being an actual historical reality.

2. Evaluate Rogers' arguments that humans could not have been amoral and then have decided to become moral – the idea that morality is a human invention.

3. Discuss the differences (based on your present understanding) between psychological egoism (as something people do) and ethical egoism (as something people ought to do).

4. Discuss the differences between contemporary Hobbesian contractarianism and Kantian contractarianism.

5. Explain why many ethicists feel that Hobbesian contractarianism is not a satisfying moral theory.

Chapter 7
Kantian Ethics

Introduction

Immanuel Kant was born in Königsberg, East Prussia in 1724. He was raised in a Christian family (German Pietists) and held a firm belief in God and morality. Kant was very interested in morality, so much so that as Schneewind observes:

> Kant invented a new way of understanding morality and ourselves as moral agents. The originality and profundity of his moral philosophy have long been recognized. It was widely discussed during his own lifetime, and there has been an almost continuous stream of explanation and criticism of it ever since. Its importance has not diminished with time.[1]

Kant wrote several books that either included material on morality or were dedicated to the topic: *Critique of Practical Reason, The Metaphysics of Morals, Anthropology from a Pragmatic Point of View,* and *Religion within the Boundaries of Mere Reason.* Perhaps his best-known material on morality is one of his earlier works entitled: *Groundwork of the Metaphysics of Morals* (published 1785). It is his thinking in this work that we will be concerned with in this chapter.

"Immanuel Kant"

Kant believed that "moral philosophy should say something about the ultimate end of human endeavor, the Highest Good, and its relationship to the moral life."[2] To have something meaningful to say about the highest good and its relationship to living a moral life, Kant knew the first step had to be to establish or provide a means for determining what is and what is not moral. In his preface to the *Groundwork*, he said: "The sole aim of this present Groundwork is to seek out and establish

---

[1]   Schneewind, "Autonomy, obligation and virtue: An overview of Kant's moral philosophy," in *The Cambridge Companion to Kant,* 309.
[2]   Johnson, "Kant's Moral Philosophy," in *Stanford Encyclopedia of Philosophy.*

the supreme principle of morality."[3] In other words, how do we decide what is the moral thing to do in any given situation?[4]

Kant wanted to provide a framework for moral thinking and acting. He did so by approaching the subject differently than the moral philosophers who preceded him. "At the center of Kant's ethical theory is the claim that normal adults are capable of being fully self-governing in moral matters."[5] Such a thing is possible only because humans are rational, autonomous, moral beings. Sullivan observes that:

> According to Kant, the most important single moral fact about us is that we possess autonomy; we have the ability to make our own decisions and to live by them rather than being totally subject to determination by the laws of natural causality like other kinds of agents in the world.[6]

Of course, if Kant is going to claim that humans are capable of moral self-governance he is also obliged to explain how such self-governance could be accomplished. That is his purpose in *Groundwork*.

The Only Thing that is Intrinsically Good

Kant's opening sentence of Chapter One of *Groundwork* is: "It is impossible to conceive anything at all in the world, or even out of it, which can be taken as good without qualification, except a *good will*."[7] What did he mean? What is a good will? For Kant, a good will is one's desire to do the right thing. The human will is that aspect of our nature with which we determine our actions. To *will* a thing is to decide it, to want to bring it about. I can *will* that I should respond with respect and courtesy each time I encounter another person. I can *will* that I keep each promise  that I make. Kant is making the bold claim that the only thing that is good in and of itself, the only thing that is intrinsically good, is a good will – a *will* that *wills* one to do the right thing. A person with a good will is a person who wants, in each case, to do the right thing, the moral thing.

---

3   Kant, *Groundwork of the Metaphysics of Morals,* 392, xiii.

4   By the time Kant contemplates moral philosophy, the ancient focus on the kind of person one ought to be has evolved into an analysis of the nature of morality and how to determine appropriate moral behavior. The basic question has shifted from *what kind of a person ought I to be* to *what is the right thing to do*?

5   Schneewind, "Autonomy, obligation and virtue: An overview of Kant's moral philosophy," 309.

6   Sullivan, *An Introduction to Kant's Ethics,* 154.

7   Kant, *Groundwork,* 1: 393, 1.

Kant is not saying that the only thing that is good is a good will. He knows that are many things that are good. He goes on in his opening paragraph to say, "Intelligence, wit, judgment and any other talents of the mind we may care to name, or courage, resolution, and constancy of purpose, as qualities of temperament, are without doubt good and desirable in many respects." He goes on to explain, however, that they can be bad and hurtful. Any of those kinds of things can also be used badly. Thieves might be intelligent and courageous. But their intelligence and courage, if used for immoral purposes become bad things. Thus those "contingently" good things (things that can be good or bad depending on how they are used) cannot be intrinsically good. Only a good will is intrinsically good.

Kant also points out that the good of a good will is not dependent upon consequences in any way. If one wills (intends) to do good, it is good (because it is the product of a good will) even if the results are less than desirable. In Kant's view, one may will to always tell the truth. In the process of being a truth-teller, however, one may tell a truth that results in something very bad happening to someone else. For Kant, that bad outcome is irrelevant. The will to be a truth-teller and the subsequent actual truth-telling cannot be diminished by negative consequences.

For Kant, a good will is good all the time and is good in and of itself. It is intrinsically good.

A Good Will and the Will to do One's Duty

Another of Kant's foundational ideas in his quest for *the supreme principle of morality* (in addition to having a good will) is that one does what one does because it is one's *duty* to do so. Duty is such an integral part of Kantian moral philosophy that his framework for moral philosophy is often referred to as *Deontological Ethics*. The Greek word for duty is *deon*. Thus, deontological ethics has to do with seeing or emphasizing the relationship between morality and the doing of one's duty. Morally speaking, to do the right thing is always one's duty, regardless of the circumstances. But what, exactly, does Kant mean by duty? He means doing the right thing simply because it is the right thing to do, not because one benefits in some way by doing the right thing. He uses the example of a grocery store owner to clarify his meaning.

It certainly accords with duty that a grocer should not overcharge his inexperienced customer; and where there is much competition a sensible shopkeeper refrains from doing so and keeps to a fixed and general price for everybody so that a child can buy from him just as well as anyone else. Thus people are served *honestly*; but this is not nearly enough to justify us in believing that the shopkeeper has acted in this way from duty or from principles of fair dealing; his interests required him to do so.[8]

Kant explains that the shopkeeper who deals honestly with his customers may look like one who is doing his duty. But this may not the case. Duty, as Kant explains it, requires a response that is not based on any kind of self-interest. If one's actions are to qualify as dutiful there can be no benefit that results from the action. One can run an honest business out of duty or out of self-interest. Kant's point is that an observation of honesty does not equal an observation of dutiful morality because one may be acting entirely out of self-interested motives.

"Duty as One's Only Motive"

Morality and motive, then, are linked in a crucial way. Why one does what one does determines whether or not one has acted in a moral manner. Suppose, for example, person X returns a lost wallet (with a good amount of cash in it) simply because that is the right thing to do (duty), while person Y returns the wallet out of self-interest, hoping for a reward. According to Kant, person X acted morally while person Y did not. Person Y did a right thing, a good thing, but his actions were not moral because his motive was not one of duty but of self-interest. So for Kant, an action can be socially appropriate and acceptable but not necessarily moral because morality depends on motive. Clearly, Kant is setting a very high standard of morality.

"Justice: What's The Right Thing to Do?"

As morality and motive are crucially linked, so are morality and freewill. Kant was a scientist who enthusiastically embraced the idea of a Newtonian mechanistic cosmos. The problem with embracing that paradigm is that it does not appear to leave room for freedom of choice. The parts of a mechanism do not choose what to do, they do what they are designed to do. If humans are part of a mechanistic cosmos, how can they have free will? Kant believed that human autonomy stood apart from the mechanistic nature of the material

---

[8]   Kant, *Groundwork*, 1: 397,9.

cosmos.[9] Humans, as thinking beings are dualistic in nature. We are embodied minds. The material body may be part of the mechanistic cosmos, but the immaterial mind (the will) is not. Since it is not material in nature it is not subject to mechanistic determinations. The mind is free to choose. Humans have freewill.[10] For Kant, this is an essential feature of human morality. There can be no morality or immorality without freewill. To be moral or immoral we must be free to choose.

What is it, then, that connects all of these threads: intention, motive, and freewill? It is rationality. Where animals are guided by instinct (even "thinking" animals) humans are guided by rationality. The human being is a rational-moral being. Rationality and morality co-exist and are interdependent. If the only thing that is intrinsically good (intrinsically moral) is a good will (the determination to do what is right simply because it is the right thing to do), then goodness or morality exists in relation to what we rationally *will* (determine) to do. For Kant, rationality and morality co-exist. Where you find one you find the other, and where you do not find both you do not find either. So when Kant says *the only thing that is itself good is a good will,* he is saying a lot.

Determining What is Moral

Kant has laid a foundation to build on. He has said that a good will is the only intrinsic good. He has linked morality and motive and he believes that rational, autonomous (self-determined) beings are capable of determining moral standards.[11] But how do they do so? What does Kant suggest as a framework for moral thinking and acting?

"The Categorical Imperative"

He suggests what he calls the *categorical imperative*. Kant believes that *moral claims* result in *moral imperatives*. What are moral claims and what are moral imperatives? A moral claim is a moral statement. You ought to

---

9   O'Neill, "Kantian Ethics," in A Companion to Ethics, 176.

10   This is my own Cartesian explanation of human nature as it applies to the issue of freewill. And while I am not suggesting that Kant would have explained things in this way, I do believe he held the same basic opinion – that the human will (the mind) is autonomous, that it is free to choose (self-determined) and not subject to mechanistic determinations.

11   I would enjoy (if it was possible) visiting with Dr. Kant about the idea of the rational autonomous humans *discovering* morality instead of *determining* it. I would to think he would be open to the idea.

do this or that, or you ought not do this or that. The statement, *murder is wrong*, is a moral claim. The statement, *a merchant ought to run an honest business*, is a moral claim.[12] Moral claims contain an implicit imperative, that is, a specific statement about what one ought or ought not do. These implicit imperatives can, and must become explicit. They must be articulated utilizing what Kant calls a *maxim* and will result in either a *hypothetical* or a *categorical* imperative (which is reflective of *the* Categorical Imperative).

What is a maxim? A maxim has to do with "the intentional aspect of one's will."[13] It is a statement that describes an act one intends to perform. An example of a maxim would be: *Whenever I make a promise, I will keep my promise.* Or another might be: *Whenever I can benefit in some way by lying, I will lie.* A maxim has to do with one's intention, one's goal; Kant would say with one's *end*, meaning the end result one intends to accomplish. The *end* of the maxim, *Whenever I make a promise, I will keep my promise,* is that I will be a promise keeper and not a promise breaker. Notice that maxims do not suggest what should be done but what one intends to do. That raises an important question for Kant: "How does one determine whether or not what one intends to do is moral?" That is where *imperatives* come into play. Kant identifies two kinds of imperatives: *hypothetical* and *categorical*.

An imperative is a command. "Close the door," is an example of an imperative. A *hypothetical imperative* is an imperative that applies to you given your subjective end, your personal intention or goal. For instance, the statement, "If you want to lose weight you must eat healthy food and exercise," is an example of a hypothetical imperative for a person who wants to lose weight. However, it does not apply to everyone. If one does not have the goal of losing weight, the imperative does not apply. Thus, it is hypothetical. It may or may not apply to you, depending on your subjective end or goal.

A *categorical imperative*, however, is one that expresses what ought to be done because it is the right thing to do. A categorical imperative carries with it a moral obligation, obligating everyone, not just those who have corresponding subjective goals. A categorical imperative is a universal law, applying to everyone, all the time. Personal maxims must be weighed against categorical imperatives to determine whether or not the personal maxim is moral.

[12] Glasgow, "Kant's Principle of Universal Law," in *Conduct and Character: Readings in Moral Theory*, 154.

[13] Glasgow, 153.

The Universal Law Formulation of the Categorical Imperative

As Glasgow points out, Kant believed that there was one Categorical Imperative (with a capital C and a capital I) that represented the *supreme principle of morality* he was identifying in *Groundwork*. But he also believed that there were other categorical imperatives (small c and i) that could be derived from *the* Categorical Imperative. Those derivative imperatives are also binding on us regardless of our personal aims or intentions.[14] His main concern, however, in *Groundwork* is to identify, as he called it, the supreme principle of morality – *the* Categorical Imperative.

"Ethics – Kant"

While Kant believed there was only one Categorical Imperative, he believed it could be expressed in more than one way. This has caused significant confusion over the years, since what Kant considers as different expressions of the same idea sound to many (myself included) like completely different imperatives. The issue will become clear as we consider two of Kant's formulations of the Categorical Imperative.

As Paton outlines Kant's material he identifies Kant's first explanation of the Categorical Imperative as the Universal Law Formulation.[15] Kant's first formulation of the Categorical Imperative is: *"Act only on that maxim through which you can at the same time will that it should become a universal law."*[16]

Notice that the Categorical Imperative functions along with one's personal maxims. Utilizing the Categorical Imperative is a process. One begins with one's maxim (whatever it happens to be about) and then asks himself if he can truly say that he would like to see the action he is contemplating become a universal law, an action that all people were required to carry out. For instance, utilizing my maxim above, "Whenever I make a promise I will keep my promise," I must ask myself, am I willing that this maxim become a universal law? Would I want it to be the case, would I want it to be universal law, that everyone would have to keep their promises? I can honestly say yes to that question. I would be happy living in a society of promise-keepers. Kant would say, then, that my maxim is moral and I may proceed in carrying it out. If, however, I consider my other maxim, "Whenever I can benefit in some way by lying, I

14 Glasgow, 156.
15 Paton, 29.
16 Kant, *Groundwork*, 2:421, 52

will lie," would I be comfortable having that maxim become universal law? I would have to say, no. I would not want to live in a society where everyone lied every time they thought it was to their advantage. Kant would say that my maxim regarding lying was not moral and that I should not act on it.

Why would Paton refer to this as the Universal Law formulation of the Categorical Imperative? Because in Kant's view, this basic Categorical Imperative (the supreme principle of morality) amounts to a Universal Law. Every person, every autonomous rational agent, ought to form a maxim for each proposed act or behavior and test it against the Categorical Imperative to know whether or not their maxims are moral. For Kant, this is not a hypothetical that depends on the subjective end one has chosen. It is an obligation the moral law places on every person.

The End in Itself Formulation of the Categorical Imperative

The Universal Law formulation (as Paton calls it) is only one way to express the idea of the Categorical Imperative, the supreme principle of morality. Another way to express it, according to Kant, is: *"Act in such a way that you always treat humanity, whether in your own person or in the person of any other, never simply as a means, but always at the same time as an end."*[17] As noted earlier, this alternative expression of the Categorical Imperative has caused a good deal of concern. Why does Kant think he has said the same basic thing in this second expression of the Categorical Imperative as he did in the first when it sounds to many people like he has said something very different? I've no idea. But somewhere in his massive intellect Kant connected the two expressions so that they generated the same supreme principle of morality – the Categorical Imperative, the Moral Law.

Whether or not we agree with Kant that each expression of the Categorical Imperative says the same thing in different ways, we can accept and appreciate what he intends in this specific formulation (which Paton identifies as The End in Itself Formulation of the Categorical Imperative). It is this: that people have intrinsic moral value and because they do they must be treated accordingly. People, Kant insists, cannot be treated as a means to our own ends, but must be treated as an end in themselves. What does that mean? Suppose that a guy named Bill, a recent retiree, knows an older woman, Betty, who can't drive, has no family nearby, is lonely and is also rich. Suppose Bill befriends and spends time with Betty (even though he does not really care to

17   Kant, *Groundwork*, 2:429, 67.

be around her), doing nice things to ingratiate himself to her, including driving her to the doctor and other important appointments. Suppose also that after a time Bill mentions that his old car is breaking down a lot and is no longer dependable. Suppose that Betty offers to buy Bill, her helpful friend, a new car (since he drives her to so many places). Bill accepts and she writes Bill a check for the amount of the car he wants. What has Bill done? Bill has used Betty as a means to an end – to get a new car.

Kant would say that this was an immoral act because Betty was used as a means to Bill's end rather than being valued as an end in herself. But why is this immoral? Do we not use other people as a means all the time? Yes. When I go to Walmart to shop and go to the checkout line, the clerk scanning my items becomes a means to my end – buying the things I need at Walmart. And I become a means to the clerk's end – having the job of helping customers buy the things they need. I am a means for the clerk and the clerk is a means for me. Why is this wrong? In this scenario it is not wrong. Why not? Because each of us is aware of the situation and freely chooses as an autonomous self-determined person to participate in the process. We each make an informed decision to be involved. But in Betty's case she was not aware that she was merely being used as a means to an end. She assumed Bill's friendship was genuine. It wasn't. It was self-serving. That is why Bill's actions were immoral, according to Kant.

How would one recognize another person as an end in him or herself? By acknowledging each individual's intrinsic moral worth and treating that person accordingly. By respecting his or her right to be informed and aware of all aspects of a situation so that he or she can make an informed decision regarding participation. For instance, if Lori needs $50 and she knows that Ed has the $50 she needs, if Lori asks Ed to *loan* her $50 even though she knows she will not be able to pay it back, Lori is using Ed as a means to her end – getting $50. If, however, she asks for a *gift* of $50, perhaps even explaining that she will not be able to pay it back, Ed is being treated as an end in himself, because he is being given the opportunity to make an informed decision as to whether or not to participate in Lori's project – getting $50. According to Kant, one approach is moral; the other is immoral.

Consider how often this kind of a scenario occurs. Each time a politician makes a promise he (or she) knows he can't keep, but makes the promise in order to achieve his goal, to get elected, he is using the voting public as a means to his end. Each time a presidential candidate says he is going to reform Washington, knowing full well he can't, he is violating this formulation of the Categorical Imperative. He is engaging in an immoral act. And so are we each time we fail to treat an individual as an end in him or herself.

There are actually a couple more formulations of the Categorical Imperative, but these two are sufficient for us to get Kant's point: that there is a supreme principle of morality, a moral law, that through rational analysis using the Categorical Imperative is accessible. Because a moral law exists, the normal rational person can discover what is moral and what is immoral.

As Kant developed his moral theory, the idea that a moral law exists was not new. What was new was the idea that in order for it to be rational it must be free of specific content. It must not be (cannot be) a list of specific rules (laws). As Schneewind explains, "The moral law itself, Kant holds, can only be the form of lawfulness itself."[18] *The moral law is the idea that lawfulness exists, that moral absolutes exist.* As rational autonomous agents, humans use reason to discover what is moral. An autonomous agent cannot, in Kant's view, be told what is moral or immoral, but must determine that reality for himself. As noted earlier (in a footnote), I believe Kant would have been comfortable with replacing the word *determine* with the word *discover*. Rational autonomous agents must discover what is moral, for otherwise they are not autonomous. Thus, the moral law cannot contain specific content (this act is right, this act is wrong), but must be a basic concept that a rational autonomous agent can use to discover specific moral realities. Thus, the moral law, the supreme moral principle, is exemplified as the basic Categorical Imperative: "*Act only on that maxim through which you can at the same time will that it should become a universal law.*"

It is important that this not be understood as some form of relativity. Kant was not suggesting that morality is relative. He believed that when the rational will (mind) engaged the Categorical Imperative it would discover a fundamental moral reality, things that are right and things that are wrong – moral absolutes, if you will. Kant believed in the existence of moral absolutes. Rational agents have to discover them. Moral absolutes exist and are discoverable. One such absolute (whether he referred to it as such or not) would be his second formulation of the Categorical Imperative: "*Act in such a way that you always treat humanity, whether in your own person or in the person of another, never simply as a means, but always at the same time as an end.*" That is a moral statement and it is an absolute statement. It is a statement of a moral absolute. Kant embraced the idea of moral absolutes.

---

[18]   Schneewind, 320.

"Kantian Ethics in Less than 6 Minutes"

Summary

Kant believed that humans are self-determined autonomous beings who must determine (or discover) through a rational process what is moral. The only thing that is intrinsically good, Kant thought, is a good will – the desire (the will or determination) to do what is right in each instance. This, of course assumes that there is a right thing to do, that there is a moral reality that stands separate from the subjective interests of individuals. As for why one would want to do the right thing in each instance, Kant believed that motive and morality were interdependently linked and that a duty-oriented motive was that which generated moral actions. Behavior driven by self-interest may not be immoral, but it certainly cannot be described as moral behavior. Morality involves doing the right thing simply because it is the right thing to do. Doing the moral thing is one's duty.

How does one determine what the moral thing to do is? In Kant's system each individual articulates a maxim for proposed actions or behaviors: *when I make a promise I will keep my promise*, or, *when lying produces a benefit for me, I will lie*. Each maxim, then, must be tested against the Categorical Imperative: *"Act only on that maxim through which you can at the same time will that it should become a universal law."* For Kant, this Categorical Imperative is basic and is the embodiment of the supreme moral principle that he is seeking to establish in the *Groundwork*: that lawfulness exists, that moral absolutes exist. It is a fitting expression of a functional moral law that can be utilized in a meaningful way by self-determined autonomous beings.

Kant believed that the Categorical Imperative, the Moral Law or the Supreme Moral Principle, could be articulated in more than one way. Another of Kant's formulations of the Moral Law is: *"Act in such a way that you always treat humanity, whether in your own person or in that of any other, never simply as a means, but always at the same time as an end."* Again, maxims must be articulated and analyzed against this imperative. Maxims such as, *I will manipulate people in order to get whatever I want*, or *I will interact with others in a way that respects their autonomy and intrinsic worth*, can be evaluated and determined to be either moral or immoral in light of this second formulation.

Kant's insights concerning the Moral Law were not that individuals were creating moral law in a subjective, relativistic manner, determining what is or is not moral. Instead, through a rational process they discover what is, in fact, either moral or immoral. For Kant, morality is a reality that exists independent of humans. Humans do not create it; humans discover it. And because morality exists independent of humans, moral absolutes exist independent of humans. Using Kant's system, those absolutes can be discovered.

Kant's duty-oriented moral system has much to commend it and appears to have significant value for contemporary moral philosophy.

Thought and Discussion Questions

1. Explain your insights into Kant's idea that only a good will is intrinsically good.

2. Discuss the merit of Kant's linking of morality with motive.

3. Explain how the articulation of personal maxims aids one in using the Categorical Imperative to determine (discover) morality.

4. Discuss the difference between hypothetical and categorical imperatives.

5. Discuss the idea that if there is a Moral Law that there must also be moral absolutes. What is the significance of this?

Chapter 8
Utilitarianism

Introduction

What has come to be known as Classical Utilitarianism is a moral theory proposed by Jeremy Bentham[1] is his book entitled *An Introduction to the Principles of Morals and Legislation*, first printed in 1780 and formally published in 1789. Social conditions in England at that time left a lot to be desired. Slavery was considered to be an economic necessity by many, women had few if any rights, there was a huge gap between the wealthy and the poor, and the legal system was not so much designed to solve legal problems or administer justice as it was to make lawyers rich. For the average working person in that new Industrial Age (many of whom were women and children), wages were low, hours were long, working conditions were deplorable and advocates concerned with social justice and change were few. One of the few advocates of social reform in late 18th and early 19th century England was Jeremy Bentham.

"The Children Who Built Victorian Britain 1/4"
"The Children Who Built Victorian Britain 2/4"
"The Children Who Built Victorian Britain 3/4"
"The Children Who Built Victorian Britain 4/4"

Generally speaking, Bentham proposed a system of moral decision-making and action based on the anticipated consequences of a number of possible courses of action. The right thing to do, Bentham argued, in any situation is that which brings the greatest amount of happiness to the greatest number of people.

Jeremy Bentham

Jeremy Bentham was born in 1748. His father was a lawyer, as his father had been. At age twelve Bentham entered Queen's College. He graduated at age sixteen and began studying law. He became fully qualified to practice law, but never did. He was

---

[1]   Driver, The History of Utilitarianism," in *Stanford Encyclopedia of Philosophy*.

more concerned with social reform, and in 1780, with the printing of *An Introduction to the Principles of Morals and Legislation*, proposed a theory that remains one of the main theories for moral philosophy today – Utilitarianism.[2]

"Jeremy Bentham: Man and Myth"

While not the first to discuss the ideas that serve as the foundational concepts of Utilitarianism, Bentham's formal proposal and specific methodology set it apart from other similar theories.[3] One of the ideas that set Bentham's theory apart from others is that he specifically wanted a moral framework that made no reference to God or religious concerns.[4] The morality or immorality of any act would be determined, not by reference to a list of rules, but solely on the basis of the consequences of the act. If an act resulted in good consequences it was moral, if it resulted in bad consequences it was immoral. How did Bentham justify this approach to moral philosophy? He argued that:

> Nature has placed mankind under the governance of two sovereign masters, *pain* and *pleasure*. It is for them alone to point out what we ought to do, as well as determine what we shall do. On the one hand the standard of right and wrong, on the other the chain of causes and effects, are fastened to their throne … They govern us in all we do … The principle of *utility* recognizes this subjection, and assumes it for the foundation of that system …

> By the principle of utility is meant that principle which approves or disapproves of every action whatsoever, according to the tendency which it appears to have to augment or diminish the happiness of the party whose interest is in question; or what is the same thing in other words, to promote or to oppose that happiness … By utility is meant that property in any object, whereby it tends to produce benefit, advantage, pleasure, good, or happiness … or … to prevent the happening of mischief, pain, evil, or unhappiness to the party whose interest is considered … A thing is said to promote the interest, or to be for the interest of an individual, when it tends to add to the sum total of his pleasure or, what comes to the same thing, to diminish the sum total of his pains …

> An action then may be said to be conformable to the principle of utility, or, for shortness sake, to utility, (meaning with respect to the community

---

[2]   Sweet, "Jeremy Bentham," in *Internet Encyclopedia of Philosophy*.
[3]   Driver, "The History of Utilitarianism," in *Stanford Encyclopedia of Philosophy*.
[4]   Bentham, *An Introduction to the Principles of Morals and Legislation*, Chapter 2.

at large) when the tendency it has to augment the happiness of the community is greater than it has to diminish it … of an action that is conformable to the principle of utility one may always say either that it is one that ought to be done, or at least that it is not one that ought to be done. One may say also, that it is right and should be done, that it is a right action, at least that it is not a wrong action. When thus interpreted, the words *ought*, and *right*, and *wrong*, and others of that stamp, have a meaning, when otherwise, they have none.[5]

Bentham's belief is that people are ruled by their quest to experience pleasure or happiness and avoid pain or unpleasantness as far as possible. From one point of view he is right. People prefer to have pleasant experiences rather than unpleasant ones, and we usually make decisions and behave in ways that will enhance the possibility of pleasure and diminish the possibility of pain. This is referred to as *psychological egoism*: the view that people are motivated by self-interest. But Bentham is not merely observing that people are very self-interested, he is advocating that the desire to experience pleasure and avoid pain ought to be the basis for determining what is moral or immoral. Instead of the words "pleasure" and "pain" he prefers the words "happiness" and "unhappiness," but he means pleasure and pain. And his point is, that which generates happiness, or the greatest amount of happiness is to be judged as moral. That which results in unhappiness is immoral, or at least not the right thing to do. He refers to this is the *principle of utility*.

"Classical Utilitarianism and Distributive Justice"

The idea that the purpose of life is the pursuit of happiness was not a new idea when Bentham proposed it. Socrates, Plato and Aristotle had embraced the idea of *eudaimonia* as the appropriate goal of life. And while *eudaimonia* can be translated as happiness (as noted in Chapter Two), Socrates, Plato and Aristotle meant something very different than Bentham meant. *Eudaimonia* (thriving or flourishing are better translations than happiness) is rooted in and grows out of *arête*, excellence or virtue. The excellent person will be the one who thrives or flourishes and will, therefore, be happy. Bentham's idea of happiness is more closely aligned with the hedonistic perspective of Epicurus[6] – the absence of pain and the satisfaction of one's physical desires, including intellectual enjoyment. Bentham is proposing that whatever results in that kind of happiness is moral.

---

[5] Bentham, Chapter 1.
[6] Mill would later argue that this was not the case. I will cover that point in the section on Mill.

"Origins of Classical Utilitarianism"

John Stuart Mill

Bentham's younger disciple and associate was John Stuart Mill. Mill (1806-1873), also a British philosopher, is considered one of the leading thinkers of the 19th century. His book *Utilitarianism* (published in 1863) is a defense of Utilitarianism as a viable moral theory. Almost immediately after Bentham published his theory, it came under attack. Eventually, Mill, the leading Utilitarian of the next generation, attempted to address the challenges.

His defense of Utilitarianism (in Chapter One of his book) begins with three interesting affirmations: 1) that Socrates advocated Utilitarianism (a questionable claim at best), 2) that moral philosophers who claim that the principles of morality are clearly evident have failed to produce a list of these clearly evident principles (a claim that is again questionable, depending on which moral philosophers he has in mind), and 3) that Kant's Categorical Imperative can lead to all sorts of "outrageous" immorality. To this last charge I would reply that it is theoretically possible for a person who is morally bankrupt to misuse the Categorical Imperative. For instance, a person could conceivably say that their maxim, "Whenever it is to my advantage I should lie, steal, and kill," should be adopted as a universal law. Kant is assuming, however, that most people are not morally bankrupt and are looking for a simple way to determine moral behavior. Mill's accusation against Kant's moral theory is unrealistic and without merit.

In Chapter Two of *Utilitarianism*, Mill begins his actual explanation/defense of the theory. He begins by noting that:

> Every writer, from Epicurus to Bentham, who maintained the theory of utility, meant by it, not something to be contradistinguished from pleasure, but pleasure itself, together with exemption from pain ... The creed which accepts as the foundation of morals, or the Greatest Happiness Principle, holds that actions are right in proportion as they tend to promote happiness, wrong as they tend to produce the reverse of happiness. By happiness is intended pleasure, and the absence of pain; by unhappiness, pain, and the privation of pleasure ... pleasure,

and freedom from pain, are the only things desirable as ends; and that all desirable things (which are as numerous in the utilitarian as in any other scheme) are desirable either for the pleasure inherent in themselves, or as means to the promotion of pleasure and the prevention of pain.[7]

"John Stuart Mill – Utilitarianism"

Mill is very clear. The Utilitarian focus is the same as the Epicurean focus: to avoid pain and experience pleasure. Opponents of Utilitarianism argued that to make pleasure the foundational idea of a moral system was to cater to animalistic nature. It had been said, evidently, that Utilitarianism was a "doctrine worthy only of swine." Mill's response is, in effect, that such an accusation is an insult to human nature. Humans not only have physical appetites that need satisfying, but higher level appetites, intellectual pleasures, that must also be satisfied. Mill explained:

There is no known Epicurean theory of life which does not assign to the pleasures of the intellect, of the feelings and imagination, and of the moral sentiments, a much higher value as pleasure than to those of mere sensation … It is quite compatible with the principle of utility to recognize the fact, that some *kinds* of pleasure are more desirable and more valuable than others. It would be absurd that while, in estimating all other things, quality is considered as well as quantity, the estimation of pleasure should be supposed to depend on quantity alone. Now it is an unquestionable fact that those who are equally acquainted with, and equally capable of appreciating and enjoying, both [physical and intellectual pleasures], do give a most marked preference to the manner of existence which employs their higher faculties.[8]

Mill is affirming that in calculating pleasure one must calculate the qualities of pleasures, not just the quantities. Some pleasures generate more happiness because

---

[7] Mill, *Utilitarianism*, Chapter Two.
[8] Ibid.

they generate more pleasure, or result in pleasure that is qualitatively different – better, more pleasurable. Epicurus had made a similar argument.

It is important, I think, to be fair to Bentham and Mill, to remember that the focus of Utilitarianism was originally social reform. In making laws that will govern a society, one of the questions politicians and lawmakers ought to ask is, *What will make the greatest number of people happy?* Common sense would dictate that such a question be asked. Good leaders will ask questions of that sort. But will they not also ask, *What is the right thing to do?* The answer Utilitarianism provides when that question is asked is, *The right thing to do is whatever makes the greatest number of people happy.* The right thing to do, from a Utilitarian point of view, is whatever minimizes unhappiness and maximizes happiness. Can Epicurean hedonistic happiness really be the foundation of morality?

That question bothered Mill, and his response to it is not a good one. Mill cites a Mr. Carlyle, who had evidently argued that true happiness was unattainable and perhaps even beyond the right of human expectation. In response, Mill argues that humans have every right to desire and pursue happiness. And while he does again differentiate between mere physical gratification and the higher kinds of pleasures, he is still advocating a hedonistic kind  of happiness and equates it with the *eudaimonistic* kind of thriving (flourishing) that the Classical philosophers advocated.[9] That, of course, is simply an unrealistic comparison. Epicurus was talking about a different kind of happiness than Socrates, Plato and Aristotle had discussed.

In Chapter Three of *Utilitarianism*, Mill argues, essentially, that happiness is the appropriate foundation for morality because God wants people to be happy. If we think metaphorically (analogically) of God as a parent, then it is not unwarranted to say that God wants his children (human beings) to be happy. What parent wants his or her children to be unhappy? But that does not add up to happiness being the determining factor in what is moral or immoral. Happiness is only one desire (goal) parents have for children. We also want them to be healthy, kind, strong, compassionate, just and so forth. Sometimes that which leads to strength and justice, for example, does not generate happiness (at least in that moment). If there are considerations other than hedonistic happiness for biological parents, then, certainly, for God there must be other considerations as well. Mill seems to have missed this point.

---

[9]   While Mill does not actually use the world *eudaimonia* in his argument it is clear that is what he has in mind.

Another feature of Utilitarianism that is crucial to the goal Bentham envisioned for it is that each person must be considered equally. No one can receive special consideration. Here is how Mill explained it:

> The happiness which forms the utilitarian standard of what is right in conduct, is not the agent's own happiness, but that of all concerned. As between his own happiness and that of others, utilitarianism requires him to be as strictly impartial as a disinterested and benevolent spectator. In the golden rule of Jesus of Nazareth, we read the complete spirit of the ethics of utility. To do as one would be done by, and to love one's neighbor as oneself, constitute the ideal perfection of utilitarian morality. As the means of making the nearest approach to this ideal, utility would enjoin, first, that laws and social arrangements should place the happiness, or (as speaking practically it may be called) the interest, of every individual, as nearly as possible in harmony with the interest of the whole.[10]

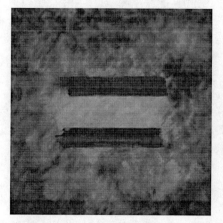

Complete equality; no impartiality allowed. On the surface this sounds, not only acceptable, but commendable as well. Mill denies an egotistical approach (which is without a doubt commendable) by suggesting that according to Utilitarianism it is not one's own happiness that is considered, but the happiness of all concerned. It seems apparent that he is thinking in terms of utilizing the principle of utility in terms of a social collective rather than individual personal ethical decision-making. Social policy, for instance, ought to be considered and enacted from this impartial perspective. But as appropriate as this may sound on the surface, is it really a viable option? We will consider it more closely in the next section.

A final consideration in this section is Mill's assertion of what is ultimately behind (or underlying) Utilitarianism as a moral theory. He says:

> The ultimate sanction, therefore, of all morality (external motive apart) being a subjective feeling in our own minds, I see nothing embarrassing to those whose standard is utility, in the question, what is the sanction of that particular standard? We may answer, the same as of all other moral standards – the conscientious feelings of mankind.[11]

[10]   Mill, *Utilitarianism*, Chapter Two.
[11]   Mill, *Utilitarianism*, Chapter Three.

Mill is saying that not only is Utilitarianism subjective in nature, but all morality is subjective in nature. In Mill's view, humans decide what is and what is not moral. Notice how different this is from Kant's view that an objective moral law exists, which also means that moral absolutes exist, a morality that is discoverable by individuals utilizing one of the formulations of the Categorical

Imperative. From Mill's subjective point of view, however, the mechanism people use to determine what is and what is not moral is a happiness calculation: whatever action generates the greatest amount of happiness for the greatest number of people is moral. Are Bentham and Mill correct? Does the principle of utility provide a satisfactory foundation for moral thinking and acting? A number of ethicists are adamant that it does not.

Utility and Morality

My purpose in this section is to consider whether or not Utilitarianism (the principle of utility) provides a satisfactory framework for moral thinking and acting. James and Stuart Rachels provide a concise summary of the issues involved:

> Classical Utilitarianism, the theory of Bentham and Mill, can be summarized in three propositions: (a) Actions are to be judged right or wrong solely by virtue of their consequences; nothing else matters. (b) In assessing consequences, the only thing that matters is the amount of happiness or unhappiness that is created; everything else is irrelevant. (c) Each person's happiness counts the same. Thus, right actions are those that produce the greatest balance of happiness over unhappiness, with each person's happiness counted as equally important.
>
> This theory has profoundly influenced both ethicists and social scientists. Most ethicists, however, reject Utilitarianism, due to a slew of objections.[12]

---

[12]   Rachels, *The Elements of Moral Philosophy*, 109.

What are some of the objections ethicists have raised regarding Utilitarianism? One has to do with the assumption that hedonistic happiness is or can be the foundation for morality. As noted above, there is a great deal of difference between the *eudaimonistic* kind of happiness (a thriving or flourishing rooted in an excellent character) proposed by Aristotle and the hedonistic kind of happiness (rooted in sensual and intellectual pleasure) proposed by Epicurus. The kind of *happiness* Bentham and Mill

proposed could include a number of things that are clearly immoral. For instance, suppose Fred, a man living in the South in the early 1960s who embraces utilitarian ethics, is in a small town when a black man rapes a white woman. White citizens are outraged and lynch mobs are roaming the streets brutalizing black men. Fred, realizing that a quick arrest and conviction would put a stop to the vigilantism and thus result in the greatest amount of happiness for the greatest number of people, goes to the local police and says he was in the vicinity of the rape when it occurred and can identify the man. He gives a description and an arrest is made. Tensions in the community are momentarily eased, and at the trail Fred provides eyewitness testimony as to the man's guilt. The (innocent) man is convicted and imprisoned and the community is restored to the harmony it knew before the ugly incident. An innocent man suffered (the man convicted was not guilty of the crime) because another man lied. But a lot of people were made happy. According to Utilitarianism, Fred's lie was a moral act.[13] Can that possibly be correct? I think not.

"Utilitarianism and its Critiques"

Another example of how the principle of utility falls short of providing a viable foundation for moral thinking and acting involves, not a theoretical example like the one above, but an actual court case: York v. Story (1963). In October 1958, Ms. Angelynn York reported an assault to the Chino, California police department. An officer took her statement and told her he needed photographs of her bruises and scratches as evidence. He took her to a private room and asked her to undress. She questioned him, but he explained it was standard procedure and was necessary. Ms. York complied and the officer required her to assume a number of different positions on the table in the room. Again Ms. York questioned him because the positions he instructed her to take

---

[13] Rachels, 111-112. Rachels explains that this theoretical example was first offered by McCloskey.

did not seem necessary for him to get the photographic evidence he needed. Again he insisted and took a number of photographs. Later, the officer told Ms. York that for some reason the photographs did not come out right so he had destroyed all of them. Instead, the officer had showed the pictures to other police officers. Also, other officers got hold of the photographs and made additional copies, circulating them around the police department. Eventually, Ms. York discovered what had happened and filed suit in court, claiming that her rights had been violated. She won her case.

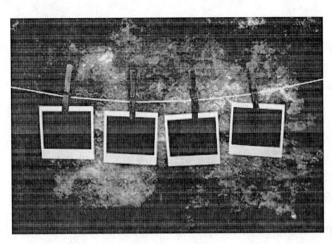

What the officers did was judged illegal, but what of the morality involved? The men who viewed the photographs received pleasure from doing so. A comparatively large number of people were given pleasure while only one person was made unhappy. According to the principle of utility, what the police officers did was not immoral because more people were made happy than were made unhappy.[14] Again, can this possibly be a correct understanding of morality? Most people would say, no.

And what of the idea of everyone being treated equally and impartially? It sounds good on the surface, but in reality is problematic. For instance, in our society we designate a number of parking spaces near the entrances to businesses as handicapped parking spaces. Only handicapped people can legally park in those spaces. This is clearly not equal, impartial treatment. The handicapped get special treatment. We justify this by saying that because of their handicap they deserve special consideration. Even if this special consideration sometimes annoys some people, as a society we believe this unequal treatment is justified. However, from a Utilitarian point of view, no individual or group of individuals ought to get special consideration, for any reason. Everybody must be treated equally.

Additionally, the no impartially rule of Utilitarianism is problematic from a personal point of view. We all have people who are, to us, special and to whom we give special consideration. For instance, my wife and my children and my grandchildren get more of my time, energy, and money than anyone else. And my friends get more consideration than strangers. I have never known or encountered anyone who did not think and act in this manner.

Suppose, for instance, that at the college where my wife and I teach there is a tornado (which happen occasionally in Iowa) and there is damage to the building. My wife and I would likely be in different places on campus when the tornado hits. When able to get out of where I was, I would go looking for my wife. In searching for my wife to rescue or care for her if she was hurt, I might pass lots of injured people. Only after I

---

[14]   Rachels 112-113.

found her and attended to her needs would I turn my attention to others. Most spouses (and parents) would feel morally justified in behaving in this manner. The fact is, while all people are created equal, we do not, and should not interact with people impartially. As a matter of morality, those closest to us deserve our special attention and care. From a Utilitarian point of view this is not acceptable.

Another basic complaint against Utilitarianism is that it requires you to anticipate the consequences and act according to what you anticipate will be the case. Act A is likely to generate result B and Act C is likely to generate result D. Result B will produce more happiness than result D; therefore, act A is the moral act that ought to be completed. The problem is that it is very difficult to accurately anticipate outcomes. The saying, *hindsight is 20:20* is appropriate here. It is easy to look back and see what has happened. It is difficult to look ahead and anticipate what will happen; yet, this is what Utilitarianism requires.

Utilitarianism requires that you do what promotes the greatest good for the greatest number of people. All that matters are the consequences. On the surface this might sound like a good idea, but consider the following scenario illustrated in what is known as the *Trolley Problem*. In one version of this moral dilemma you are standing next to a trolley or train track. A train is coming down the track. On the track ahead are five people

(trapped in a car that is stuck on the track) who will be killed if the train continues down the track. Where you happen to be standing there is a switch that will divert the train onto another track before it hits the car with the five people in it. However, on that track there is a man working, situated in such a way that he will not see the train approaching him. You have to make a decision. You can throw the switch, diverting the train onto the other track and save the five people, but in the process will kill the one man on the other track. What do you do? According to Utilitarianism, the moral thing to do is to throw the switch and save the five people – the greatest good for the greatest number of people. What about the one man who dies? He is a casualty of the greatest good.

"Justice: What's The Right Thing to Do? 1/2"

In a slightly different version of the problem, you are standing on a bridge above the track and see the train moving toward the five people. On the bridge next to you is a large fat man whose body mass would be sufficient to stop the train, keeping it from killing the five people. According to Utilitarianism, it would be necessary for you to push the fat man off the bridge onto the tracks below to stop the train before it hits the five people.

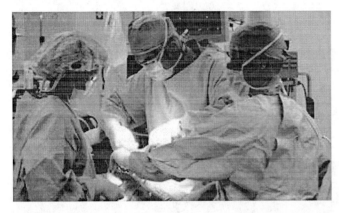

Illustrations like these (though they are only theoretical) illustrate how difficult it would be to carry out the principle of utility in any consistent manner. Do not the rights and/or needs of the few, or even of the one, need to be considered? Can it possibly be acceptable to intentionally destroy one life in order to save another ... or five others? If we begin down that road where do we end up? Could it be that doctors could one day decide to kill one healthy, but unimportant person to harvest his or her organs for transplant in order to save five other sick, but important people? Such behavior is consistent with the principle of utility.

"Justice: What's The Right Thing to Do? 2/2"

Other illustrations are possible but these seem adequate to make the point: Utilitarianism as a stand-alone framework for moral thinking and acting is problematic. Those embracing the theory, however, have not given up easily. In light of the criticisms of the theory an additional form of Utilitarianism has been developed: Rule Utilitarianism.

Act Utilitarianism and Rule Utilitarianism

Act Utilitarianism is Utilitarianism in its basic form. The principle of utility says, *An action is right if it promotes happiness and wrong if it promotes unhappiness.* According to Darwall, this is a statement of what is referred to as Act Utilitarianism, which he defines specifically as: "An act is right if and only if, of those acts available to the agents in the circumstances, it would produce the greatest total net happiness."[15] Since Act Utilitarianism is simply basic Utilitarianism the objections discussed in the section above apply to Act Utilitarianism.

---

[15]   Darwall, "Utilitarianism: Act or Rule?" in *Conduct and Character*, 125.

Because of those objections, a slightly different form of Utilitarianism has been developed: *Rule Utilitarianism*. In contrasting Act and Rule Utilitarianism, Hooker (though he refers to Rule Utilitarianism as Rule-consequentialism) explains that:

> Rule-consequentialism claims instead that the individual acts of murder, torture, promise-breaking, and so on, can be wrong even when those particular acts bring about better consequences than any alternative acts would have. For rule-consequentialism makes the rightness and wrongness of particular acts, not a matter of the consequences of those individual acts, but rather a matter of conformity with that set of fairly general rules whose acceptance by (more or less) everyone would have the best consequences. And, this acceptance of fairly general rules forbidding murder, torture, promise-breaking, and so on, would clearly have better consequences than everyone's accepting fairly general rules permitting such acts.[16]

It does not take a detailed analysis to see immediately that Rule Utilitarianism involves a significant departure from the basic principle of utility as suggested by Bentham and defended by Mill. In short, Rule Utilitarianism is not Utilitarianism at all. I will not attempt to define what it is, but what it isn't seems readily apparent.

"Ethics Utility Act and Rule"

Summary

Utilitarianism is the idea that life is about being happy and the way to determine what is moral or immoral is to anticipate the consequences of an act to determine if it will generate more happiness than unhappiness. It sounds simple, and appealing. Yet as described above, it is rife with problems. Making morality dependent on a hedonistic form of happiness can lead to all sorts of problems, as illustrated above in the cases of Fred the lying witness and Ms. York the victim of indecent behavior. Anticipating consequences ahead of time is difficult to do, and treating everyone impartially is not appropriate in all circumstances. There are just too many problems with Utilitarianism for it to serve as a viable moral theory. This is not to say that we must not be concerned with the consequences of our actions. Of course we should be concerned with the consequences of our actions. But to say that consequences are all that matter is to go too far. To determine morality solely on the basis of anticipated consequences and what generates the most happiness is to make morality (right and wrong, good and bad) dependent on desire and whim.

[16] Hooker, "Rule-Consequentialism," in *Conduct and Character*, 133.

Thought and Discussion Questions

1. Identify the feature of Utilitarianism that you find appealing and explain why.

2. Explain what the principle of utility is and how it works.

3. Explain your thinking regarding that aspect of Utilitarianism that requires that all people be treated impartially.

4. Explain what you consider to be the most serious weakness of Utilitarianism.

5. Identify the basic differences between Kantian Ethics and Utilitarianism.

Chapter 9
Ethical Egoism

Introduction

Ethical Egoism is the idea that whether or not an act is moral or immoral depends on whether or not the act under consideration serves one's own best interests. Ethical Egoism says that self-interested acts are moral. In its strongest form, it suggests that acts that do not serve one's own best interests are immoral, for one is morally obligated to put one's own interests ahead of everyone else's.

Ayn Rand (1905-1982) was an ethical egoist. Hicks provides an excellent brief statement of her egoist theory:

> The Provocative title of Ayn Rand's *The Virtue of Selfishness* matches an equally provocative thesis about ethics … Rand's view is that … self-interest, properly understood, is the standard of morality and selflessness is the deepest immorality … Self-interest, rightly understood, according to Rand, is to see oneself as an end in oneself. That is to say that one's own life and happiness are one's highest values, and that one does not exist as a servant or slave to the interests of others. Nor do others exist as servants or slaves to one's own interests. Each person's own life and happiness is his ultimate end. Self-interest rightly understood also entails *self-responsibility*: one's life is one's own, and so is the responsibility for sustaining and enhancing it. It is up to each of us to determine what value our lives require, how to best achieve those values, and to act to achieve those values.[1]

There is much to commend in Rand's theory. From one point of view it has great appeal to individualistic, autonomous Western people. The idea that my life is important and that I am responsible for making something of myself has been part of the American spirit from the earliest pioneer days. Yet when we think deeply about the implications of Ethical Egoism and the claims it makes about what is moral and immoral and why, one is left with the uneasy feeling that something is amiss. Something about Ethical Egoism doesn't feel or sound quite right. Why? Is it because we, generally speaking, have been taught that being concerned for others is right and appropriate and a theory that says we should only be concerned for ourselves (be completely selfish) just seems wrong? Or is there really

---

[1] Hicks, "Ayn Ailssa Rand," in *Internet Encyclopedia of Philosophy*.

something inherently wrong with the idea? When Rand wrote about *The Virtue of Selfishness* could she have been right? Is it right (moral) to be entirely self-interested?

"Ayn Rand Mike Wallace Interview 1959 1/3"
"Ayn Rand Mike Wallace Interview 1959 2/3"
"Ayn Rand Mike Wallace Interview 1959 3/3"

Psychological Egoism – What Humans Do

One would be hard pressed to find a philosophical discussion of Ethical Egoism without some discussion also of a related idea known as *Psychological Egoism*. Psychological Egoism is the idea that "all actions are done either solely or ultimately for the sake of self-interest."[2] Psychological Egoism is a *descriptive* theory in that it is an attempt to describe human behavior. It is saying that when people do what they do, they do so out of self-interested motives. The theory says we behave the way we do because it is in our best interest to do so. The question is, *Is the theory of Psychological Egoism correct?* Do all of our actions (entirely and only) derive from self-interested motives? To answer this question it is imperative that we understand exactly what the theory proposes. Psychological Egoism is not suggesting that we sometimes act in self-interested ways, or that even most of the time we are self-interested. The theory claims that humans are entirely self-interested all the time: that we only act in ways that we believe will be beneficial to us.

There is little doubt that humans quite often (perhaps the majority of the time) act in self-interested ways. When we are hungry we eat; when we are tired we rest; when we are lonely we seek out the company of others. We educate ourselves and spend enormous amounts of energy and money becoming who and what we want to be. We teach our children that they can become who and what they want to be. We work hard to provide ourselves with a comfortable lifestyle. We are, by nature, self-interested people. But is self-interested *all* we are? That is the question.

---

[2] Shoemaker, "Egoisms," in *Conduct and Character*, 21.

Psychological egoists maintain that *all* we are is self-interested, that everything we do comes back around to some benefit to ourselves. Can this be right? Are *all* of our decisions and actions *entirely* and *only* based on what is best for us? I think very few people would answer that question in the affirmative. Most of us are aware of having made decisions and acted in ways that were based not on our own interests but those of others – parents and spouses quite often act in ways that benefit others instead of themselves. Psychological egoists, however, would likely reply that we are just fooling ourselves if we believe that. If you look closely, they would say, analyzing carefully, you will see that there is some benefit to you in all you do. Thus, all you do you do with your own best interests in mind.

"Philosophy Topic: Psychological Egoism (Friends)"

I believe there are several problems with responses of this sort. First, a decision I make or an action I take cannot be rooted in self-interest if I am unaware of a benefit I might realize from the decision or action. For instance, suppose I am on the bank of a river and see a child in distress being swept downstream. Without stopping to analyze the situation I jump into the river and get to the child and rescue him. Suppose then that in a few minutes frantic parents arrive and in their gratitude offer me a reward for my good deed. Whether I accept or decline the reward is irrelevant. When I jumped into the river to rescue the child, I could not have known a reward would be offered. My decision to act could not have been rooted in self-interest. In fact, since I am not a strong swimmer and the river had a swift current, jumping into the river might have been dangerous for me. My action might have been the very opposite of what was in my own best interest.

A psychological egoist might counter this argument by saying that I might have had a pre-existing desire for attention and praise and jumped in, possibly jeopardizing myself, in anticipation of personal glory. While I suppose that such a thing might be theoretically possible, for the psychological egoist to be able to prove his or her point about personal motives he or she would have to have some sort of evidence. Just making the assertion that such motives could exist is not evidence or proof – which brings me to the second problem with the claim of Psychological Egoism: psychological egoists cannot possibly know people are always and only self-interested. Motives are internal. They are part of the content of the mind that is entirely private and unavailable to anyone other than the individual who has them. When I tell a psychological egoist that when I jumped into the river to save the child I had no personal benefit in mind, he cannot know otherwise. He can speculate. He can claim. He can accuse. But to claim to *know* why people do what they do is ultimately beyond our ability to know unless they tell us.

The classic example of selfless rather than self-interested behavior is the soldier who throws himself on a grenade to save others from the effects of the explosion. What personal benefit does the soldier realize from giving his life to save others? If he dies in the process it would be very difficult to assign a personal benefit to his action. Yet, amazingly, psychological egoists attempt to do that very thing.[3]

"Philosophy Topic: Psychological Egoism"

It is essential to remember that Psychological Egoism is a theory that can be asserted, but not proven.[4] In the end, whether or not an individual has motives (at least occasionally) that are not rooted in his or her own best interests can only be determined by that individual – who is, after all, the only one who knows what his or her motives really are. For the psychological egoist to say that people who claim they are not entirely and only self-interested are either lying or caught up in self-deception, appears not only to be a very questionable assertion, but a very arrogant one. The reality is that Psychological Egoism, as it is stated in its strong form, is an unsound theory.

Ethical Egoism – What Humans Ought To Do

While Psychological Egoism is a theory about what people *actually do.* Ethical Egoism is an ethical theory about what people *ought to do.* Ethical Egoists argue that people ought to do is only those things that are in their own best interest. Keeping the difference between the two theories in mind is essential as we proceed. Why? Because what people actually do and what they ought to do are two different things.

"Egoism"

---

[3] See Shaver, "Egoism," in *Stanford Encyclopedia of Philosophy*.
[4] Ibid. In that article, Shaver makes reference to empirical research projects that support that people do, in fact, act out of motives that are not rooted in self-interest.

Theories regarding Ethical Egoism can be traced all the way back to the time of Plato, even though the term Ethical Egoism did not come along until much later. In Book 2 of *Republic*, Plato's character Glaucon, in a discussion with Socrates about justice, proposes theories that we identify today as Psychological Egoism and Ethical Egoism. Glaucon argues that people are entirely self-interested and would do whatever they wanted (that is, behave immorally) if they thought they could get away with it. To

illustrate his point he tells the story of a shepherd who was the ancestor of a man from Lydia named Gyges. This shepherd was the servant of the king, caring for the king's sheep. One day this shepherd found a gold ring. He kept it, and in the course of wearing it discovered, quite by accident, that if he twisted the ring around on his finger so that the top of the ring was in the palm of his hand, he became invisible. He happened to be at the palace reporting to the king when he made the discovery. So while there, with his new power of invisibility, he slipped into the Queen's chamber and seduced her. The two of them then attacked and killed the king and the shepherd took over the kingdom.

Glaucon then goes on to argue that if two such magical rings existed and one was given to an unjust or immoral man, and the other to a just or moral man, that the moral man would use his power of invisibility to do the same kinds of things the immoral man would do. Glaucon's argument is, "No one believes justice to be good when it is kept private, since whenever either person thinks he can do injustice with impunity, he does it. Indeed, every man believes that injustice is far more profitable to himself than justice."[5]

Before he finishes his argument, Glaucon advocates not only Psychological Egoism but Ethical Egoism as well, suggesting that the egoistical person who sees to his own interests, even if it involves immoral actions, is happier than the moral man who is not entirely self-interested. Is Glaucon right? I think Glaucon is wrong. Why? Because the larger context of the discussion (between Glaucon, Socrates, and others) had to do with justice (morality) not happiness. Basically, his argument is, since being immoral makes one happier than being moral (which he asserts but does not prove), immorality, he concludes, is better than morality. In doing so, Glaucon makes hedonistic happiness more important than morality. But even if an egoistical person is *hedonistically happier* than a non-egoistical person, that does not mean that his behavior has been moral. As noted in the previous chapter on Utilitarianism, hedonistic happiness cannot be the basis for or the definition of morality. Just because an act makes someone happy or gives him pleasure does not make the act moral.

[5]   Plato, *Republic* 2.358e-2.361d.

"The Ring of Gyges: Morality and Hypocrisy"

Remember, Ethical Egoism is the idea that one *ought to*, that one is *morally obligated to*, always put his or her own best interests ahead of the interests of all others. In the strongest version of Ethical Egoism it is considered immoral not to always put one's own interests ahead of all others.[6] As noted earlier, Ayn Rand's belief was that the only way to respect oneself and life is to put one's own interests ahead of the interests of all others. Can this be right? Are parents who put the interests of their children ahead of their own disrespecting or devaluing their own personal worth? Are they behaving immorally? Is the soldier who sacrifices himself to save his comrades somehow devaluing his own worth and life? Is that soldier behaving immorally? Is the adult child who sacrifices her own interests in order to care for an aging parent devaluing her life and worth by making that sacrifice? Is she betraying herself? And is doing so an act of immorality? Of course not. Ethical Egoism flies in the face of common sense and advocates a level of selfishness that would make human interaction very unpleasant if large numbers of people embraced the theory. Should people put their own interests ahead of everyone else's all the time? I don't believe so. I would not want to live in a society where people embraced Ethical Egoism.

Self-interest vs. Selfishness

However, to reject Ethical Egoism as a viable theory for moral thinking and acting is not to reject the concept of appropriate self-interest. We are by nature self-interested people. When we are hungry we eat, when tired we rest. There is nothing wrong with seeing to one's needs. One can be self-interested without being selfish. Self-interest is not a problem until it degenerates into self-absorption.

When Jesus stressed the importance of loving one's neighbor, he said that we ought to love others as much as we love ourselves. Self-love (self-interest) is not inappropriate or problematic in any way … as long as it is not allowed to degenerate into self-absorption, which is manifested in selfish behavior.

[6] Moseley, "Egoism," in *Internet Encyclopedia of Philosophy*.

Being appropriately self-interested without becoming self-absorbed and selfish requires a good deal of introspection and self-discipline. Occasional selfishness should not produce too much alarm. But when selfishness begins to define our personality and impact our relationships with others it is time for a change. Why? Because selfishness is harmful to oneself and to others. If human beings have intrinsic worth and value, it is essential that we recognize it, in ourselves and in others. Not to recognize it is to deny its existence. To fail to recognize another's worth is to devalue that person, which is harmful to that person. How does one recognize another's worth? To verbally acknowledge another's worth without in some way demonstrating it is an empty gesture. How can we demonstrate that others do have worth and value equal to our own? By (at least some of the time) placing their

interests above our own. Telling someone you love them is good. Showing them is better. Telling someone you value them is good, showing them is better.

Self-interest is essential for human survival, health, and happiness. But it cannot be allowed to degenerate into self-absorption and selfishness.

END

"Self Love vs Selfishness"

Is Altruism Possible

Altruism is the opposite of egoism. It is putting the interests of others ahead of one's own interests. This morning (June of 2012) on the news I heard a story about a successful businessman in Kentucky. A local K-Mart was going out of business and all the merchandise was being sold at discount prices. By the last day of the sale much of the merchandise was already gone, but there were still items left, mostly clothing, household and personal items. The businessman decided to buy all the merchandise that was left. It took five cashiers working for several hours to check out all the items. The bill came to $20,000.00. The businessman then, instead of selling the merchandise for a profit (which he could easily have done), donated it all to a local charity to be distributed to families in need. This is an example of altruism. How so? Because the businessman could have sold the merchandise and made a profit, but he decided to give it to people in need. He put their interests ahead of his own.

"Kentucky Man Buys Kmart Inventory"

Why would the businessman do such a thing? A psychological egoist might say he did it to make himself feel good, or to enhance his status in the community. Thus, his action was not motivated by altruistic concerns, but by his own self-interest. The businessman, when interviewed by the television reporter, said he did it because there were good people in his community who were in need. He had the means to help them, so he did. He was not acting in his own best interest, but in the interest of others. The only reply a psychological egoist has to that claim is to say the man is either lying or is self-deluded. As noted earlier, the psychological egoist is certainly not able to prove such a claim, and in making such a claim appears to be needlessly harsh and arrogant.

Can anyone be entirely altruistic? Probably not. We are self-interested people and we cannot always put the needs of others ahead of our own. But it is certainly possible to be both self-interested and others-interested. This is what Jesus meant when he said to love others as much as you love yourself. The moral person is both self-interested and others-interested. The man in the story above is a successful businessman. His success allowed him to meet his own needs and those of his family, and also have the means to help others. Far from being immoral, as the strong Ethical Egoism position suggests, the man's actions were, within the framework of most other moral theories, supremely moral.

Can there be an Obligation to Help Others

In the story above, the Kentucky businessman had the means to help and wanted to help, so he helped. But did he have an *obligation* to help? Was he morally obligated to help others? Would his not helping have been an act of immorality?

If there is a morally right thing to do and a morally wrong thing to do, are we obligated to do the right thing and obligated not to do the wrong thing? If morality exists, and if humans are moral beings, then we are obligated to act morally and to not act immorally. If there is a morally right thing to do and we do not do it, we have behaved immorally. If there is an immoral behavior to be avoided and we do not avoid it, we have behaved immorally.

This is not rocket science and is really not that hard to figure out. But every time I ask my ethics students, *do we have an obligation to help others*, there is a lot of hemming and hawing. The concept of *obligation* (as in moral obligation) is a big one. Here is how I usually ask the question. It is Friday night. You've worked hard all week. You have paid all your bills and have met all your financial obligations. You have some extra money so you are going to treat yourself to a movie and some popcorn. Outside the theater, a

group representing a charity that provides nutrition and health care for children in Africa has a table and display set up and is asking for donations. The photos on their display are heart wrenching and their material explains that nearly 2 million children die each year from preventable diseases. You have extra money. You *can* help. But are you *obligated* to help?[7] The response is usually, no, you are not obligated. You can help if you want to, but you are not obligated to. Why not? Well, because you can't be obligated to help other people. Why not? Well, because then you'd have to be helping other people all the time. This is not sound reasoning, but it is usually the typical response.

At some point in the conversation I take an informal poll, asking how many think that if you are standing outside that theater and have an opportunity to help that you also have an obligation to help? Usually, only a few hands go up – usually women.[8] Why do we hesitate so when confronted with the moral obligation to help others? Perhaps we are more self-interested than we think.

"Peter Singer 'The Life You Can Save' at Happiness & Its Causes 2012"

Do we, in fact, have a moral obligation to help others *if we can*? I believe so. It is said that a *can* implies an *ought*. If I can help, I ought to help. It is not just an option; it is an obligation. If all people have intrinsic worth and value and if doing good is the moral thing to do, then if I have the means to do good, I ought to do so. I have a moral obligation to help those I can help.

---

[7]   Borrowed from Rachels, 62-63.
[8]   That fact will be significant in the next chapter when we discuss the differences between male and female moral thinking.

Summary

The theory of Psychological Egoism says that people behave in self-interested ways. The theory of Ethical Egoism claims that people ought to behave in an entirely self-interested manner, that it is morally right to do so, and that each person is morally obligated to put his or her interests ahead of the interests of others.

Generally speaking, people do behave in their own best interest. We do what we think is best for us; we do what we believe will make us happy. However, just because we are appropriately self-interested most of the time does not mean that we are only self-interested all the time and that we do nothing based solely on the needs and interests of others. The simple reality is that most people manage to be both self-interested and others-interested. The theory of Psychological Egoism does not appear to be true.

The theory of Ethical Egoism, the idea that people have an obligation to be only and entirely self-interested, appears to be less than adequate as a viable framework for moral thinking and acting, for it leaves no avenue for demonstrating the worth and value of other human beings. It is rooted in self-absorption and selfishness and would, if embraced by a majority in any society, produce a society that few people would want to be part of.

Instead, a healthy measure of altruism, balanced with an appropriate measure of self-interest produces a society of people whose own needs are met and who are able to affirm the worth and value (the humanness) of others by acknowledging an obligation to help if they have the means to help.

Ethical Egoism, as a moral system, offers nothing useful as a framework for moral thinking and acting.

Thought and Discussion Questions

1. People are often (or even mostly) psychological egoists. Explain why that fact does not mean that people ought to be Ethical Egoists.

2. Explain the difference between being self-interested and being self-absorbed. Why is this important in a discussion of Ethical Egoism?

3. Explain your insights into altruism and its role in a functional moral theory.

4. Discuss the idea of having an obligation to help others, including the idea that a *can* implies an *ought*.

5. Identify what you think is the best illustration that people are not always and only self-interested. Elaborate and explain.

Chapter 10
Care Ethics

Introduction

Care Ethics, sometimes also referred to as Feminine Ethics or the Feminine Ethics of Care, can be difficult to define depending on whether one is focusing on the feminist aspect or the care aspect of the theory. From a feminist point of view, Feminist Ethics is about "an attempt to revise, reformulate, or rethink traditional ethics to the extent it depreciates or devalues women's moral experience."[1] Or, if one chooses to focus more specifically on the moral theory itself, rather than focusing on the perceived injustices done to women by men thinking like men, care ethics "implies

that there is moral significance in the fundamental elements of relationships and dependencies in human life.[2] In other words, care ethics seeks to provide a framework for moral thinking and acting that is rooted in human interaction and relationships, focusing specifically on the relationship involved in giving and receiving care. The focus in this chapter will be mostly on the theory itself and whether or not it can serve as a viable framework for moral thinking and acting. However, to fully understand the theory and its implications we must also consider the feminist arguments associated with the theory. The issue has to do with whether or not men and women think differently about morality and moral issues. The issue is *not* whether or not men and women may arrive at different conclusions about what is moral and what is immoral, but whether or not there is a difference, perhaps a profound difference, in how they think about morality in general, a difference in how they approach analyzing and solving moral dilemmas.

In general, do men and women think differently? Most people would say, yes. Specifically then, do men and women think differently about moral issues and dilemmas? It is a valid and intriguing question.

Kohlberg's Stages of Moral Development

Lawrence Kohlberg was a psychologist whose specialty had to do with the development of moral reasoning. Kohlberg's research led him to conclude that children go through three distinct stages of moral development as they grow, each stage involving two phases.

---

[1] Tong and Williams, "Feminist Ethics," in *Stanford Encyclopedia of Philosophy*.
[2] Sanders-Saudt, "Care Ethics," in *Internet Encyclopedia of Philosophy*.

Level 1 involves what Kohlberg calls *Preconventional Morality*. At this level, Kohlberg sees children going through two stages: *Stage 1*, the Obedience and Punishment Orientation – obeying rules (being moral) in order to avoid punishment for doing a bad or wrong thing; and *Stage 2*, Individualism and Exchange – pursuing one's own interests and allowing others to do the same. In this stage, punishment remains a concern, but it is a risk one takes in pursuing one's goals.

Level 2 is identified as *Conventional Morality*. At this level, *Stage 3* has to do with Good Interpersonal Relationships – good behavior has to do with good motives and feelings such as love, empathy, trust, and concern for others. *Stage 4*, Maintaining Social Order, involves young people beginning to see society as a whole and the importance of obeying laws, respecting authority, and performing one's duty.

Level 3 is *Postconventional Morality*. At this level, *Stage 5* has to do with the concept of a Social Contract and Individual Rights. Society is viewed in a more theoretical manner. What rights and values should society promote and uphold? Finally, at *Stage 6*, the focus is on Universal Principles – that individuals have rights and that disputes must be settled through just processes.[3]

"Dr. Kohleberg's Theory of Moral Development"

For Kohlberg, these stages represent the changes that occur in a child's thinking about morality as he or she matures. The more mature the child is, the higher his or her level of moral thinking will be.

Heinz's Dilemma

One of the interview tools Kohlberg used to study children so he could determine where on his scale of moral development they were, was a story indentified as Heinz's Dilemma. Kohlberg would tell the story about Mr. Heinz, which involved a difficult situation where Heinz chose to act in a certain manner. Kohlberg then ask the children if Mr. Heinz should or should not have acted as he did and why. The *why* part of the question was the most important aspect of the interview, providing Kohlberg with the

---

[3]   Kohlberg, *The Philosophy of Moral Development*, 409-412.

insights he was searching for. Kohlberg's purpose was to discover the level of the child's moral reasoning. The story, paraphrased, goes something like this:

Mr. Heinz's wife is very sick with a kind of cancer and a new medicine that a chemist/pharmacist has discovered can cure it. The ingredients to make the medicine cost the chemist $200. He makes the medicine and then sells it for $2000. He is the only one who has the medicine that can save Mrs. Heinz. Mr. Heinz goes to the chemist and explains that he has only been able to scrape together (borrowing from family and friends) $1000 and asks the chemist to sell him the medicine for that much right now and he (Heinz) will pay the rest later. The chemist says, no. He invented it and deserves to make a profit off the sale of the medicine. Mr. Heinz pleads with the chemist, but to no avail. Finally, in desperation, Mr. Heinz breaks into the chemist's lab and steals the medicine for his wife.

"Moral Development"

Kohlberg then asked: Should Mr. Heinz have done that? Kohlberg was not really interested in whether the child said yes or no. Because whatever the child said, the next question was, why? That's what Kohlberg was looking for – the reasoning process behind the answer. This would identify the level of the child's moral reasoning.

In one such interview, discussed by Carol Gilligan, two eleven year old children were interviewed, a boy named Jake and a girl named Amy.

When Jake was asked about Mr. Heinz's decision to steal the medicine, Jake reasoned that Mr. Heinz had done the right thing. After all, there was a human life involved and Mr. Heinz's wife was worth more than the $1000 difference in the amount of money the chemist wanted and the amount Mr. Heinz had. A human life is worth more than money. The chemist can get his money later. If Mrs. Heinz dies, Mr. Heinz can't get her back.

When Amy was given the same scenario and question, her response was different. She did not think Mr. Heinz should have stolen the medicine. He should have kept trying to borrow more money and kept talking with the chemist until some agreement was reached. Mr. Heinz took a considerable risk in stealing the medicine. What if he got arrested and went to jail? Then who would be there to take care of Mrs. Heinz? Even if she got better from the medicine, she might get sick again and if Mr. Heinz is in jail, who would take care of Mrs. Heinz? Mr. Heinz really should not have stolen the medicine. He should have kept trying to find the additional money he needed and kept talking to the chemist until he got something worked out.[4]

In Kohlberg's view, Jake appeared to be more advanced than Amy in his moral reasoning. Amy's response appeared to be rooted in stage 3, where personal relationships are important. Amy stressed the caring relationship between Mr. Heinz and his sick wife, and the need for Mr. Heinz to continue interacting with the chemist until a solution was reached. Jake's response, however, appeared to reflect a higher level of analysis, perhaps at stage 5, where impersonal principles are significant. Jake had referred to a human life being worth more than money. Kohlberg concluded that Jake was operating at a higher level of moral reasoning than Amy.

Kohlberg's research in general (as he interpreted it) seemed to suggest that men tend to engage in higher-level moral reasoning. Was he right? Does moral reasoning involve a hierarchal scale with higher and lower levels of moral reasoning?

Feminist Objections

One psychologist and researcher who has called Kohlberg's research methods and conclusions into question is Carol Gilligan. She has noted:

I observed that women, especially when speaking about their own experiences of moral conflict and choice, often define moral problems in a way that eludes the categories of moral theory and is at odds with the assumptions that shape psychological thinking about morality and about the self. This discovery, that a different voice often guides the moral judgments and actions of women, called attention to a major design problem in previous moral judgment research: namely, the use of all-male samples as the empirical basis for theory construction. ... The selection of an all-male sample as the basis for generalizations that are applied to both males and females is logically inconsistent.[5]

---

[4]   Gilligan, *In A Different Voice: Psychological Theory and Women's Development*, 26, 28.

[5]   Gilligan, "Moral Orientation and Moral Development," in *Conduct and Character*, 278.

Put simply, Gilligan noticed that women thought differently about moral issues than men did. She also knew that Kohlberg's research, which consisted of an all-male research group, did not include female perspectives. How, then, could generalizations concerning moral reasoning be made regarding women? Kohlberg's methodology was flawed.

"Carol Gilligan on Women and Moral Development"

It also became apparent that perhaps something other than a hierarchy of lower and higher levels of moral reasoning needed to be developed, something that would reflect the valid otherness of female moral reasoning, something that would not suggest that the way men tend to think about moral issues is somehow superior to the way women tend to think about moral issues.

Male and Female Ethical Perspectives

What are the differences between the ways men and women think about moral issues? Mackinnon has prepared a chart that illustrates what some of the perceived (or supposed) differences between male and female moral reasoning might be:

Female Ethical Perspective	Male Ethical Perspective
Personal	Impersonal
Partial	Impartial
Private	Public
Natural	Contractual
Feeling	Reason
Compassionate	Fair
Concrete	Universal
Responsibility	Rights
Relationship	Individual
Solidarity	Autonomy[6]

It is clear, however, as one's reads Mackinnon's comments that she is not convinced that this representation is entirely accurate. It does appear, however, generally speaking, that while men tend to analyze moral issues from a rational-justice

---

[6] Mackinnon, *Ethics: Theory and Contemporary Issues*, 7th edition, 145.

orientation, women tend to analyze moral issues from an emotive-relational orientation. This does not mean that women are not rational or logical in their moral deliberations. It means that their rationale and logic involve more emotive and relational features than does the rationale and logic used by men.

"Ethics of Care 1/4"
"Ethics of Care 2/4"
"Ethics of Care 3/4"
"Ethics of Care 4/4"

Care Ethics

Nel Noddings is one of the foremost advocates of Care Ethics.[7] Building on one of Hume's assertions, that morals are rooted in feelings or sentiment,[8] Noddings argues that women approach moral concerns from a perspective that grows out of their natural urges to be caring. Their ways of thinking about morality necessarily include a relational feature that is (or ought to be) essential in moral thinking. She identifies the *one caring* and the *one cared for*. The dynamic for making moral decisions must involve the giving and receiving of care that is at the heart of the many relationships that characterize the female life.

"Inside the Academy: Nel Noddings"

Noddings argues that there is a kind of natural goodness that is associated with the caring relationship. That goodness, however, she acknowledges, is not necessarily a kind of moral goodness, for animals maintain caring relationships (a mother bear caring for her cubs, for example) that are not considered moral in nature. But the good of a caring relationship certainly can involve a moral good. The example she chooses to illustrate how this natural caring serves as a foundation for moral thinking and acting involves questions related to abortion.[9]

---

[7] The following brief overview of Noddings' position is based on Chapter 4 (An Ethic of Caring) from her book, *Caring: A Feminist Approach to Ethics and Moral Education.*

[8] A very questionable assertion. If Hume is correct, morality is entirely subjective. This issue will be addressed at length in Chapter Twelve.

[9] A detailed analysis of the abortion issue will be presented in Chapter Fourteen. However, to understanding the nature of Noddings' position the reader may want to review that material in connection with this section.

In the scenario Noddings develops, she assumes that the "incipient embryo" under consideration is simply "an information speck" (that is, a clump of cells containing DNA that acts as an instruction manual for building a baby) and that the issue of how to respond to this information speck is a non-moral issue to begin with.[10] It is the relational aspects of what is and what will be that generates the morality associated with the decision to keep or abort the information speck. Since this information speck is, in the case of the woman under consideration, the result of a loving (caring) relationship, the woman feels a connection with, and has a deep interest in the future of the baby that the information speck will produce. Thus, she wants to keep the speck and nurture it. The moral decision that grows out of her natural urges to care and nurture is to not have an abortion. However, jump forward twenty years. The baby that the information speck became is now a mature young woman who is pregnant with her own information speck. But unlike her mother, she is unsure of the love between herself and the father of the speck. She is frightened and uncertain about her future and that of the speck. She makes a moral decision to abort the speck. For Noddings, each woman has made a moral decision based on her specific feelings given the unique situation each was involved in.

"Suter Science Seminar – Caring: How We Become Attached"

In her presentation, Noddings includes a discussion of obligation that is designed to demonstrate just how natural caring generates moral obligations. She attempts to argue that what she is proposing is not relativistic, but is based on solid universal principles. However, her foundational idea is that of Hume, that morality is rooted in feeling, in sentiment. I would suggest that if that is the case, if morality is rooted in or based on feelings, then the only universal principle involved is that morality will be subject to the subjectivity of individual emotions and situational contexts. Noddings' insistence that what she is proposing is not subjective seems incredible. Obviously it is entirely subjective.

---

[10]   There are two assumptions at work here: 1) that a fertilized egg is not a person but only an information speck – to state this position as a fact and not an assumption is completely irresponsible – and 2) that what to do with the "information speck" is not a moral issue. The second assumption can only be valid if the first assumption is valid and there is no possible way to reach a definitive conclusion regarding the personhood of a fertilized egg. So Nodding makes two statements as if they are facts when they are nothing more than assumptions and opinions.

As a stand-alone moral theory Care Ethics leaves a lot to be desired. It is entirely relativistic and provides nothing substantive in the way of defining morality[11] or of clearly differentiating between good and evil. This is not to say that caring should not be part of a functional moral theory. Of course it should. From one point of view, what Noddings describes as caring, Jesus described as love. A moral person loves or cares about other people and moral decisions will be impacted by the fact that we love (or care for) others. But the idea that women (universally) have caring urges that by themselves provide a paradigm for moral thinking and acting is a theory that is unsupported by anthropological and sociological data. Studies have revealed that female biology alone does not generate *natural caring urges*.[12] Both males and females are capable of being nurturing and caring. But does being a caring person by itself provide a functional paradigm for moral thinking and acting? I do not believe it does.

Others have voiced similar concerns regarding Care Ethics and have suggested that instead of thinking of Care Ethics as a stand-alone moral theory, caring should be thought of as one virtue in a Virtue Ethics theory of morality. Halwani makes one such proposal:

> My suggestion now is to think of care as a virtue, as one virtue, albeit an important one, among those that go into constituting a flourishing life. As a virtue, care would not simply be a natural impulse, but to use Noddings' terminology, also ethical (in Aristotelian terms, it would not be a natural virtue, but one harnessed by reason). This position allows us to maintain what is most desirable about CE [Care Ethics]. First, consider CE's insistence on the idea that human beings are not abstract individuals who morally relate to each other following principles such as justice and nonviolation of autonomy. One of VE's [Virtue Ethics] main claims is that we are social animals who need to negotiate the ways we are to deal and live with each other. With this general

[11]   Halwani points out that Noddings does argue that to be moral one must be a caring person. This, Noddings refers to as the "ethical ideal," (Halwani, "Care Ethics and Virtue Ethics," in *Conduct and Character*, 300. This however, falls far short of a substantive definition of morality.

[12]   Shepard, 273-275. In many cultural contexts women are more caring and nurturing than men. But this is not universally the case. The question, however, is, "is the nurturing "nature" of women a result of biology or of social expectation? Are females taught to be nurturing?" If there is an aspect of nurturing and social expectation in female nurturance, then Noddings' argument that Care Ethics is related to the "natural" female urge to care rests on a questionable assumption.

claim about our sociality, VE also claims that without certain types of relationships we will not flourish. Without friends and family members, human beings will lead impoverished lives, being unable to partake in the pleasures of associating with people with whom they can trust and share their joys, sorrows, and activities. It is not just that intimate relationships are instrumental to flourishing, but that they are part and parcel of a flourishing life: the ends and goals of intimate others constrain the very ends and goals of the agent, and the very conception of the agent's life: intimate relationships "are not external conditions of [virtuous] activities, like money or power. Rather they are the form virtuous activity takes when it is especially fine and praiseworthy." VE, then, gives pride of place to CE's insistence on the sociality of human life and to its emphasis on the importance of certain types of relations such as those of friendship and family.[13]

I think Halwani (and others who have made similar proposals – such as James Rachels) have seen that as a stand-alone theory Care Ethics is problematic. But as part of the more comprehensive theory of Virtue Ethics, caring can be an important virtue. Whether one calls it caring or loving (in the sense of the *agapé* love of Jesus' moral system) the idea of loving-caring relationships must permeate our lives if we are to be moral, happy (flourishing) people.

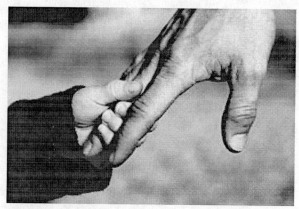

I would also add that in the context of Virtue Ethics (at least a form of it that is similar to Aristotelian Virtue Ethics) some of the subjectivity of standard version of Care Ethics is eliminated.

Summary

Feminists argue that women think differently about moral concerns than do men. At this point few people would disagree with them. Women think differently (from a different perspective, with different considerations) than men. It should not be surprising that women think differently about morality. Their thinking is both rational and logical, but may have a much stronger focus on the importance of interpersonal relationships in the process of moral thinking and acting than a typical male focus that may be more rooted in universal principles and the concept of Justice.

Theorists like Carol Gilligan and Nel Noddings have made significant contributions and drawn attention to the feminine voice in moral philosophy. With its focus on interpersonal relationships and the giving and receiving of care, Care Ethics has offered some important observations and enhanced ethical theory. However, as a stand-alone

---

[13] Halwani, "Care Ethics and Virtue Ethics," in *Conduct and Character*, 301-302.

theory it appears to be less than adequate. It is entirely subjective (despite Noddings' claims to the contrary) and lacks substantive methods for determining morality. Rather than a stand-alone theory of moral philosophy, Care Ethics may work as a component of Virtue Ethics.

Thought and Discussion Questions

1. Discuss Gilligan's charge that Kohlberg's research methods were faulty. What was the problem and how can it be remedied?

2. Kohlberg's basic hierarchy of moral reasoning appears logical and consistent. Why does it not lead to correct conclusions regarding the differences for example, between Jake's and Amy's moral reasoning skills?

3. Noddings used two examples of possible abortions to illustrate how Care Ethics allows women to make ethical decisions. Rogers is not impressed with her illustrations. Why not?

4. Describe the relative strengths and weaknesses you see in Care Ethics, especially as a stand-alone moral system.

5. Explain how caring might work as part of a larger, more comprehensive moral theory.

Chapter 11
Contemporary Virtue Ethics

Introduction

As we have already seen, the idea that morality is related to or grows out of the kind of a person one is predates Socrates. Virtue Ethics, articulated most clearly in the ancient world by Aristotle, is one of the oldest, if not the oldest, forms of moral philosophy. But by the time of the Enlightenment a paradigm shift had occurred.[1] Instead of asking, "What kind of a person ought one to be?" the question became, "What is the right thing to do – in this or that circumstance?" Virtue Ethics was replaced as the dominant ethical theory by either Kant's Deontological approach or Bentham's Utilitarian approach. Other less dominant theories were also proposed and embraced by some, but Deontological or Consequentialist theories had the larger number of advocates.

"The Enlightenment 1/2"
"The Enlightenment 2/2"

Why did this shift occur? I believe the underlying reason (or at least one of them) was that from the time of the Renaissance into contemporary times the world has been in a continual process of becoming a much more complex place to live. New ideas, new technologies, and new social and personal realities generated new circumstances that presented new ethical dilemmas. People wanted and needed to know how to 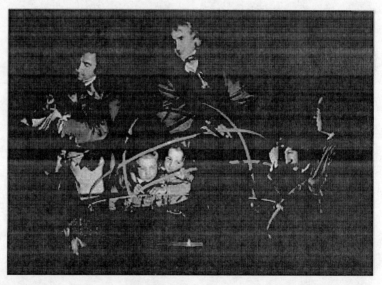 respond. Confronted with new situations and new moral dilemmas, they asked, "What is the right thing to do?" It appeared that the old framework of virtue ethics, focused on the kind of a person one ought to be, did not offer much guidance for specific responses to the new situations people were encountering. The old question, "What kind of a person should I be?" was replaced with a new question, "What should I do?" so the old system needed to be replaced with a new system. Or so it seemed.

---

[1] Hursthouse, "Virtue Ethics," in *Stanford Encyclopedia of Philosophy.*

As the complex world continued to evolve, becoming even more complex and confusing, it appeared that there needed to be a simple test to determine right and wrong. Kant proposed the Categorical Imperative, Mill, the Principle of Utility.[2] Each system allowed for one to determine in a definitive manner what behavior is right or wrong in any given situation. Great! Now people could discover right and wrong, good and bad. But each system, Deontological or Consequentialist, approached moral concerns from very different perspectives, and what one system advocated the other denounced.[3] Also, each system, as they were understood and practiced, had little to say about the moral development of the individual. The paradigm shift that took moral philosophy in a new direction may have met a need in one area, but it left a void in another. By the middle of the 20th century, some moral philosophers began to feel like another paradigm shift was necessary. Ethics, it seemed, had stalled and needed to be revived.

END

Ancient Virtue Ethics

To review briefly, Aristotle had proposed that life had a purpose, a goal toward which it moved: the realization of a person's potential, which would lead to happiness. The ancient Greek concept of happiness, however, was different from ours. For Aristotle, the idea of happiness (*eudaimonia*) meant flourishing or thriving. To achieve that goal, one had to be an *arête* kind of a person, an excellent person: one who over the course of his life developed traits that resulted in him being an excellent person. For Aristotle, the character of an excellent person involved a group of traits that represented a mean between two extremes. The list of traits that Aristotle believed to result in *arête* included the traits listed below:

The Deficiency	The Virtuous Mean	The Excess
Cowardice	Courage	Foolhardiness
Lack of restraint	Temperate	Ascetic self-denial
Stinginess	Liberality	Wasteful extravagance
Pettiness	Magnanimous	Ostentatious exhibitionism
Overly humble	Proud	Vainglorious arrogance
Indolent	Ambitious	Overreaching
Disagreeable	Good Tempered	Overly affable
Unfriendly surliness	Friendliness	Overly accommodating
Deceitfulness	Truthfulness	Exaggeration

---

[2] There were other theories that were developed. One influential paradigm was Social Contract Theory. Another was Ethical Egoism. We have discussed each of these.

[3] Kant advocated intention and duty, Bentham advocated happiness and consequences. Kant said consequences are irrelevant; Bentham said intention is irrelevant.

The Deficiency	The Virtuous Mean	The Excess
Humorless	Wittiness	Buffoonery
Shamelessness	Modesty	Bashfulness
Callousness	Just	Vengeful

Look at and think carefully about the traits in the middle column – The Virtuous Mean. Think about the kind of person a man would be if those traits characterized him. Most of us would like to be friends with that kind of a person. Most of us would like to be that kind of a person. Clearly, Aristotle believed that to be a person who would flourish in life (who had a good life and was happy) one had to be a certain kind of a person – a good person, a person who got along well with others and was respected and liked.

"Virtue Ethics Summarized"

But what about moral behavior? What about knowing how to live a moral life? If the middle column represents the kind of person a virtuous person is, then the other two columns represent the kind of person the virtuous person will not be. The virtuous person, for example, who is just will not be calloused (and all the things associated with it – cold, unfeeling, uncaring, unsympathetic, and so forth) or vengeful (and all the things associated with it – intolerant, mean-spirited, violent, and so forth). If the virtuous man is truthful, he will not be a liar. The list of what a virtuous man is also serves as a list of things he is not. It becomes a moral code of how to live, and not to live, in order to be an excellent person.

Also, we must remember that for Aristotle, the virtues could not be attained and lived apart from reason. Humans are rational animals, according to Aristotle. To live a fully human life one must live a life of reason. Reason (*phronesis*, practical wisdom) is the foundation and driving force behind the development of each virtue. A virtuous person is also a rational person, and for Aristotle the highest form of rational endeavor was contemplation – the kind of philosophical contemplation that characterized his life.

To be sure, Aristotle's approach to moral philosophy did not involve anything like Kant's Categorical Imperative or the Bentham's Principle of Utility. But I believe if we could ask Aristotle about how his system helped one figure out what is the right thing to do in a given circumstance, he would reply that an excellent person, who is also a rational, contemplative person, will know, in any given circumstance, what is the right thing to do.

Aristotle was confident that his moral theory was complete and accomplished its intended purpose.

Contemporary Virtue Ethics

Anscombe's paper generated a flurry of activity among ethicists. In the years that followed, papers and books, for and against Virtue Ethics, contributed to the ongoing discussion concerning the viability of Virtue Ethics as a satisfactory moral theory for contemporary society. Put simply, can a moral theory developed 2,500 years ago provide a meaningful framework for moral thinking and acting in the modern world? Perhaps. Perhaps not.
Maybe it would need to be tweaked just a bit. Has it been? Is Contemporary Virtue Ethics substantially different from Aristotelian Virtue Ethics? In some ways, yes; in others no.[4] One of the differences will be in what we include in our list of virtues that would lead to or result in an excellent life in contemporary society. Rachels has developed a list of virtues that most contemporary people would agree are essential traits for achieving excellence in life.

Virtues Valued in Contemporary [Western] Society

Benevolence	Fairness	Reasonableness
Civility	Friendliness	Self-confidence
Compassion	Generosity	Self-control
Conscientiousness	Honesty	Self-discipline
Cooperativeness	Industriousness	Self-reliance
Courage	Justice	Tactfulness
Courteousness	Loyalty	Thoughtfulness
Dependability	Moderation	Tolerance[5]

---

[4] The substantial difference is that some of Aristotle's conclusions regarding manual labor, slavery and women have been rejected. See Simpson, "Contemporary Virtue Ethics and Aristotle."

[5] Rachels, "The Ethics of Virtue," in *Ethics: History, Theory, and Contemporary Issues*, 697.

Rachels' list has twice as many items in it as Aristotle's. Why? Perhaps because contemporary life is more complex and it takes more virtues to be an excellent person today than it did 2,500 years ago. But perhaps the difference is simply two different moral philosophers, each developing his own list, one being more specific than the other. I doubt that Aristotle would be unhappy with Rachels' list. Other than some of Aristotle's culturally shaped views that can no longer be embraced (noted above) the basic differences between ancient and modern Virtue Ethics appear to be insignificant.[6]

Weaknesses of Virtue Ethics

What strengths and weakness have been observed regarding Virtue Ethics? One of the weaknesses of Virtue Ethics is that it appears to be somewhat *relativistic*. It is difficult to reach a consensus as to what traits ought to be included in a list of virtues. In addition, when a list is finally agreed upon and then compared to a list prepared in another culture, the lists will be different. Traits that are considered valuable in one culture might not be considered valuable or even appropriate in another. Take honesty as an example. In the West, being honest and telling the truth

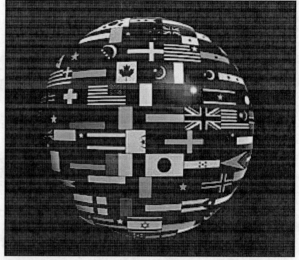

is considered, not only the moral thing to do, but is essential to the effective functioning of society. Though no one is entirely honest all the time, we value and emphasize the need for truth-telling. We teach our children not to lie, to be honest, to tell the truth. A Western list of virtues would almost certainly include honesty. There are many cultures in the world, however, where this would not be the case. In those cultures (I am not going to identify them), what is valued is having the upper hand, the advantage. If lying provides one with an advantage, then the right thing to do is to lie. It appears, then, that Virtue Ethics would not have universal applicability. However, I believe that if ethicists from different cultures sat down and worked together, a list of basic virtues valued in all those cultures could be complied and used effectively in multicultural contexts.

[6] Simpson discusses some basic differences between theory and practice in ancient and modern Virtue Ethics (in "Contemporary Virtue Ethics and Aristotle") but these have little impact on the ideas of the basic theory.

Relativism can also be a concern from a *class* or *status* perspective. For instance, Bertrand Russell complained that Aristotle's list of virtues lacked traits such as benevolence or philanthropy. I have to disagree with Russell on this specific point, for I believe that Aristotle's virtues of liberality and magnificence allow for benevolence and philanthropy. Aristotle did not specifically require either, but that sort of generosity ma y certainly be allowed under those virtues. However, having said that, it must still be acknowledged that just as cultural differences can impact what virtues are valued, so, too, status or class differences can impact what traits are valued. However, again, if ethicists representing different class or status groups worked together, I believe they could produce a list of virtues that people within those various groups could embrace as valued virtues.

A second perceived weakness of Virtue Ethics has to do with *the lack of a specific methodology for discovering the right thing to do* when faced with an ethical dilemma. Kant's Categorical Imperative and Bentham's Principle of Utility provide issue-by-issue guidance for determining morality. Virtue Ethics does not have an equivalent mechanism. But I believe this "weakness" is more perceived than real. The value of Virtue Ethics (ancient or contemporary) is that the virtuous (or excellent) person (*arête* – which includes *phronesis,* practical wisdom) will be one who, because of the kind of person he or she is, will do the right thing in each case. The excellent person, guided by practical wisdom will know what is the right thing to do. A special mechanism for discovering the right thing to do is unnecessary for the virtuous person. After all, Kant's Categorical Imperative is, in reality, quite simple. It consists of simple questions designed to clarify moral or immoral behavior: *"Would it be good if everyone did what you are thinking about doing?"* Or, *"Does this way of behaving give other people the respect they deserve?"* Bentham's Principle of Utility is just as basic: *"Will this action generate more of less happiness?"* A person guided by practical wisdom (the virtuous person) would probably think to ask those kinds of questions in figuring out how to respond or behave in a given situation, so I'm not convinced the criticism is as serious an issue as some might suppose.

A third criticism of Virtue Ethics has to do with *conflicts between the virtues.* The classic example here is the possible conflict between the virtues of honesty and kindness. A wife asks her husband: *Do these jeans make my behind look big?* Suppose her husband is both an honest man and a kind man and suppose that the jeans have nothing to do with the size of her behind. Should he be honest or should he be kind? Perhaps, in this situation, he can't be both. Or, in a different scenario, suppose the wife, having just returned from the salon with a new hairstyle asks: *What do you think?* What if he thinks it is the silliest hairstyle he has ever seen on a mature woman? Does he opt for honesty or kindness? It is possible that in some cases one virtue might conflict with another. In such cases it is important to remember that the virtues are qualities that represent tendencies in behavior, not hard fast rules that cannot be contextualized. A person can be an honest person but in a given situation decide not to say what he is thinking. He can choose to be tactful and kind without failing to be honest.

"Abe Lincoln Geico Commercial"

Questions can be raised regarding a few perceived weaknesses of Virtue Ethics. I believe, however, that they can be answered and that serious objections are lacking.

Strengths of Virtue Ethics

Having considered the weaknesses of Virtue Ethics, what strengths can be identified? One of the strengths of Virtue Ethics is *its holistic nature*. Virtue Ethics is rooted in and aims for rationality as the guiding or controlling factor in life, but Virtue Ethics does not ignore the emotive and appetitive aspects of life. Whether ancient or modern Virtue Ethics is being considered, the emotive aspect of human nature and the appetites associated with one's physical needs are part of the bigger picture. Ascetic self-denial is not necessary, but self-control and personal discipline (rooted in rationality) keep the appetites and emotions in check. One lives a balanced life, a life of moderation between extremes.

A second strength of Virtue Ethics is its *focus on character*, on the kind of person one ought to be. Though contemporary moral philosophy often asks, *"What is the right thing to do?"* Virtue Ethics suggests that the person who is an excellent person (because of his character) will be likely to do the right thing in a given situation simply because he is an excellent person who habitually does the right kinds of things. Morality is about more than knowing what to do in a given situation. It is about the kind of life one lives on a day-to-day basis. Virtue Ethics (like ancient Hebrew and early Christian moral philosophy) focuses on this aspect of morality: what kind of a person ought one to be?

A third strength of Virtue Ethics is its *focus on interdependence*. Humans are interdependent, relational beings. We live in societies, interacting with one another. We do so based on a shared and agreed upon standard of morality. Virtue Ethics is built on the insight that in order to be appropriately and successfully interdependent we must develop character traits that facilitate interdependence and relationship. The focus in Virtue Ethics is on the kind of person one is in relation to other people.

Finally, a fourth strength of Virtue Ethics is that it *allows for partiality* in our relationships with others. Kant and Mill both stressed the importance of, and need for, impartiality in moral considerations. Yet, relational beings who enjoy different levels of intimacy (from family, to close friends, to acquaintances) must be allowed to exhibit partiality, for partiality is part of the nature of loving relationships. Virtue Ethics allows for partiality of this nature.

Rachels' Observation

At the close of his presentation entitled, *The Ethics of Virtue*, James Rachels says, "For these reasons, it seems best to regard the theory of virtues as part of an overall theory of ethics rather than as a complete theory in itself."[7] Some of his reasons are similar to the questions discussed in the section above on the Weaknesses of Virtue Ethics. Even though I do not believe the "weaknesses" constitute significant challenges for Virtue Ethics, I do agree that given the contemporary interest in specific answers to specific moral dilemmas that Virtue Ethics might serve more effectively as part of a larger moral theory than as a stand-alone theory. This will be discussed in more detail in Chapter Thirteen.

Summary

The moral system known as Virtue Ethics may predate Socrates. Aristotle is the theory's most ardent and thorough proponent. Virtue Ethics is rooted in the idea that the goal or purpose of life is to flourish (*eudaimonia*), and that the way to accomplish that is to be an excellent or virtuous (*arête*) person – that is, one who has developed the traits of character considered admirable and praiseworthy and that will result in the kind of happiness associated with *eudaimonia*. This approach to moral philosophy is best articulated by the question, "What kind of a person ought one to be?" This was the basic approach to moral philosophy from the time people began doing moral philosophy. But by the time the Enlightenment was getting underway, the basic question of moral philosophy, "What kind of person ought one to be?" had shifted to, "What is the right thing to do?" For nearly 300 years that question shaped moral philosophy differently, taking it in different directions than it had gone before.

---

[7] Rachels, "The Ethics of Virtue," *Ethics: History, Theory, and Contemporary Issues*, 705.

By the mid-1950s it became apparent that moral philosophy needed a course correction. Anscombe wrote an article in 1958 that provided the impetus for change. She suggested a return to Virtue Ethics. Over the next few years a number of papers and books were published about the viability of Virtue Ethics as a framework for contemporary moral philosophy.

What became the new, contemporary version of Virtue Ethics is not substantially different from ancient Virtue Ethics. The most striking difference (from a practical point of view) between the ancient and contemporary versions is the list of virtues considered essential for living an excellent life. The contemporary version, like the ancient version, has some weaknesses, especially when viewed from a modern perspective. But those weaknesses are not serious enough to abandon the theory. Its strengths more than compensate for its weaknesses. Those strengths include its holistic nature, its focus on character, its focus on interdependence, and that it allows for partiality.

While Virtue Ethics has much to commend it, it does appear to lack what contemporary society wants in a moral theory – a specific methodology for determining right and wrong. It may be, then, that Virtue Ethics, instead of functioning as a stand-alone theory may work best as part of a larger, more comprehensive ethical theory.

Thought and Discussion Questions

1. Discuss your thinking on the difference between the two questions, "What kind of a person ought one to be?" and "What is the right thing to do?" What is the significance of each question? What are the strengths and weaknesses of each question?

2. Analyze and discuss the similarities and differences between Aristotle's list of virtues and Rachels' list.

3. Discuss the implications of the contemporary list being longer and different than the ancient list.

4. Review the sections above that discuss the weaknesses and strengths of Virtue Ethics. Discuss what you consider to be its most serious weakness and its greatest strength. Explain why.

5. React to Rachels' suggestion that Virtue Ethics be part of a more comprehensive moral system.

Section Summary
Chapter 1-11

We have covered a lot of ground so far. We have discussed:

Ancient Hebrew Moral Philosophy
Greek Moral Philosophy
Jesus' Moral Philosophy
Early Christian Moral Philosophy
The Moral Philosophy of Augustine and Aquinas
Kantian Ethics
Utilitarianism
Ethical Egoism
Care Ethics
Contemporary Virtue Ethics

Several of these systems have approached moral philosophy by asking the question, *"What kind of a person ought one to be?"* while several others have asked, *"What is the right thing to do?"* Those that focus on character share in common the idea that living life according to wisdom (Aristotle spoke in terms of *phornesis* – practical wisdom) allows one to live morally and effectively, in a way that brings success and satisfaction in relational interdependence with others. The systems that focus on knowing what to do in specific circumstances allow one to ask and answer specific questions (what is the right thing to do in this or that situation), providing him with insights into morality as it relates to specific moral dilemmas.

As the socio-cultural landscape in the West changed over time the old question, *what kind of a person ought one to be*, no longer appeared to be sufficient. The world was changing and questions about morality were being asked that had not been asked before. Specific questions (especially new and complex ones) needed specific answers. The ethical focus shifted from character to behavior, from being to doing. In time, however, morality without an emphasis on character revealed its own inadequacies. Metaphorically speaking, Western society had been untied from its moorings and found itself adrift in a tumultuous sea of moral dilemmas. Perhaps the ancient focus had been best after all? Perhaps we needed to go back to what had been? And so a moral system rooted in character, Virtue Ethics, was proposed once again and generated a great deal of interest. However, while to doing orientation of more modern systems had proven not entirely satisfactory, it had met an important need – specific methodologies designed to provide specific answers to specific moral questions. Perhaps what modern society needs is some combination of the two, some combination of the old and the new, a system that addresses both being and doing.

A system that addresses both being and doing is what I hope to provide in Chapter 13. But before I get to that we will need to discuss morality in general – what it is and how we ought to think about it. And we need to discuss moral relativity and moral absolutes. Having discussed those things in Chapter 12, we will be prepared to consider a moral system that addresses both being and doing in Chapter 13.

Chapter 12
Defining Morality

Introduction

Moral, morality, immorality: we use the terms all the time. But what do they mean? What is morality? What makes an act moral or immoral? A typical dictionary might define moral as *pertaining to or concerned with the principles of right conduct, the distinction between right and wrong*. A dictionary of philosophy might go into more detail, but in the end will reflect the same idea: *morality has to do with what is right or wrong, good or bad*. Thus, behaving in a *moral* manner is good, and behaving in an *immoral* manner is bad. The average person probably knows that. The difficulty in discussing morality is in defining what kinds of behaviors are good and what kinds are bad. How does one distinguish between good and bad? We need to know what the essence of good is so that when we see it we recognize it for what it is – good. We also need to know what the essence of bad is so that when we see it we recognize it for what it is – bad. This is where defining morality begins to be challenging.

Morality and Humanness

Perhaps one way to understand morality, that is, to develop insights into the kinds of things that make an act moral or immoral, is to think in terms of the kind of beings we are. We are human beings. What does it mean to be human? Aristotle noted that being human means being *rational*. Humans are capable of logical analysis and abstract conceptualization. This cognitive capacity is one of the things that separates us from the lower animals. We can think in ways they cannot.[1]

We are also *self-determined* beings.[2] We are free to make choices. We determine what we will and will not do, the kind of person we will and will not be. We are not

---

[1]   For me, included in or along with rationality is the kind of self-awareness unique to humans. We are not only aware, we are aware of being aware. I call this 2nd level awareness.
     Peter Van Inwagen has dealt effectively with the Free Will issue in his book, *An Essay on Free Will*. Readers who are not fully convinced that humans are self-determined can read his material.

[2]   It is possible to embrace an idea or principle ideally but not always live up to it in our personal behavior. I believe this is often the case in our valuing of other people. We value human life, but we do not always act like we do in our relationships with individuals.

mechanistically determined, despite what materialist philosophers attempt to argue. We are not slaves to instinctive drives, behaving like dogs or cats. We choose. And we can freely choose to do good – an idea that will become crucial to my argument as it proceeds.

Another feature that is distinctive to humans is *morality*. Because we are rational beings we are also moral beings. We think about right and wrong, good and bad, justice and injustice, morality and immorality. We put a lot of effort into teaching our children to be good instead of bad. Along with rationality and self-determination, morality is an aspect of our human nature.

These three features: *rationality*, *self-determination*, and morality make us a unique species. They also make us responsible. They obligate us to be who and what we are capable of being. If we *can* think, we *ought* to think. If we *can* choose, we *ought* to choose. If we *can* be moral, we *ought* to be moral – someone has observed that *a moral can implies a moral ought.*

Humans are also *valuing* beings – we value things. What kinds of things do we value? We value things (objects) that are dear to us: the photo of a loved one, a childhood toy that brought us happiness, a tool that helps us accomplish an important task, things that were expensive or hard to come by, things that serve as symbols for important concepts – a wedding ring, for instance. We value all sorts of things, but the things we value most are things that have *intrinsic value* – the things (though not physical objects) that have value in and of themselves, apart from any personal sentimental value we might attach to them. For example, we value justice. We value freedom. We value beauty. We value love.

What else do we value? We value humanness. We understand the intrinsic value of being rational, moral, self-determined human beings. So we value humanness; we value human life because of what it means to be human.

How does our *thinking* regarding what is valuable impact our *behavior* regarding what is valuable? How do we act in relation to the things we value? For the objects we value, we safeguard them, display them, care for them, and cherish them. We do not damage them, forget them or toss just them away. Why not? Because we value them. For the concepts we value, we hold them in reverence, sacrifice for them, embrace them, fight for them, and enjoy them. We do not denigrate them, ignore them, relinquish or reject them, invalidate them, diminish them, or allow others to do so. What about the people we value? How do we behave toward them? We respect them, honor them, love them, care for them, sacrifice for them, fight for them, enjoy being with them, share with them, confide in them, and trust them. We do not devalue them by disrespecting them in word or deed, by abusing them physically or emotionally, by ignoring them, by manipulatively using them merely as a means to our own selfish end, or by allowing others to do so. When we value someone there are things we do and things we do not do – simply because we value them.

But beyond the specific value we attach to personal relationships with specific people, do we value human beings in general? I believe we do, at least in principle, even if we do not always behave as if we do.[3] We recognize the value that resides intrinsically in each human being. Human life is worth reproducing. Human life is worth nurturing. Human life is worth preserving. Human life is worth defending. Human life is worth cherishing. Why? Because there is  something of value there. There is rationality. There is self-determination. There is morality. And while there is individual autonomy, there is also an interconnectedness, an interdependence. There is a relational feature to life that allows for love, compassion, kindness, courage, sacrifice, purpose, achievement, and meaning. In short, there is humanness and humanness has value.[4]

Some might object to this line of reasoning, suggesting that I am arguing that things have value because we value them. Since we value humans, humans have value. If a thing has value simply because we value it, it does not have intrinsic value.[5] Intrinsic value would exist whether or not people recognize a thing's worth and value it appropriately. That is certainly true. I am not suggesting that humanness has value simply because we value it, but that it actually has intrinsic value. How so? To be human is to be capable of valuing and being valued. A valuing existence has value in and of itself, irrespective of any specific considerations, positive or negative, that might be part of that existence. Just as being human involves being rational, self-determined, and moral it also involves valuing. Because humans are rational, self-determined, moral, and valuing beings, humans have intrinsic value.

[3] Some have argued that life itself has intrinsic value. I disagree. Cancer is alive. It has no value at all. Flies are alive. They have instrumental value as part of our eco system, but they do not have intrinsic value. However, because of their rationality, self-determination, and morality humans (and any other species that has those characteristics) have intrinsic value.

[4] Intrinsic value, that which has value in and of itself – such as a human being, is distinguished from instrumental value, the value a thing has because we consider it valuable or useful in some way. A hammer has instrumental value as a tool that aids in the accomplishing of a task, but a hammer has no intrinsic value.

[5] There is no Footnote here.

What Makes an Act Moral or Immoral

It is when we understand the intrinsic value of humanness that we are in a position to determine what makes an act moral or immoral. I propose that *morality involves recognizing the intrinsic value of humanness (one's own and that of others), along with actions, reactions, and interactions that reflect an appreciation of human value. Immorality involves a failure to recognize the intrinsic value of humanness (one's own and that of others), along with a subsequent failure to act, react and interact in ways that reflect an appreciation of human value. Thus, an act is moral if it recognizes and or enhances human value, and is immoral if it fails to recognize or in some way diminishes the value of humanness.*[6]

This way of thinking about what is moral and immoral can be referred to as *metamorality*, that is, it is the underlying or foundational concept of morality that allows us to begin thinking about moral character and moral behavior. The metamorality must be in place as an underlying concept before we can begin to think about how it will express or manifest itself in one's character (one's habitual way of being) and in specific behaviors in response to specific moral dilemmas. While *metamorality* is an appreciation of humanness, *morality* is that appreciation expressed, generally, in one's character, and specifically, in actions related to given situations.

For instance, if I have an underlying appreciation for humanness that expresses itself in my character, my habitual behaviors will be those that reflect that appreciation. I will interact with people in ways that are consistent with my appreciation of their humanness. I will be respectful, courteous, honest, kind, charitable, and so forth because I value what they are – a human being. My character will also reflect the value I have for myself as a human being. In valuing the humanness of others, I value my own. In devaluing the humanness of others, I devalue my own. If I am a moral person, my characteristic behavior will reflect an appreciation of or for humanness. Likewise, in specific situations, concerns, or crisis where specific needs arise, if I am a moral person my behavior toward my fellow human beings in those specific instances (my sympathy, my willingness to help, and the way I go about helping) will

---

[6] Some may object, suggesting that I am arguing a form of *speciesism*, that humans value humanity simply because we are human and value our humanity. That is not what I am suggesting. I am arguing that the nature of humanness (what it is to be human) has intrinsic value. I would say that any species with the same essential features that comprise humanity (rationality, self-determination, morality, etc.) would also have intrinsic value. This argument will be very important in the third section of the book, *Contemporary Ethical Dilemmas*, where we will be looking at specific moral dilemmas, attempting to determine right and wrong behavior in relation to each of those concerns.

reflect my appreciation of their humanness. If I value humanness, my character in general and my actions in given situations will reflect that value.

So then let us reconsider the standard definition of morality: *pertaining to or concerned with the principles of right conduct, the distinction between right and wrong.* What are the principles of right conduct? The principles of right conduct involve *recognizing the intrinsic value of humanness (one's own and that of others), along with actions, reactions, and interactions that reflect an appreciation of human value.* If we ask about distinguishing between right and wrong, or ask the question that is asked in the section heading, "What makes an act moral or immoral?" we can say, *an act is moral if it recognizes and or enhances human value, and is immoral if it fails to recognize or in some way diminishes the value of humanness.*

This, I believe, provides us with a place to begin as we attempt to construct a viable moral theory. It is a foundation to build on. But before proceeding, there remains an important question that must be considered. It has to do with whether or to what degree morality is relative.

START

Is Morality Relative?

Are there some things that are always right, regardless of context and circumstances? Are there some things that are always wrong, regardless of context and circumstances? If you say, "Yes," then you are affirming the existence of moral absolutes – things that are absolutely right or absolutely wrong irrespective of any other issues or concerns. If you say, "No," then you are denying the existence of moral absolutes, which means that morality is relative; that is, that what is right or wrong depends on the situation or circumstances or the place or time. Is morality relative? Is morality absolute? Or could it be that there are some moral issues that are relative and some that are absolute?

The idea that morality is relative to place, time, and circumstances is not new. The ancient Greek historian, Herodotus, tells a story about the Persian king, Darius, and an experiment he set up between the Greeks and the Callatians (a tribe of Indians) regarding burial practices. Wanting the spirits of their dead relatives to enter and live in them, the Callatians ate their dead, while the Greeks burned the bodies of their dead. Each cultural group was horrified at the thought of treating their dead the way the other group  treated theirs. For the Callatians, burning the dead bodies of their loved ones would be horribly disrespectful. For the Greeks, eating the bodies of their loved ones would be just as horrible. Who was right? The conclusion was that neither was right and neither was wrong but that *custom* (cultural tradition) *is the lord of all*. In other words, universal absolutes that govern behavior do not exist. Time, place, and circumstance determine what is right and what is wrong. The Sophist, Protagoras, also espoused relativism, claiming that, o*f all things, man is the measure*. For Protagoras, since people determine what is right and wrong, what is right and wrong differs from one group of people to another.

However, even in ancient Greece, relativism of this sort was not the dominant paradigm. Neither Plato nor Aristotle advocated cultural and moral relativism of this type. It was not until modern times (the mid 1500s) that the idea of cultural and moral relativism became more popular.

Is morality relative? Or does a universal moral code exist? Few ethicists today advocate absolute moral relativity. But for many ethicists, the existence of a universal moral code is also considered questionable. Can a case be made for moral relativity?

"Is Morality Relative?"

Cultural and Moral Relativity

In the context of moral philosophy, cultural relativity is the idea that there are no universal moral rules (no moral absolutes) that are binding on all people in all times, places and circumstances. Each culture determines what is right or wrong in that culture. Thus, in one culture it might be considered moral to lie if it provides one with

some advantage, while in another culture lying might be considered immoral whether or not it might be advantageous. In one culture it might be moral to commit infanticide, while in another infanticide would be considered immoral.[7] Obviously, in attempting to define morality and discover what makes an act either moral or immoral, whether or not morality can consist of universal standards is a crucial consideration. What are the arguments for and against cultural relativism?

---

[7]   It has been argued that some interpretations of Ethical Egoism could involve moral relativity on a personal level. Most discussions of moral relativity, however, involve the relativity at the cultural rather than the personal level.

Those who advocate absolute cultural relativism usually offer three arguments. The first has to do with *cultural diversity*. The argument here is not just that cultures are different. Of course they are. Each culture has its own ways of doing things: language, food, clothing, family structures, and so forth. There is a tremendous amount of this kind of cultural diversity in the world. Diversity of this sort is not what proponents of cultural relativity have in mind. The diversity they have in mind has to do with moral issues: infanticide, euthanasia, marital fidelity, bribery, and other such issues. Specifically, the argument from cultural diversity is that, *because there is moral diversity it is obvious that there is no single universal moral standard to which all people are accountable. The moral diversity that we see in the world requires that we see our own moral system as merely one system among many.*

Is this a sound argument? A brief analysis of it will demonstrate that it is not. The moral diversity that exists from culture to culture does not even suggest, let alone make it obvious, that there is no universal moral code. The moral diversity that exists from culture to culture may be due to several factors. Just because cultures do not observe the moral standards of a universal moral code does not mean that a universal moral code does not exist. For instance, people who practice infanticide

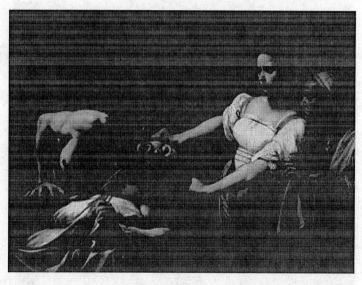

may not consider that infanticide to be murder and therefore immoral. They may be aware the murdering of an adult to be immoral but not the killing an infant. Or it may be that they simply do not care that others consider it is immoral. People often do that which is immoral, knowing full well that it is immoral, but not caring that it is. To argue that since not all cultures observe a universal moral code, it is obvious that no universal moral code exists is like arguing that since people do not observe the speed limit, it is obvious that there is no speed limit. The argument does not stand; it is not sound.

The second argument designed to support absolute cultural relativity is often referred to as *the untenability of moral objectivism*. The phrase *moral objectivism* refers to a moral code that is objective (and therefore universal) rather than one that is subjective (relative) and therefore not universal. This argument is really just an extension of the cultural diversity argument. Specifically, the argument is that the idea of a universal moral code is untenable – there simply can't be a universal moral code. Why not? Because, the argument goes, cultural relativism exists. Since cultural relativism exists, there can't be a universal moral code. Also, the argument assumes that it has been demonstrated that a universal moral code does not and cannot exist because there is no God who could give one. No God, therefore no universal moral code. Stated succinctly, the two-part argument can be put like this: since God does not exist to give a universal moral code and since cultural diversity exists, moral relativity exists.

Is this argument sound? Again, a brief analysis of the argument demonstrates that it is not sound. First, while some believe that God does not exist it has not been demonstrated that God does not exist. In fact, there is only one positive argument against the existence of God, the problem of evil, and that argument is easily answered. Other arguments against the existence of God are merely assertions that there is no evidence that God exists. This assertion is incorrect. Many positive arguments can be made for the existence of God.[8] Belief that God does not exist is an arbitrary assumption that is embraced in spite of evidence to the contrary.

"Does Evil Disprove God?"

Second, even if there is no God it is not the case that there cannot, therefore, be a universal moral code. There could be a universal moral code based on the intrinsic value of humanness. I will discuss this idea in more detail in the section below on Moral Absolutes. Whether or not all cultures recognize all features of the moral code is irrelevant. The code can exist whether or not people are aware of or acknowledge its existence.

The aspect of the argument that rests on the presence of cultural diversity has already been addressed. The argument, therefore, is not sound. It has not demonstrated that a universal moral code is untenable. The claim that a universal moral code is untenable is based on assumptions that have not been proven. Thus, the argument is not sound. There is nothing untenable about the idea of a universal moral law.

The third argument in favor of absolute moral relativism is that *acknowledging that morality is relative promotes tolerance*. This argument merely assumes that morality is relative and then says that being relative is a good thing because it promotes tolerance. However, we have seen that the first two arguments are unsound. Neither proves the case for moral relativity. Therefore one cannot simply assume moral relativity and then say it is a good thing. There is no argument here. There is only assumption and assertion.

---

[8]   See Rogers, *Proof of God: Inquiries into the Philosophy of Religion, A Concise Introduction.*

The assertion that moral relativity is good because it promotes tolerance of moral systems other than our own appears to be based on the assumption that all moral codes ought to be tolerated. Is that a good assumption? Certainly not. Ethnocentrism is the belief that only one's own culture or ethnic perspective is valid and deserving of respect. It (like racism) is an ugly belief and must be eliminated. We must be able to acknowledge and validate the perspectives and practices of other cultural groups – generally speaking. But must we tolerate everything they do? The suggestion that absolute moral relativity is good because it promotes tolerance rests on the assumption that morality is relative and that all practices are moral (because each culture determines what is moral in that culture) and ought, therefore, to be tolerated by those who live by a different moral code. Why must they be tolerated? Because one moral code is just as valid as any other. Why would one make that assumption? Why would one assume that a practice such as infanticide could ever be moral? Why would one assume that ethnocide (as practiced by the Nazis against Jewish people during WWII) could ever be moral? Yet, if morality is, in fact, absolutely relative, then we ought to tolerate things such as infanticide and ethnocide. Can that possibly be right? No, it cannot.

"Culture and Ethnocentrism"

In thinking about the three "arguments" in favor of moral relativity, we see that actually there is only one argument – the argument based on cultural relativity. And, as we have seen, that argument is not sound. It does not even come close to proving that morality is absolutely relative. What we really have is one unsound argument and two assertions rooted in unsound assumptions. Those who advocate absolute cultural relativism have not made their case. What is the alternative? The alternative to absolute cultural relativism is to understand that a universal moral code does exist, that moral absolutes exist. The alternative to absolute cultural relativity is to understand that cultural relativity is not absolute, but is *relative*. Social norms do vary from culture to culture and there is nothing wrong with that – to a degree. There are some things cultural groups get to decide for themselves and some things they do not get to decide. What kinds of things are culturally relative and what kinds of things are not? And how can we know the difference? To answer these questions we must first consider moral absolutes.

Moral Absolutes

What are moral absolutes? Moral absolutes are behaviors that are either always right in every instance and can never be wrong, or always wrong in every instance and can never be right. A universal moral code is made up of moral absolutes. There are two questions concerning moral absolutes that must be addressed. The first is, "If moral absolutes do exist, where did they come from?" The second is, "If moral absolutes exist, what are they?"

As to the first question, regarding the origin of moral absolutes, moral absolutes have existed simultaneously along with rationality, self-determination and valuing. As long as there has been rationality, self-determination, and valuing, there has been morality. They are co-existing realities. As to the second question, regarding what these moral absolutes are, moral absolutes are acts that either enhance or devalue humanness: *an act is moral if it recognizes and or enhances human value, and is immoral if it fails to recognize or in some way diminishes the value of humanness.* To determine specifically what kinds of things would be moral absolutes, one would need to ask if a given act enhances or devalues humanness.

It is really not that difficult. Think about it for a moment. Does murder enhance or devalue humanness? Murder is a violent act that ends the life of another person. It is the ultimate devaluing of the murdered person. Thus, murder is immoral.

Consider child molestation. In the act of molestation the child becomes merely an object for the adult's personal pleasure. The child is not treated as a human being with intrinsic value. The child's dignity is stripped away as he or she is manipulated and used. Child molestation leaves children feeling confused, betrayed, angry, and distrustful. It is degrading and devaluing. Child molestation, therefore, is immoral.

Consider bullying. The person being bullied, usually a child or adolescent being picked on by peers or those a few years older, is called names, is made the butt of jokes and may be physically intimidated or abused and is certainly emotionally abused. The bullied person is rejected and ridiculed and made to feel worthless. Being bullied leaves one feeling the opposite of being valued. Bullying is designed to tear down, not to build up. Bullying is degrading and devaluing. Bullying, therefore, is immoral.

Consider stealing. Stealing from another person, whether it is his or her wallet or purse, means of transportation, words, or artistic productions (music or art), diminishes his or her humanity by saying, in effect, you do not matter. Your personhood, your presence, your rights are irrelevant. I can take what you have and I will. To diminish the personhood of another, to make a person feel irrelevant, to make a person feel disregarded and violated devalues his or her humanness. Stealing, therefore, is immoral.

"Internet Piracy"

Consider rape. Rape usually involves a man raping a woman. Rape is an act of violence where a woman's personhood and autonomy are taken from her. Her dignity is stripped from her and her value as a human is diminished in an act that, in effect, says: your will is irrelevant, you are irrelevant. I will do to you what I please. Rape can have serious physical and emotional consequences. Rape diminishes one's humanness. Rape is, therefore, an immoral act.

Consider animal cruelty. A person who is cruel to animals (that is, who causes an animal to feel pain or to suffer when there is no greater good involved in the act – medical research, for example) causes a living thing to suffer needlessly. Intentionally perpetrated needless cruelty devalues sentient life by lowering the quality of life. Causing needless pain and suffering for sport or personal pleasure devalues the humanity of the one causing the pain. The one causing the needless suffering says, in effect, I do not care about the feelings of a living creature. I do not care that I lower the quality of life of a living creature. I do not value life in general. Animal cruelty devalues the humanity of the one committing the cruelty. Animal cruelty is, therefore, immoral.

"The Face of Dogfighting: One Dog's Incredible Journey"

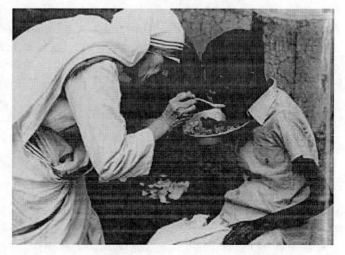

Consider, however, an act of kindness, such as feeding a hungry person or giving a thirsty person something to drink. The person giving the food or drink feels compassion. His or her act communicates the worthiness and value of the person in need. Two human beings are interacting in a healthy, caring manner that elevates the humanness of the one giving and the one receiving. The value of humanness is confirmed. An act of kindness shown to another person is a moral act.

Consider honesty. When one is honest, one is affirming a belief in the value of truth, of the importance of honesty in personal interaction. Honesty is a feature of intimacy. It involves a transparency that promotes trust. Honesty enhances the interconnectedness of humanity, allowing people to work together in harmony. Honesty elevates humanness. Honesty is moral.[9]

Assessing what an act does to the humanness of another (or to one's own humanness) determines the morality of the act. Utilizing this method, one can identify moral and immoral behaviors and begin to compile a list of such behaviors. For instance, in the examples above I have identified both moral and immoral behaviors:

Moral Behaviors	Immoral Behaviors
Kindness	Murder
Honesty	Child molestation
	Bullying
	Stealing
	Rape
	Animal cruelty

This list is only partial, serving as an example of how the process can work. In an actual list there might be as many moral behaviors as there are immoral behaviors. The problem in creating any list of this type is that people will disagree as to what should be on the list. For instance, in my list I have included bullying as an immoral act. Others might object, saying that while bullying may not be nice, it is not immoral. This, of course, depends on how one defines and determines morality. As I have defined morality, relating it to the valuing of humanness, bullying would be an immoral act. What about animal cruelty? Does being needlessly cruel to an animal devalue the humanity of the one committing the act? I believe it does. Others may argue that it does not. That topic and others like it would need to be part of an ongoing dialog in an attempt to arrive at a clear understanding of morality as it relates to humanness.

[9] Being honest does not require that one always say exactly what one thinks. Sometimes saying exactly what one thinks can be unkind. A College professor, for instance, can be honest without telling one of his students that his or her work resembles what a sloppy fifth grader might turn in. One does not have to be unkind to be honest. Tactfulness and honesty are not mutually exclusive.

One of the complaints that is often raised against the existence of moral absolutes is the challenge of identifying what they are. Identifying what is moral and immoral is always going to be challenging. But that does not mean that some basic understanding cannot be achieved or that at least a short list of moral and immoral behaviors cannot be developed. It may be a challenging and time consuming process, but understanding what is and what is not moral is important enough to be given whatever time and energy is required to sustain an ongoing dialog. At one time in Western culture, slavery was considered moral by many, if not most, people. Today that is no longer the case. Given enough time and dialog, people can and do change their minds about important issues. The civil rights and feminist movements are additional illustrations of how attitudes toward what is moral or immoral can change given enough time and dialog. Just because something is difficult does not mean that it cannot be accomplished and that the project, therefore, ought to be abandoned.

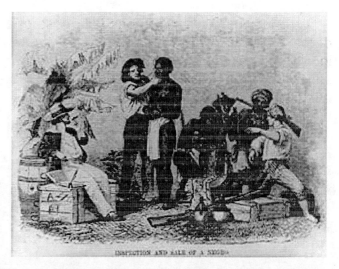

Why is it important to pursue the development of an agreed upon moral code? Because not having one is problematic. Cultural diversity is a reality, and for the most part is not only acceptable, but healthy and necessary. Each group of people must be allowed to govern themselves and determine their own cultural reality – up to a point. There are many things about day-to-day life that do not involve issues of morality: clothing styles, food preferences, transportation and communication technologies, housing preferences, family structures (preferences for either nuclear or extended families for instance), approaches to education, and so forth. In these *non-moral* areas, cultures must be free to determine their own behaviors. In matters such as these cultural relativity is entirely appropriate. I refer to this as *relative relativity*. It is a form of cultural relativity that has to do with non-moral concerns. Relative relativity is a limited form of relativity. It is not *absolute relativity*. Those who advocate moral relativity are advocating absolute relativity, arguing that cultures have the right to determine morality in their culture without consideration to anything beyond their own cultural beliefs.

History demonstrates that absolute relativity is dangerous and leads to unconscionable behavior. Consider the ancient Hindu custom of Satee (widow burning). Because of their religious beliefs, if a husband died, his wife also had to die in order to accompany him into the next life so she could continue caring for his needs. Many Hindu women (understandably) resisted the idea and the process. The widows who resisted would be tied to her dead husband's funeral pier and burned alive while her husband's body was being burned. This custom had been practiced for thousands of years. When the British came to India they objected to the practice. The Indian response was that this was their cultural practice and had been accepted since ancient times. As cultural outsiders, the Indians argued, the British had nothing to say about the practice. The British disagreed and outlawed the practice. For the British, there was a universal moral code that transcended cultural privileges and rights. The Indian people were claiming the right to kill widows based on absolute cultural relativism. From their perspective, it was their culture, their practice, and no one else's business. Were they right? Did they have the right to burn widows alive because that was their custom? Or were the British right? Either way, the historical reality is that the belief that each culture has the absolute right to determine what is or is not moral led to the practice of widow burning.

"India: Forgotten Women"

Consider the Nazi's in mid-twentieth century Germany. The Nazi's hated Jewish people and wanted them out of their society. The Nazi's considered the Jewish way of life a threat to the German way of life. The Nazi's final solution to the Jewish problem was to kill six million men, women, and children, to engage in *ethnocide* in an attempt to rid their society of the perceived threat. After the war, as "war criminals" were rounded up and put on trial in Nuremberg, the Nazi defense, as the Indian defense had been centuries before, was rooted in the idea of absolute cultural relativism – the German culture, a German problem, a German solution, and no one else's business. The rest of the Western world disagreed. Germany could not engage in ethnocide. There was a higher moral law that transcended the cultural perspective of Germany. Was Germany right? Could they exterminate the Jewish people if they wanted to? Or were the Allies right? Was there a higher moral law that transcended the cultural practices of Germany? Either way, history demonstrates that the idea that morality is absolutely relative gave birth to an unconscionable practice.

"The Nazis – A Warning from History"

Consider infanticide. In the early 1960s, China already had the largest population on earth. In 1966, Chairman Mao Zedong initiated a number of strict policies designed to stabilize China's society. One of the policies was the one child rule. Each couple could only have one child. To break the rule and have additional children would result in severe consequences that would make it nearly impossible to survive. So each couple would have only one child. The problem was that in China it is the responsibility of the oldest son to care for his aging parents. Daughters could not accept responsibility for aging parents. When daughters married they became part of their husband's family and could not be responsible for their parents. That meant that if parents wanted someone to care for them in their old age they must have a son, not a daughter. Since they could only have one child, that one child had to be a boy. But what if their baby was a girl? The situation was horrible. The result was that millions of girl babies were either killed or tossed out to die simply because they were girls instead of boys. Infanticide. When news of the practice spread, the Western world was outraged. China was severely criticized. Fortunately the Cultural Revolution last only 10 years or so and the practice subsided. But the Chinese defended their actions on the basis of absolute cultural relativism – our culture, our problem, our solution, and none of your business. Were the Chinese right? Was the West right? Was China's infanticide moral? Or is there a moral code that transcends cultural perspectives? Either way, history once again demonstrates that the idea that morality is entirely relative leads to horrible results.

Though many additional illustrations could be offered, these three are sufficient to make the point: absolute cultural relativity leads to unconscionable acts. None of these examples are theoretical case scenarios. They are historical fact. Attempting to deny the ultimate results of absolute relativity is futile. However, it is important to note that my argument against moral relativity is not these unconscionable historical consequences (although they do factor in), but that fact that a universal moral code exists because morality is part of being human. *Humans do not determine morality, they discover it as they come to understand what it means to be human, as they learn how to value humanness.* Objective moral standards exist and must be respected if our humanness is to be meaningful.

END

Summary

In this chapter, I have argued that the definition of morality grows out of the definition of humanity. When we understand what it is to be human, we can understand what it is to be moral. Approaching morality from this perspective, the Principle of Essential Humanness, we can say that *morality involves recognizing the intrinsic value of humanness (one's own and that of others), along with actions, reactions, and interactions that reflect an appreciation of human value. Immorality involves a failure to recognize the intrinsic value of humanness (one's own and that of others), along with a subsequent failure to act, react and interact in ways that reflect an appreciation of human value. Thus, an act is moral if it recognizes and or enhances human value, and is immoral if it fails to recognize or in some way diminishes the value of humanness.*
One of the key questions related to morality is whether it is absolute or relative. Few ethicists advocate absolute moral relativity. Those who do so usually offer three arguments: cultural diversity, the untenability of moral objectivism, and the promotion of tolerance. We looked at each of these arguments and discovered that each is unsound and does not support absolute cultural relativity.

We looked at several specific behaviors to assess their morality or immorality as the behavior relates to humanness. From the examples discussed, we developed a partial list of moral and immoral behaviors. We also discussed historical examples of what can happen when morality is considered to be absolutely relative – sooner or later unconscionable acts are the result.

Thought and Discussion Questions

1. Discuss Rogers' idea that morality is part and parcel of being human as are rationality and self-determination.

2. Discuss Rogers' idea that the definition of morality must be tied to humanness and value. Include a discussion of metamorality.

3. Discuss the three arguments offered in support of absolute moral relativity and Rogers' response to each of them.

4. Discuss the validity or invalidity of Rogers' three historical illustrations of where cultural relativity leads.
5. If you disagree with Rogers' view and definition of morality, lay out your own view and definition of morality.

Chapter 13
Critical Ethical Eclecticism

Introduction

Aristotle proposed an ethical framework, known today as Virtue Ethics, rooted in the development of character traits that resulted in being an excellent person, which in turn allowed one to flourish or thrive in life. Jesus proposed an ethical framework rooted in love for God and for others, involving the highest form of love, a love focused not on feeling but on behavior, stressing that we love others as much as we love ourselves. Centuries later, Kant proposed an ethical framework rooted in doing one's duty based on what he called the Categorical Imperative, an Imperative that could be expressed in more than one way, but that provided one with the means to determine what is and is not moral. Bentham proposed Utilitarianism, a form of consequentialism built on the Principle of Utility, the idea that the quest for happiness is fundamental to life and that which brings happiness to people is moral.

Over the centuries there have been many ethical theories proposed. The ones I've just noted are, perhaps, those that have been most influential in Western society. Each of them has something useful or helpful about it. Even those that I have critiqued in previous chapters and determined inadequate (as a viable or stand-alone theory) have some feature about them that can be useful when faced with a moral dilemma. But none of them appear to be satisfactory in all situations. Each of them appears to fail in some respect, especially when it comes to determining what is the moral thing to do in a given situation.

In this chapter, I want to suggest a functional moral paradigm that will provide answers to the numerous and complex moral questions of contemporary Western society. In other words, I want to propose a theory that will not fail to provide one with the answers one needs to work through a moral dilemma. Whether or not I accomplish my goal is for the reader to decide.

The Basic Features of a Functional Moral Paradigm

What would a fully functional moral paradigm look like? What features would it need to be viable, to provide one with an effective framework for moral thinking and acting in contemporary society? It would need five features. A functional moral theory would need:

1. *A thorough and effective definition/explanation of morality.* It is impossible to think about morality, to discuss morality, and to determine what the moral thing to do in any given situation is if we do not know what morality is. So a functional moral theory must begin by explaining what morality is, which includes an explanation of what makes an act moral or immoral.

2. *A proper focus on the development of moral character.* From the very beginning of moral philosophy the focus was on the kind of person one ought to be. Only recently (the past few hundred years) has the focus shifted to behaviors in specific circumstances. While the question, *what is the right thing to do*, is a good and valid question, so is the question, *what kind of a person ought one to be?* Both questions deserve to be asked and answered. However, when considering what the proper behavior in a given situation might be, it is apparent that one who is of high moral character, one who habitually does the right kinds of things in general, will be likely (perhaps more likely) to do the right thing in a specific situation. Thus, a functional moral theory will be one that focuses on the development of moral character.

3. *A mechanism for discovering the moral thing to do in a given situation.* While a proper focus on moral character is an essential feature of a functional moral theory, so is the inclusion of a mechanism for determining the moral thing to do in a given situation. A person may be of the highest moral character and find himself completely confounded when confronted by a moral dilemma to which he has not given much thought. A moral theory that stresses only moral character and provides no mechanism for determining right action in given situations is incomplete. Therefore, a functional moral theory will include a mechanism for discovering the moral thing to do in a specific situation.

4. *A proper focus on motive and intention.* Why one does what one does is of crucial importance. Two people can perform the same act, say, giving money to a poor person. One can do it out of compassion for the poor person, wanting to help, the other can do it for  appearances sake, to impress and generate positive regard from others. The end result for the poor person is the same in either case, but the givers gave for very different reasons. One motive was altruistic, the other egoistic, one others-centered, the other self-centered. But if the outcome for the poor person is the same, why does motive matter? Because motive and intention provide the foundation for human behavior. What we do (action) and why we do it (motive)

are connected because we are rational self-determined people. We decide who and what we are and we do so for reasons. Reasons (motive and intentions) matter. So a functional moral theory will provide a proper focus on motive and intentions.

5. *A proper focus on consequences.* As important as motives and intentions are, consequences are equally important. What happens is as important as why it happens. A moral theory that focuses only on motive and intention is lopsided. There must be a focus on consequences as well. Humans act for reasons. And actions have consequences – that matter. What happens to me matters; and what happens to you matters. Why? Because as human beings, we matter. So what happens to us – consequences – also matters.

These five features must be present in a moral theory if it is to be viable in contemporary society as a means for moral thinking and acting. The problem is, of all the theories we have reviewed and evaluated thus far, none of them contain all these features. Each of them contains one or more of these features, but none contains all of them. The task, then, in offering a truly functional moral theory is to suggest a moral framework that does contain all five features. That will be my task in the following section.

Critical Ethical Eclecticism:
A Functional Moral Paradigm

What is Critical Ethical Eclecticism? How does it work? Why is it any more "functional" than any other ethical theory? My goal here is to answer all three of these questions.

What is Critical Ethical Eclecticism? Critical Ethical Eclecticism (CEE) is an ethical theory or moral framework that makes use of a number of other ethical theories to create a new composite theory that (hopefully) will not suffer from the shortcomings of the other individual systems. By combining the best features of other theories, along with a definition of morality that links it to humanness, CEE will (hopefully) offer a more balanced framework for moral thinking and acting.

The word *ethical* in the name CEE is present for obvious reasons – it is an ethical theory. The word *eclectic* is also obvious – the theory borrows from and is composed of different aspects of other theories. But why include the word *critical* in CEE? By *critical* I refer, not to criticizing other theories, although that is sometimes necessary, but rather to a critical, careful and thoughtful analysis of: 1) what contemporary society needs in a moral theory (what features must be included in a functional moral theory), and 2) what features of already existing moral theories can be borrowed to create a composite theory that will work well in contemporary society.

How does CEE work? The paragraph above offers a brief explanation, but some additional clarification may be helpful. Perhaps it might be best to consider CEE in light of the five essential features of a functional moral theory discussed in the previous section. CEE is a functional moral theory because:

1. *CEE includes a thorough and effective definition/explanation of morality.* As discussed in the previous chapter: morality involves recognizing the intrinsic value of humanness (one's own and that of others), along with actions, reactions, and interactions that reflect an appreciation of human value. Immorality involves a failure to recognize the intrinsic value of humanness (one's own and that of others), along with a subsequent failure to act, react and interact in ways that reflect an appreciation of human value. Thus, an act is moral if it recognizes and or enhances human value, and is immoral if it fails to recognize or in some way diminishes the value of humanness.

The key here is that this is not merely a definition that says morality has to do with the concepts of right and wrong, which tells us nothing very helpful about morality, but one that equates morality with humanness in a way that allows for the specific identification of that which is moral or immoral based on how an act values and enhances or devalues and diminishes humanness.

2. *CEE includes a proper focus on the development of moral character.* Ancient moral philosophers were on to something important with their focus on becoming a person who lived an effective life because one lived according to the dictates of wisdom (ancient Hebrew moral philosophy); or because one became an excellent person, thereby flourishing and thriving (ancient Greek moral philosophy); or being a loving person who treats others the way one would like to be treated (the moral philosophy of Jesus). The idea that one who is a person of high moral character, who habitually does the right kinds of things, will be one who is likely to act morally  when confronted with a moral dilemma is, I believe, a valid and useful idea. The kinds of things one does grows out of (is correlated to) the kind of a person one is. A good person is likely to do good things. If we, as a society, are concerned about people doing the right thing, the moral thing in any given situation, then we need to be concerned about the development of individual moral character.

Aristotle and Jesus understood this, and their moral philosophy had a great deal to do with the development of moral character. How does moral character develop? Socrates asked this same question. The answer is, it must be taught. Again, Aristotle and Jesus agreed on this point: the development of moral character is part of an effective enculturation or socialization process. The kind of moral character needed in contemporary society is one that stresses the linkage between morality and humanness. Moral character must: 1) be rooted in and related to our essential humanness, 2) reflect the interrelational and interdependent nature of our essential humanness, and 3) be rooted in an appreciation of the intrinsic value of each human being, reflected in the way we interact with others. Insights regarding the moral character of individuals must be associated with the linkage between morality and humanness.

CEE stresses the need for a foundational moral character built on the linkage between morality and humanness, emphasizing the need for the further development of specific character traits such as those stressed by Jesus and his followers (love, patience, kindness, and so forth) as well as those advocated by Aristotle and proponents of contemporary Virtue Ethics. In other words, CEE borrows from Jesus and Aristotle,[1] stressing the importance of moral character as a foundational feature of a functional moral theory. One of the key components of Critical Ethical Eclecticism is Virtue Ethics.

3. *CEE includes a mechanism for discovering the moral thing to do in a given situation.* Being the kind of person one ought to be has a lot to do with doing the right thing, the moral thing, in any given situation. But without some mechanism for analyzing specific situations and the options involved, one is left without clear guidance as to what to do or not do in situations where the moral thing to do is not obvious. This is one of the complaints against Virtue Ethics – it contains no mechanism for making specific determinations of right and wrong. CEE avoids this weakness by including a mechanism for making specific determinations.

---

[1]   A number of ethicists are under the impression that Christian ethics is not essentially Virtue Ethics. They are mistaken. However, their mistake is easily forgiven, for so many Christian Ethicists (also mistakenly) work out of a Divine Command Theory perspective, failing to understand the "virtue" foundation of the moral philosophy of the apostles Peter and Paul, to say nothing of Jesus' own focus on the development of appropriate moral character – which is, in effect, virtue ethics. Jesus advocated what might be called a Golden Rule Ethic of Love, but that ethical framework was built on the foundation of an appropriate moral character – the kind of person one ought to be. Jesus advocated a form of virtue ethics. Thus, it is accurate for me to say that CEE borrows a focus on Virtue from Jesus and Aristotle.

The mechanism CEE uses is the definition/explanation of morality described in number 1 above: *morality involves recognizing the intrinsic value of humanness (one's own and that of others), along with actions, reactions, and interactions that reflect an appreciation of human value. Immorality involves a failure to recognize the intrinsic value of humanness (one's own and that of others), along with a subsequent failure to act, react and interact in ways that reflect an appreciation of human value. Thus, an act is moral if it recognizes and or enhances human value, and is immoral if it fails to recognize or in some way diminishes the value of humanness.* This explanation of morality, *The Principle of Essential Humanness*, allows one to analyze a behavior (or potential behavior) and determine whether it is moral or immoral depending on whether it values and enhances or devalues and diminishes humanness.

At this point it might be appropriate to address the difference between a *rule-oriented process* and an *analysis-oriented process*. A rule-oriented process is one that involves a list of rules – do this, don't do that. It does not involve any kind of critical thinking. It is a simple process. A child can determine what to do or not do if right and wrong is contained in a list of rules. The problem with rule-oriented morality (such as the Divine Command Theory) is that the list of rules has be to continually updated if it is to remain relevant to evolving needs. For instance, consider the Ten Commandments of the Old Testament. It is a good list, as far as it goes. But what does it have to say regarding euthanasia, animal rights, environmental issues, human cloning and other contemporary ethical concerns? Absolutely nothing. If one is asking about adultery or stealing, the Ten Commandments have something to say. If one is asking about human cloning, they have nothing to say. In that regard the list is outdated and inadequate. For many contemporary ethical concerns, the list is irrelevant. All rule-oriented approaches to moral philosophy are subject to this weakness.

What CEE offers as a mechanism for discovering what is and is not moral is an analysis-oriented process. It is a process that requires rational people to engage in critical thinking to discover (not determine, but *discover* – the difference is crucial)[2] what is moral. Both Kant and Bentham offered something similar. Kant's Categorical Imperative (either formulation), "*Act only on that maxim through which you can at the*

---

2   Morality is not subjective, not relative. It is objective. Moral absolutes exist. That which is moral is inexorably connected to and associated with the intrinsic value of humanness. Those things that enhance rather than diminish humanness in any given situation must be "discovered" through the rational process.

same time will that it should become a universal law,[3] or *"Act in such a way that you always treat humanity, whether in your own person or in the person of another, never simply as a means, but always at the same time as an end,"*[4] is an analysis-oriented process for discovering moral or immoral behavior. Bentham's Principle of Utility, *"that principle which approves or disapproves of every action whatsoever, according to the tendency which it appears to have to augment or diminish the happiness of the party whose interest is in question,"*[5] is also an analysis-oriented process for discovering moral or immoral behavior. Where Kant offered the Categorical Imperative and Bentham offered the Principle of Utility, CEE offers the Principle of Essential Humanness: *morality involves recognizing the intrinsic value of humanness (one's own and that of others), along with actions, reactions, and interactions that reflect an appreciation of human value. Immorality involves a failure to recognize the intrinsic value of humanness (one's own and that of others), along with a subsequent failure to act, react and interact in ways that reflect an appreciation of human value. Thus, an act is moral if it recognizes and or enhances human value, and is immoral if it fails to recognize or in some way diminishes the value of humanness.*

If the goal of CEE in this regard is similar to Kant's or Bentham's (offering a mechanism for discovering morality), why not use those frameworks instead of offering a third alternative? As has been noted in Chapter Eight, Utilitarianism as proposed by Bentham (a very specific form of Consequentialism), is based on hedonistic happiness and is in my view, for the reasons offered in Chapter Eight, unacceptable as a framework for moral thinking and acting. As for Kantianism, while I hold Kant's system in very high regard, it does not appear to be helpful in all cases. Also, Kant believed that only intention and duty were important, that consequences were beyond one's control and thus unimportant. I disagree. While consequences cannot be the sole determinate of morality (as Bentham and Mill suggested), they cannot be ignored.

For these reasons, then, instead of using Kant's Categorical Imperative (either version of it) or Bentham's Principle of Utility, CEE offers a third alternative. CEE utilizes one universal principle (the Principle of Essential Humanness), articulated in a precise manner, which allows one to utilize an analysis-oriented process to discover moral and immoral behavior. In this regard CEE follows the lead of Kant and Bentham.

3   Kant, *Groundwork*, 2:421, 52.
4   Kant, *Groundwork*, 2:429, 67.
5   Bentham, *An Introduction to the Principles of Morals and Legislation*, Chapter 1.

4. *CEE involves a proper focus on motive and intention.* As noted earlier, what people do is important. Equally important is why they do it. Motive matters. Intention matters. In this regard Kant and Bentham disagreed. Kant believed that motive and intention were important and that consequences, since they are beyond our control, are not important in differentiating between moral and immoral. Bentham, however, believed consequences were all that mattered. Intentions are not important, but only results. Here all I can say is that I think Bentham was simply wrong. And I believe that thoughtful reflection on day-to-day experience will support that contention. How often do we ask people, why did you do that? Quite often, actually. Why do we ask? Because we want to know what their reason was for acting as they did. We want to understand their motive. We want to understand their intention. Why? Because often, in day-to-day life, a person's motive or intention for what they do makes their action either acceptable or unacceptable. Consider the inept husband who is attempting to compliment his wife on her outfit. He might say, "I like that outfit. It doesn't make you look fat." At first his wife may be annoyed, but she might then realize that he was trying to compliment her, even though he did it badly. Because he was trying to say something nice, she will not (hopefully) become angry with him. Why not? Because of his motive, his intention. He did not mean to insult, but to compliment. Because of his intention, his blunder will be overlooked. In the everyday world, intention and motive matter. And so, too, in the realm of ethics, intention and motive matter.

Kant believed that because we cannot control what happens we cannot be held accountable for what happens. But we are fully capable of managing our motives and intentions. Therefore, Kant argued that we are responsible for our intentions and must be sure that they are morally appropriate. To a degree, I agree with Kant and will have more to add on the subject in the next section. For now, the point is that a functional moral theory will involve an appropriate focus on motives and intentions. Why we do what we do matters, especially when it come to determining morality.

Suppose, for instance, that one evening while my wife and I are watching our favorite TV show someone knocks on our door. It is our neighbor Betty and she is in a panic. I bring her into the house. On the verge of hysteria, Betty explains that she just witnessed a murder a few blocks across town and the killers are aware that she witnessed what they did. They are after her. One of them looked familiar to her and she is worried that they know where she lives. She wants us to hide her. I agree and tell my wife to take Betty down into the basement and try to calm her while I call the police. A little unsettled myself, I sit down to think for a moment before I call the police. Before I can call, there is another knock at the door. Two rough-looking men are there and one of them explains that they are Betty's cousins from out of town and have come to visit her. She isn't home and she's not answering her cell phone. They want to know if I know where she is. I hesitate a moment, shake my head and say, "No, I haven't seen Betty all day." They hesitate a moment before thanking me for my help. They turn to leave and I close the door. I call the police and when they arrive Betty tells them her story and goes with them to the police station.

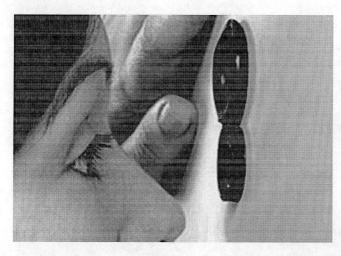

Later, as I'm reflecting on the event I realize that I lied to the killers. I lied, telling them I had not seen Betty. But I'm an honest man. I don't lie. Lying is wrong – morally unacceptable. But surely in this case and others like it, lying is acceptable because I lied to save a life. Those men would have killed Betty if they had found her. By hiding her and lying to the killers, I saved her life. Surely that made the lie justifiable. Valuing Betty's humanness took precedent over, was more important than, the need to be honest with those who would devalue Betty's humanness by depriving her of life.

Most people, I think, would agree that in such cases that kind of a lie is justifiable. But Kant did not. He even told the same basic story and arrived at the conclusion that to lie to the killers would be morally wrong. I disagree with Kant. Why? Because my motive for lying, my intention, was to save a life. I was not deceiving them for any personal gain. I was concerned for the life of another. My motive justified my behavior. Because of why I lied, my lying was not immoral. Motive matters.

CEE includes a proper focus on motive and intention. This feature is borrowed from Kant, even though I apply it differently than Kant did.

5. *CEE involves a proper focus on consequences.* Motive and intention are important, but so are consequences. Kant's point about our not being able to control outcomes and therefore not being responsible for outcomes is valid. But because we cannot control outcomes all the time does not mean that we should not be concerned about outcomes, or that consequences have nothing to do with the rightness or wrongness of an act. Of course they do. Consider the example offered above, where Betty is being pursued by killers and I lie to them about knowing where she was. I lied. But my lie is justifiable. Why? In the section above I said it was because my intention was to save her life and that my intent or motive justified the deception in that case. I believe that explanation is appropriate. But one can view the same situation from the perspective of consequences. My lying to the killers saved Betty's life. The

result (consequences) of my lie was that Betty's life was saved. Consequences, in some cases, determine the rightness or wrongness of an act.

The role of consequences in determining morality (at least in some instances) demonstrates the value and preferability of an analysis-oriented mechanism for discovering morality over a rule-oriented mechanism. A list of rules is static, inflexible. If lying is on the list as an immoral act, then lying is wrong, all the time – even in cases such as the Betty dilemma. But can that possibly be the case? Was I wrong to deceive the killers to save Betty's life? A functional moral theory must be one that is appropriately flexible so that issues such as intention and consequences can be factored into an analysis of the morality of an act.

Considering the consequences of an act may be more subtle than it might first appear. Consider, for instance, Kant's first formulation of the Categorical Imperative – *Act only on that maxim through which you can at the same time will that it should become a universal law.* What is Kant really asking us to do here? He is saying that when one is anticipating an action and asking whether such an act would be moral or immoral, we  must ask if we would be happy (comfortable) if the proposed action was required of everyone. For instance, if I am considering committing a robbery because I am short of cash, I should ask myself, would I want everyone to commit robbery whenever they were short of cash? If my answer is no, I would not want everyone committing robbery whenever they were short of case, then I should not commit a robbery either. But why not? What is Kant's point? It grows out of a consequentialist perspective. He is asking, what would the world be like if people committed robbery every time they were short of case? He is asking what the consequences would be if everyone robbed each other all the time.

Consider Kant's second formulation of the Categorical Imperative – *Act in such a way that you always treat humanity, whether in your own person or in the person of another, never simply as a means, but always at the same time as an end.* Why does Kant think treating people merely as a means to an end is wrong? Because of what it does to the person who gets used. They are hurt. Their humanness is diminished. Kant does not specifically say this, but this is clearly his intent. His concern has to do with the consequences of treating others as a means instead of giving them the respect they deserve. Consequences matter.

If consequences are so important, why not use Bentham's system of Utilitarianism? Because Utilitarianism is entirely consequentialist. It is rooted in absolute relativity and does not give appropriate attention to intent and motive. Additionally, Utilitarianism is also rooted in a hedonistic form of happiness that, for many ethicists, makes it unacceptable as a functional moral theory. However, Utilitarianism is only one expression of consequentialism. A moral theory, such as CEE, can include a proper focus on consequences without embracing Utilitarianism. One of the important features of CEE is a healthy dose of consequentialism.

It is obvious that because of the eclectic nature of CEE that individuals using the model have the freedom to select the theories they believe will provide the most valuable insights in a given situation. One person wrestling with a particular moral concern might feel that Kantian theory will be helpful while another might think in terms of Virtue Ethics and another in terms of consequentialism. Sometimes a person may utilize Kant's Categorical Imperative in combination with Jesus' Golden Rule. The whole point of CEE being eclectic is that it allows for the utilization of one theory by itself or in combination with others. CEE's foundational concept (morality rooted in the value of humanness) working in combination with the various aspects of other moral theories gives CEE a flexibility that other theories lack. CEE's flexibility is its strength.[6]

Summary

A number of important ethical systems have been suggested over the centuries. Each of them contains important and helpful features that help us understand what morality is and how we ought to live. But none of them seems entirely complete and able to meet all of the ethical needs perceived by contemporary society.

In order for an ethical system to provide a functional framework for moral thinking and acting it would need a number of features, including:

1. *A thorough and effective definition/explanation of morality.*

2. *A proper focus on the development of moral character.*

[6] Some, no doubt, will object that the eclectic nature of CEE is not a strength but a weakness, that the theory provides little in the way of moral guidance. Obviously, I would disagree. CEE's focus on morality being rooted in the value of humanness along with its mechanism for determining what is and what is not moral provides a great deal of moral guidance. In conjunction with those features, its flexibility allows it to be utilized in a wider variety of circumstances than would otherwise be the case. The most important feature of its eclectic nature is that the strengths of multiple theories can be utilized interdependently to address issues that might not otherwise be effectively addressed.

3. *A mechanism for discovering the moral thing to do in a given situation.*

4. *A proper focus on motive and intention.*

5. *A proper focus on consequences.*

Yet none of the major moral systems, from ancient times to the present, contain all of these features. It seems apparent, then, that moral philosophy (in light of the needs of contemporary society) is in need of a system that does contain each of these features. Critical Ethical Eclecticism, based on the Principle of Essential Humanness, is an ethical paradigm that is eclectic in nature, borrowing from other theories to generate a composite theory that does contain each of the five needed features, resulting, therefore, in a functional framework for moral thinking and acting.

Thought and Discussion Questions

1. Discuss each of the five essential features Rogers mentions, explaining your agreement or disagreement with each as essential to a functional moral theory.

2. Explain your views on Rogers' observations regarding rule-oriented and analysis-oriented mechanisms as those mechanisms function in relation to morality.

3. Kant focused on intention, excluding consequences, Bentham focused on consequences, excluding intentions. Rogers argues for an appropriate focus on each. Explain why.

4. Discuss your views in relation to the importance of a focus on the development of moral character in a functional moral theory.

5. Discuss Rogers' Principle of Essential Humanness.

Section Summary
Chapter 12-13

This section has consisted of only two chapters, but they are very important chapters. Chapter 12 is a discussion of what morality is and how morality can be discovered (understanding what makes an act moral or immoral) using the Principle of Essential Humanness. Another important feature of Chapter 12 is the discussion regarding moral absolutes – that morality is not subjective, not relative, but is, in fact, objective. Even a simple evaluation of the arguments offered in support of absolute moral relativity reveals that they do not demonstrate that morality is relative. An absolute morality that transcends cultural perspectives exists and can be discovered (not determined but discovered) utilizing the Principle of Essential Humanness.

Chapter 13 is a discussion of Critical Ethical Eclecticism, a framework for moral thinking and acting. CEE is a composite theory, borrowing from other existing moral theories.

The heart of any moral theory is its definition/explanation of morality and the mechanism it provides, if indeed it provides one, for determining what makes an act moral or immoral. My definition/explanation is: *morality involves recognizing the intrinsic value of humanness (one's own and that of others), along with actions, reactions, and interactions that reflect an appreciation of human value. Immorality involves a failure to recognize the intrinsic value of humanness (one's own and that of others), along with a subsequent failure to act, react and interact in ways that reflect an appreciation of human value. Thus, an act is moral if it recognizes and or enhances human value, and is immoral if it fails to recognize or in some way diminishes the value of humanness.*
If a moral theory is going to prove effective for contemporary people it will need five features. Those five features are:

1. *A thorough and effective definition/explanation of morality.*

2. *A proper focus on the development of moral character.*

3. *A mechanism for discovering the moral thing to do in a given situation.*

4. *A proper focus on motive and intention.*

5. *A proper focus on consequences.*

CEE is a composite theory that contains these five features and will serve as a functional framework for moral thinking and acting in contemporary society.

Chapter 14
Abortion

Introduction

An abortion is the termination of a pregnancy by removing the living, developing fetus from the uterus. The morality or immorality of having an abortion has been one of the most hotly debated ethical issues of the past forty or fifty years.

In some states an abortion can be performed legally up to the 24th week of pregnancy. Most however are performed during the first 14 weeks. Abortions performed after the 24th week are referred to as partial birth abortions and are illegal.[1] The most common procedure used in abortions done between weeks 7 through 15 of the pregnancy is the vacuum aspiration process. In simple terms, a tube with a vacuum hose attached is inserted into the uterus. The amniotic fluid and the fetus are suctioned out and deposited into a collection jar. The fetus is torn apart in the process. The uterine wall is then scraped to be sure any remaining fetal tissue is removed.

What is the Issue?

What is the issue (the problem) related to abortion?[2] The issue is a complicated one. If a fetus is a person, then abortion, according to many people, is murder. Killing an innocent person (someone who is not a criminal or an enemy combatant) is considered murder. However, if the fetus is not a person, but simply an organism at different stages of development, then removing that organism from a 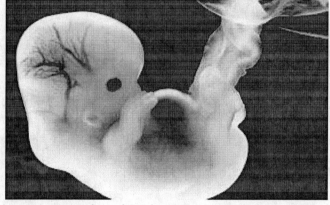 woman's body is not murder, for there is no personhood to be terminated. It must be noted that the point is not whether or not the fetus is alive. Of course it is *alive*; it is growing and developing. The issue, as it is perceived and argued, is one of personhood. When does the developing fetus become a person?

---

1. In a partial birth abortion the baby is partially delivered, the head and perhaps the shoulders being outside the mother's body. The baby is then killed, often by a crushing the skull, before the rest of the delivery is completed. Thus the name partial birth abortion. The baby is partially born before being killed.

2. For those who would like more detail than I can present in this overview, Gordon has provided a concise but thorough presentation in his article, *Abortion*, in the *Internet Encyclopedia of Philosophy*.

At what point during fetal development is a *person* present? The fertilized egg is referred to as a *zygote*. This stage, beginning at conception, lasts about 2 weeks. The zygote then becomes an *embryo*, a developmental stage that runs from weeks 2 through 8. By the 9th week the developing embryo becomes and remains a *fetus* until birth, usually between 38 and 42 weeks. The question is, at what point during this time of development between conception and birth is personhood (and the rights associated with it, such as the right to life) achieved? In other words, when does a baby become a person and have a right to life? That depends on how one defines a person.

Again, it is important to be specific. The issue is not whether or not the organism is alive. It is growing and developing, so it is alive. The issue is not whether or not the growing organism is human. Humans give birth to humans, not to monkeys or lizards, so the organism that has been developing since conception is human. The issue, as it is usually framed in the context of abortion, is when should that organism be considered a person? To answer that, we need to know what constitutes personhood.[3]

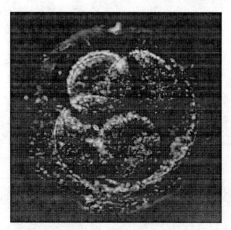

Some might suggest that if an organism is human and is alive, it is a person. A fertilized egg of human parents is human and is alive. Therefore, it is a person. A person came into being at the moment of conception. Many people advocate this position. However, some might point out that this approach does not define, in any precise manner, what constitutes personhood. It assumes a linkage between *living* [cells] and personhood. Can, or should, such an assumption be made? Assumptions of that sort are never helpful. So we must still ask, what constitutes personhood?

Since the days of the ancient Greeks, personhood has been linked with rationality. Aristotle said that *man is the rational animal*. His point was that rationality is unique to humanness. Humans are rational; animals are not. Rationality, in this sense, means a lot more than simple thinking. Animals think. But do they engage in high-level abstract conceptualization? They do not. They do not generate logical syllogisms or think in terms of abstract concepts such as justice or morality. Thus, they are not rational as humans are rational. Human are self-determined. We make choices. And many of the choices we make are moral choices. Thus, we are moral beings. Animals are not. Along with, or as part of, their rationality and self-determination, humans enjoy a level of conscious awareness that animals do not. Many animals are self-aware in that they understand their existence as separate from other individual animals. Many animals recognize themselves in a mirror – some dogs, elephants, and chimps for example. Obviously, they are aware of their specific individual existence. But humans are not only self-aware, humans are aware of being aware. I refer to this as second-level awareness. We think about ourselves as being rational, self-determined, moral beings

---

[3] Harris and Holm, "Abortion," in *The Oxford Handbook of Practical Ethics* provide a good discussion of personhood as it relates to the abortion issue.

who make morally significant choices. Our level of awareness allows us to ask, *what would I do in this or that situation?* Animals do not do this.

Personhood, then, normally is linked to rationality, self-determination, morality, and to second-level awareness. This sort of linkage is obviously associated with adult human personhood. The problem is that the developing fetus does not yet actually have (or at least does not exhibit) any of these traits. Does this mean, then, that the fetus is not a person and does not have a right to life? Some would argue that in this way of thinking about personhood a fetus is not a person, for it does not yet manifest the traits associated with personhood. But then neither do babies. Neither does an elderly person suffering from dementia, or a severely developmentally disabled person. Are we willing to say that babies, or seniors with dementia, or developmentally disabled people have no personhood and thus none of the rights associated with personhood, such as the right to life? Most people would not be comfortable advocating that babies, severely developmentally disabled people, or people with dementia can be killed because they do not exhibit the personhood of fully functional adults. Why, then, many would ask, is it acceptable to terminate the life of a fetus because the fetus does not exhibit the personhood of a fully functional adult?

Another aspect of the personhood issue has to do with potentiality. It is argued that while the fetus may not yet be a person, it is *potentially* a person. At some point in the future it will be a person. Because of its potential personhood it has the standing of a person and therefore the rights associated with personhood. Therefore, it is wrong to deprive a fetus of its life just as it is wrong to deprive a six-month old, a six year old, or a fifty-six year old person of his or her life. In this argument, the potential for personhood generates the status of personhood and the rights associated with it.

But the argument for potentiality can be tricky. Because one thing is potentially another does not mean it is the other. An acorn, for instance, is potentially an oak tree. But is the acorn an oak tree? Does it have the status of an oak tree? I have an oak tree in my yard. It is beautiful. I would not consider cutting it down. But the acorns it produces are not oak trees. They are, in my yard at least, squirrel food. Consider another example of potentiality: each human is potentially dead. But does our potential death (we will all be dead one day) mean that we should be treated as if we are dead now? Most of us would not be open to that possibility. The argument for potentiality is not clear as some think it is.

It is worth noting, however, that a number of embryologists consider the fetus a person from the time of conception. In a statement included in *Human Cloning and Human Dignity: An Ethical Inquiry*, George and Gomez-Lobo make the following comment in a footnote:

> A human embryo (like a human being in the fetal, infant, child, or adolescent stage) is not properly classified as a "prehuman" organism with the mere potential to become a human being. No human embryologist or textbook in human embryology known to us presents, accepts, or remotely contemplates such a view. The testimony of all leading embryology textbooks is that a human embryo *is – already* and not merely potentially – a human being. His or her potential, assuming a sufficient measure of good health and a suitable environment, is to develop by an internally directed process of growth through the further stages of maturity on the continuum that is his or her life.[4]

In their eight-page statement, George and Gomez-Lobo discuss fetal capacities as *basic natural* capacities and *immediately exercisable* capacities. The idea is that the basic natural capacities associated with full personhood are inherently present in the human fetus though they are not yet immediately exercisable. Given proper development, they will be. This, of course, is another form of the argument from potentiality. I mention it because it is significant that this is the position of many embryologists. As Siegel notes, this view involves a developmental continuum, from a capacity that is innate but not yet actualized to one that is fully actualized.[5]

To complicate matters further, some advocates of abortion acknowledge that a fetus is a person from the moment of conception, but argue that terminating its life is moral because the rights of the mother outweigh the rights of the fetus.[6]

"Prof. Alfonso Gomez Lobo vs Embryonic Stem Cell Research"

---

[4] George and Gomez-Lobo, *Human Cloning ad Human Dignity*, 258-266.
[5] Siegel, Andrew, "Ethics of Stem Cell Research," in *Stanford Encyclopedia of Philosophy*.
[6] Thomson, "A Defense of Abortion," in *Ethics: History, Theory, and Contemporary Issues*, 734.

Even with this brief summary of the issues related to abortion, one should be able to see that it is a complex question that requires serious critical analysis to put oneself in a position to be able to discover if it is moral to terminate the life of a fetus. In order to do that, we need to consider the merits of a number of the arguments presented for and against abortion.

What are the Arguments?

In this section I want to present some specific arguments for and against abortion and analyze their strengths and weaknesses. Then, in the following section I will discuss how Critical Ethical Eclecticism might be helpful in thinking about the abortion issue.

The first argument I want to consider is a pro-abortionist argument by Margaret Olivia Little. Little says, "I believe that early abortion is fully permissible, widely decent, and, indeed, can be honorable."[7] Why? Little's argument involves two points: 1) the *personhood* argument referred to above, and 2) what she refers to as the *gestational assistance* argument. What precisely does she argue? In her personhood argument, Little presents a standard version of that argument as it has to do with potential. A human fetus is potentially a fully functional human but is not yet one. Since it is not yet a fully formed person why should it be given the status of a fully formed person? For instance, (this is my illustration, not Little's) a newborn female is given the status of female person, but is not accorded the same range of rights a twenty-five year old female is given. She is not yet a rational, self-determined moral person and we do not treat her as if she was. When she is, we will. Until then she is denied that status. Why, then, Little wants to know, do we accord the status of a fully formed human to a being that is not a fully formed being?

Little has a point. We do not give newborns all the rights of fully formed adults (the right to vote, for instance). However, what we do acknowledge as a right of the infant is the right to life. A newborn's life may not be terminated even though, as some would argue, its personhood is only potential. Little's argument, in effect, is that in the absence of (fully functional adult) personhood, the life of the fetus may be terminated. But she does not argue that *any time* there is an absence of fully functional adult personhood life may be terminated, such as in the case of a newborn, severe developmental disability, advanced dementia, and so forth. One might ask, why is the termination of life permissible in one instance where fully functional adult personhood is absent but not in others? Her position, at least as far as part one of her overall argument goes, is inconsistent and therefore illogical.

[7]   Little, "The Moral Permissibility of Abortion," in *Taking Sides: Clashing Views on Moral Issues*, 76.

The second part of her argument has to do with gestational assistance. Her point is that we fail to understand what the process of gestation really is, and reach conclusions about it that cannot (ought not) be reached. For Little, gestation is a period of assistance, a period where a person (the mother) is saving the life of another person (the fetus) by offering a supply of blood and a heart to pump it, oxygen, food and so forth. Evidently it did not occur to Little that her second argument cannot be sound given her first argument – a lack of personhood. One person, the mother, cannot be providing assistance to another person, the fetus, if there is no other person, which would be the case, because without personhood there is no "person" to assist. She goes on, however, asserting that since the mother is *assisting* the fetus by giving the fetus access to her own life support systems, the decision to withhold the assistance is not immoral. Her argument is that one person can offer life-support assistance or not offer it. There is no moral obligation to save life if one can save life. Of course, Little simply assumes that and does not argue the point. A number of ethicists would challenge her assumption, arguing that a moral *can* (I *can* save a life) implies a moral *ought* (*thus I ought* to save a life).

Little's two-point argument fails at both points. It is not a sound argument.

Another pro-abortionist argument worthy of consideration (already noted above) is offered by Judith Jarvis Thomson. Thomson's argument, in fact, is the basis for Little's second point in her two-point argument. But Thomson's argument is so famous that it deserves specific attention. Unlike Little, Thomson does not deny the personhood of the fetus simply because it does not display the traits of fully functional adult personhood. Thompson suggests that fetal personhood be embraced. However, the mother's rights must also be embraced. The following brief excerpt provides the gist of Thomson's argument:

> I propose, then, that we grant that the fetus is a person from the moment of conception. How does the argument go from here? Something like this, I take it. Every person has a right to life. So the fetus has a right to life. No doubt the mother has a right to decide what shall happen in and to her body; everyone would grant that. But surely a person's right to life is stronger and more stringent than the mother's right to decide what happens in and to her body, and so outweighs it. So the fetus may not be killed; an abortion may not be preformed.

> It sounds plausible. But now let me ask you to imagine this. You wake up in the morning and find yourself back to back in bed with an unconscious violinist. A famous unconscious violinist. He has been found to have a fatal kidney ailment, and the Society of Music Lovers

has canvassed all the available medical records and found that you alone have the right blood type to help. They have therefore kidnapped you, and last night the violinist's circulatory system was plugged into yours, so that your kidneys can be used to extract poisons from his blood as well as your own. The director of the hospital now tells you, "look, we're sorry the Society of Music Lovers did this to you – we would never have permitted it if we had known. But still, they did it and the violinist is now plugged into you. To unplug you would be to kill him. But never mind, it's only for nine months. By then he will have recovered from his ailment, and can safely be unplugged from you." Is it morally incumbent on you to accede to this situation? No doubt it would be very nice of you if you did, a great kindness. But do you *have* to accede to it?[8]

"Judith Jarvis Thompson – The Violinist Argument"

Thomson's answer is that, no, the woman does not have an obligation to provide life support to the violinist. Neither does a mother have an obligation to provide life support to a fetus. Her right not to be hooked up to another person for nine months as that person draws life support from her, thus perhaps minimizing or even jeopardizing her own life, do not require her to support the life of that other person – the fetus. She can withdraw the support if she chooses. And the decision to do so and the act of doing so is moral – even if the fetus dies as a result.

Of course one of the main problems with Thomson's analogy is that being kidnapped and hooked up against one's will to serve as life support for another person is not at all similar to becoming pregnant as a result of consensual sex.

In her paper, Thomson deals with scenarios such as a pregnancy resulting from rape and a pregnancy where complicating medical issues endanger the mother's life. Those are separate and specific questions and I will not deal with them here. Rather, I want to focus on Thomson's main argument: the mother's rights outweighing the needs (rights?) of the fetus. Why? Why would the mother's right to decide how her body is used outweigh the fetus' right to life?

[8] Thomson, "A Defense of Abortion," in *Ethics: History, Theory, and Contemporary Issues*, 734

Even if the fetus has the right to life, Thomson argues, the mother is not obligated to provide life support, for deciding not to support life is not the same as depriving one of the right to life. The mother may decide not to provide life support by deciding to have an abortion. Such an action would not be immoral. Her argument is as follows. Suppose she is deathly ill and the only thing that will save her is that Henry Fonda (a movie star of her generation) will come from Hollywood to Cambridge, Massachusetts (where Thomson taught at MIT) and lay his hand on her forehead. If he were to make the trip and lay his hand on her head, thereby saving her, it would be a gracious gift. But Henry Fonda, even though only his touch will save her, has no obligation to travel from the West Coast to the East Coast to save her. No one would think Henry Fonda immoral for not making the trip to Cambridge to save Thomson. In a similar way, no one should think a woman immoral for not wanting to serve as life support for another person. If she did, she would be granting a gracious gift, but she is not obligated to.

Her argument makes use of another analogy, comparing the life-saving touch of Henry Fonda (or anyone else) to the life-giving relationship between a fetus and a mother. The legitimacy of the analogy, however, is doubtful. First, if someone can save a life (without violating any other significant consideration), are they not obligated to do so? As noted earlier, many ethicists advocate that *a moral can implies a moral ought*. If a doctor can save a life, is he not morally bound to do so? Thomson's assertion that Henry Fonda is not obligated to save her is an assumption that many ethicists (including me) would challenge. Second, the relationship between a mother and her baby is not really the same as the relationship between two separate people. A woman who is a doctor and provides life support for patients (let's say she administers a life-saving procedure) and who is also pregnant can testify that there is a difference between the external kind of life-support she provides for her patients and the internal kind of life-support she provides for her baby. Thomson's Henry Fonda analogy is invalid. Her argument, therefore, is unsound. In the end, Thomson's position, that ending the pregnancy by means of an abortion is not immoral, is without support.

As for anti-abortionist arguments, I want to highlight an argument made by Don Marquis. Marquis begins his presentation by discussing a variety of arguments offered by both pro and anti-abortionists, showing how each group opposes the arguments of the other, creating something of an irresolvable standoff because each side makes some valid points. Marquis then notes that, "All this suggests that a necessary condition of resolving the  abortion controversy is a more theoretical account of the wrongness of killing. After all, if we merely believe, but do not understand, why killing adult human beings such as ourselves is wrong, how could we conceivably show that abortion is either immoral or permissible?"[9]

Marquis makes a good point in suggesting that we believe killing human beings is wrong, but we may not be able to explain why. What is it that makes killing a human being wrong?[10] In answering the question he has raised, Marquis goes on to say:

> In order to develop such an account, we can start from the following unproblematic assumption concerning our own case: it is wrong to kill *us*. Why is it wrong? ...

> What primarily makes killing wrong is neither its effects on the murderer nor its effect on the victim's friends and relatives, but its effect on the victim. The loss of one's life is one of the greatest losses one can suffer. The loss of one's life deprives one of all the experiences, activities, projects, and enjoyments that would otherwise have constituted one's future. Therefore, killing someone is wrong primarily because the killing inflicts (one of) the greatest possible losses on the victim. To describe this as the loss of life can be misleading, however. The change in my biological state does not by itself make killing me wrong. The effect of the loss of my biological life is the loss of all those activities, projects, experiences, and enjoyments which would otherwise have constituted my future personal life.[11]

Marquis' argument is first, that it is wrong to kill *us* and second, that it is wrong to kill *us* because of the *effect* of the act: depriving us of our future. It is an interesting premise, but one that raises a lot of questions. For instance, who, exactly, constitutes *us*? Is the *us*, Americans? Is it white people, or educated people or poor people? Is the *us* fully formed functional adults? Or does he mean human beings in general? He means human beings. He says it is wrong to kill us because we are human beings. But why does that make it wrong? What if a race of peaceful aliens, posing no threat to us came to earth? And what if, like humans, they were rational, self-conscious, self-determined, moral beings – just not "human" beings? Would killing them be moral simply because they are not *us* – not human? No. And Marquis agrees. He addresses that issue in his material. My point is that to argue that killing *us* is wrong because it is *us* who is being killed is awkward terminology and is, by itself, problematic. It would have been nice if Marquis had explained his position differently.

---

[9] Marquis, "Why Abortion is Immoral," in *Taking Sides: Clashing Views on Moral Issues*, 71-72.

[10] The question assumes that there are valid reasons for killing human beings, such as killing an enemy combatant in war, a police officer killing a criminal in the line of duty, one person killing another in self-defense, or an accident that results in the death of an innocent person. None of these situations are at issue in this particular discussion. The issue here is the intentional killing of an innocent person. Why is that an immoral act?

[11] Marquis, 72.

But fortunately Marquis does not stop there. He goes on to explain that killing is wrong because of the effect (impact) it has on us, on the person being killed. Killing is wrong because it deprives the victim of his or her future, a future of varied experiences that will have some value, either intrinsic or instrumental. Killing people is wrong because people have futures and depriving them of their future is wrong. The implications for abortion are obvious. Terminating the life of a fetus deprives it of its future. For Marquis, this is what makes killing a fetus immoral.

Marquis is right in that killing a person deprives him of his future. But why is depriving a person (an adult or a fetus) of his future experiences immoral? This is where Marquis' theory encounters its most serious difficulty. What is there about a yet unreal (a presently non-existent) future that makes depriving a person of his future immoral? Marquis does not explain this. He argues that one's future will be of value and that depriving a person of that value is immoral, but that is as far as he goes.

His theory is problematic in that futures are uncertain. One's future depends on one's own decisions and those of others. One's future may be good or bad, and will likely be a combination of both. But for some unfortunate souls, the future may be comprised mostly of suffering. Since the future is uncertain, may not be good, may be very brief, and, depending on the choices others make, may not exist at all, it is difficult to see how depriving a person of a possible uncertain future that may be very unpleasant can be immoral.

I understand what Marquis is trying to do and generally I agree. We need to explain *why* killing a person is wrong. There is a sense in which life can be defined as the experiences one has in the process of living. To deprive a person of those experiences, present or future, just seems wrong. However, to say this is really saying nothing more than killing is wrong because it is depriving a person of life. Yes. But *why* is depriving a person of life wrong? Marquis wanted to provide an answer. Has he? Does his theory, as he believes it does, explain why abortion is immoral?

The Morality or Immorality of Abortion

The arguments offered above are representative of the arguments, or kinds of arguments, that are part of the abortion debate. As noted earlier in the chapter, the central issue for most people is whether or not the fetus is a person. We believe (whether or not we can explain why) that it is wrong to kill innocent people. If the unborn child is a person, then terminating its life is immoral. If it is not a person, then terminating its life is not immoral. The arguments regarding the personhood of the fetus are inconclusive. People have strong opinions regarding the personhood of the fetus, but proof one way or the other has not yet been produced – and may not be. What, then, is to be done? I think the answer to the abortion dilemma is to be found down the same road Marquis went down, but expressed somewhat differently than he expressed it. There needs to be some clear insights into why killing innocent humans is wrong, and

there needs to be a mechanism available so that some specific questions can be asked and answered. I think the key to the dilemma is to utilize CEE and the Principle of Essential Humanness, thinking first about the valuing of humanness in general (humanness as discussed in Chapters Twelve and Thirteen), and second in determining which of the systems or theories CEE makes use of offer a helpful perspective on whether or not abortion in a given situation is a moral or immoral response.

The foundational concept of CEE, the Principle of Essential Humanness, is that humanness, because of what it is – rationality, self-determination, morality – has intrinsic value. Humans value and humans have value, not simply because we are alive or are human, but because of what humanity entails: rationality, self-determination morality. Humans may not be the only species that have these intrinsically valuable characteristics. Whoever has these characteristics would also be intrinsically valuable. But humans do have these traits, and that makes humanness intrinsically valuable. And that which has intrinsic value ought not be devalued. To devalue or diminish that which

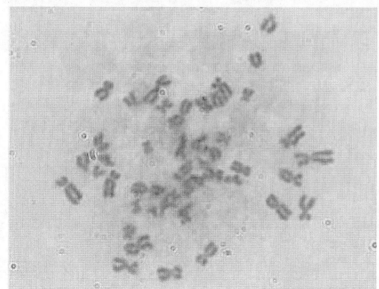

is intrinsically valuable is immoral. The killing of innocent people devalues that which is intrinsically valuable. Therefore, the killing of innocent people is immoral.[12]

This way of reasoning provides a clear explanation for why the killing of innocent people is morally unacceptable. How does this address the issue of the status of the fetus? The status of the fetus is addressed from a different perspective. Instead of addressing the issue

[12] It is important that the argument be very specific: *the killing of innocent people*, for there might be situations where killing is not an act of devaluing--such as self-defense, where an attacker would not be innocent and killing that person (if necessary) would not be immoral.

of personhood, which usually describes personhood in terms of a fully functional adult, which the fetus is not, the status of the fetus is addressed under the broader rubric of humanness and the intrinsic value of humanness. Is the human fetus human? If the fetus has human DNA, human chromosomes, and human cells, then it would be hard to say that it is not human. Is it a fully formed human, capable of everything a fully formed and fully functional human is capable of? Certainly not. However, it is still a human, and as such has intrinsic value. Why? Because of what a human is. Because of what makes a human a human: rationality, self- determination and morality. But a fetus does not yet have those traits. No, it doesn't. But neither does a six-month old baby or, for that matter, even a six-year old child. A six-year old child is not yet fully rational because it cannot engage in abstract conceptualization – a crucial feature of rationality. The ability to engage in abstract conceptualization does not develop until around age eleven. Neither is a six-year old child fully moral (capable of abstract moral thinking) or fully self-determined. Does that mean that a six-year old child is not human because it is not yet fully rational, self-determined or moral? Certainly not.[13] A human is a human regardless of whether his developmental trajectory is still moving up or has reached its peak and has begun to move in a downward trajectory.

Some might think that this sounds suspiciously like a thinly veiled version of the potentiality argument. It is not. One is not potentially a human. One cannot become a human over a period of time. One is either human or not human. I am arguing that human parents conceive human children. Having human DNA, human chromosomes, and human cells make one a human.[14] And if one is a human, then one has intrinsic value irrespective of one's developmental status. Whether I am a zygote at the beginning of the human developmental continuum or a senior who is catatonic from dementia on the other end of the human developmental continuum, I am still a human who has intrinsic value. Traits and skills that have yet to develop or those that have developed and over the years diminished and disappeared have nothing to do with the kind of being I am. And the kind of being I am is one with intrinsic value. Therefore, devaluing me, at any stage of my existence, is immoral. Terminating the life of a human fetus is to devalue the humanness of that fetus and is therefore immoral.

[13]   Neither do we consider the mentally retarded to be subhuman. They do not possess the traits often associated with personhood (rationality, moral reasoning, self-determination), but we still consider them to be human and have the intrinsic value associated with humanness.

[14]   I'm making use here of the law of the excluded middle. Either one exists or one does not exist. There is no middle state between existence and non-existence. By extension, one either exists as a human or one does not exist as a human. There is no middle state between existing as a human and not existing as a human. One is either a human or not a human.

The Principle of Essential Humanness, the foundational premise of CEE, helps us understand that the killing of innocent people is immoral. Abortion is killing an innocent person. Therefore, abortion (unless it is performed to save the life of the mother, in which case it may be thought of as an act of self-defense) is an immoral act. Killing innocent humans is simply unacceptable.

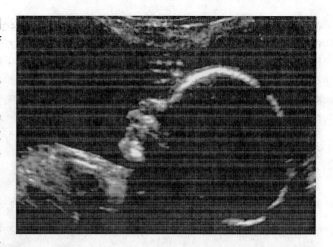

In addition to this perspective, CEE offers a mechanism for thinking about what is and isn't moral. Since CEE is eclectic in nature and draws from a select group of previously proposed moral theories, it has more to offer than a single theory can offer. In addition to considering the humanness of her developing baby, the pregnant woman who is uncertain about how to proceed needs to think about her situation from the perspectives of Jesus' Golden Rule Ethic of Love and Virtue Ethics.

Jesus proposed what I have called the Golden Rule Ethic of Love. The idea is that love (how one behaves toward others) is to guide one's actions toward others. We are to treat others the way we would want them to treat us if we were in their place and they were in ours. Mother, if you were your unborn baby, what would you want you to do? Jesus' moral system requires that we be others-centered. It is the opposite of Ethical Egoism and the self-centered egoist is not going to appreciate Jesus' admonition to consider others, such as one's unborn baby. Not to consider the needs of the yet to be born baby is the act of a self-centered person.

From a Virtue Ethics perspective, the abortion issue has to do with, or must be resolved in, the context of personal character. The virtuous person is courageous, kind, compassionate, generous and so forth. It is difficult to see how a person who has or is trying to develop the virtues in her life would, unless her life were in danger from the pregnancy, consider killing her fetus the courageous, kind, compassionate, generous thing to do.

As a paradigm for moral thinking and acting, CEE provides insights that other theories do not. And from a CEE perspective, it appears that abortion, except when the mother's life is in danger, is immoral.

Summary

The abortion issue remains one of the most divisive issues in contemporary society. Few people are ambivalent about the subject. Most are dedicated to pro or anti-abortionist agendas. For most people, on either side of the question, the issue begins and ends with arguments related to personhood and potentiality. Is the fetus a person? Even if it is not yet a person, does its potential to become a person factor into its status and whether or not abortion is moral? Pro-abortionists answer these questions in the negative; anti-abortionists answer them in the affirmative.

Some pro-abortionists, Thomson, for instance, and those who embrace her perspective, acknowledge that the fetus is a person from the time of conception, but argue that its status as a person does not outweigh the mother's rights to determine whether or not she offers her body as a life support system to the fetus, opting for an abortion instead.

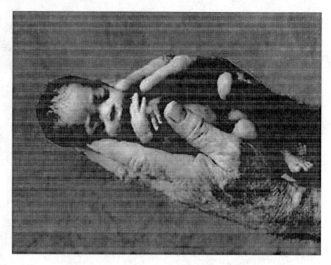

Seeing that the standard arguments do not appear to have resolved the issue to any meaningful degree, Marquis offers an alternative perspective. Suggesting that we need to understand why it is wrong to kill a human, Marquis argues that it is wrong to kill a person because doing so robs the victim of his or her future experiences. His argument, though interesting, is not entirely satisfying. I suggest, therefore, that we approach the matter from the perspective of the Principle of Essential Humanness. Humanness has an inherent value. Human parents conceive and give birth to human children. Having human DNA, human chromosomes, and human cells make one a human, not something less than a human, a human in potential waiting to develop into a human. One is either human or not human. And if one is human, one has intrinsic value because of what is entailed in humanness. To devalue the humanness of another is immoral. Killing an innocent human is devaluing his humanness. Therefore, killing an innocent human is immoral. A fetus is an innocent human, therefore, killing a fetus is immoral. Unless the mother's life is at risk (in which case an abortion can be considered an act of self-defense) abortion is immoral because it is the devaluing of humanness.

CEE does not stop at that point, however. It makes use of other moral theories through the case of Jesus' Golden Rule Ethic of Love and Virtue Ethics. Applying those theories will clarify that a pregnant woman must consider her proposed action from the fetus' perspective – it would not want to be killed – and from a Virtue Ethics perspective. CEE demonstrates that abortion, except in cases where the mother's life in at risk, is immoral.

Thought and Discussion Questions

1. Discuss your views of human personhood and how one would determine when personhood is present.

2. Discuss your thinking as it regards the potentiality of personhood in relation to the abortion debate.

3. Discuss Rogers' argument about the intrinsic value of humanness as it relates to the abortion issue.

4. Discuss the idea (based on the law of the excluded middle) that one is either a human or not and that there is no such thing as becoming a human in a developmental process.

5. Discuss your response to Rogers' conclusion that if the fetus is a human with intrinsic value, then killing it is immoral.

Chapter 15
Animal Suffering

Introduction

Animals are an intricate part of our lives – even for those who are not pet owners. Ten billion animals are killed in the U.S. each year for food. The human population of the entire planet is just over 6 billion people. Yet in the United States alone, 19,000 animals die *each minute* so we can eat meat. That's a lot of dead animals. Still, we need meat because for most of us becoming a vegetarian is simply not an option.

"McDonald's, The Meat Industry, and Chickens"

"Chicken Farm"

Another way animals play a significant role in our lives is their use in medical research. Twenty-five million animals are used in research each year (including testing of cosmetics) in the United States. The animals involved include: chimpanzees and other primates, dogs (beagles, especially), cats, rabbits, rats and mice, birds, and other animals. Many of them die as a result of the research – suffering horribly before they do. Those who survive the testing are killed.

"Fighting Animal Testing: Cruelty Free Cosmetics"

Those who oppose the use of animals for medical research point out that over 90% of the drugs that pass animal testing fail in trials involving humans. Why? Because the drugs impact animals differently than they impact humans. Thus, testing the drugs on animals appears to be pointless. Those who advocate for the use of animals in medical research are

quick to point out all the discoveries, including drugs and medical procedures, directly associated with animal research, that improve or save human lives.

"Animal Testing Ethics"

In addition to the number of animals who die each year so we can eat meat and those who suffer and die in the name of medical research, there are animals that are treated cruelly by owners; sometimes just because of thoughtless stupidity and sometimes as some form of sadistic entertainment – animal fights and so forth.

Whether we are talking about animals that die each year so we can eat meat, or in relation to animal research, or that die as a result of cruelty, the number of animals that suffer and die each year is astonishing and raises important moral questions. As Frey notes, "Certainly, the different uses we make of animals, whether as subjects for cosmetic and product testing, as the source of food, leather, and fur, and as vehicles for medical and scientific research may raise particular moral questions."[1]

What is the Issue?

The issues related to animal suffering are complex. The first clarification I need to make is that we are not discussing animal suffering in general. The world is full of suffering – animal and human. Both people and animals suffer as a result of what is referred to as *natural evil*: fires, floods, earthquakes, tornadoes and hurricanes, landslides and avalanches, cancer and other diseases, and so forth. In moral philosophy, animal suffering is not about the suffering animals endure as a result of natural evil. Rather, it is about the suffering they endure at the hands of humans – *human inflicted suffering*.

It is also important to identify what kind of animals we are talking about. The kinds of animals under consideration are those that are sentient and capable of desire and anticipation. Thus, the category is broad and includes not only primates but also dogs, cats, horses, rabbits, rats and so forth. Ants, flies, mosquitoes, and other such lower animal forms are not part of the discussion.

When humans cause other humans to suffer needlessly (unjustified suffering) it is generally considered immoral. *But is it immoral for humans to*

---

[1] Frey, "Animals," in *The Oxford Handbook of Practical Ethics*, 163.

cause the needless, unjustified suffering of animals? That is the question at the heart of the animal suffering and animal rights debates. The answer may depend on the differences between humans and animals, or the similarities between them. Those two different perspectives give rise to two very different approaches to the problem and it will be necessary to consider each perspective.

In order to narrow the topic to a manageable size and to focus on that part of the issue that many ethicists consider the most crucial aspect of the discussion, I will be focusing on the use of animals in medical research. The questions asked and answered in relation to animal suffering that results from medical research will be the same basic questions that need to be addressed in relation to other causes of animal suffering.

"Is Animal Testing Justified?"

The issue of justification is crucial in the discussion. Whether or not causing animal suffering is moral or immoral may depend on whether or not there is justification for causing it. Doctors and dentists cause human suffering (pain) all the time. However, they do so in the hope of accomplishing a greater good – better health. The suffering they cause, therefore, is justified. Is there adequate justification for the pain and suffering humans cause animals in the course of conducting medical research?

The basic question is, *is it moral for humans to cause animals to suffer?* But asking that question generates another, *do animals have a moral status (as humans do) and the rights that would be associated with a moral status?* What does this mean? Gruen explains: "To say that a being deserves moral consideration is to say that there is a moral claim that this being has on those who can recognize such claims. A morally considerable being is a being who can be wronged in a morally relevant sense."[2] For those who advocate animal rights, the idea is that animals deserve moral consideration and that we are obligated to give them the consideration they deserve. How would one go about establishing that position?

What are the Arguments?

In the discussion regarding animal suffering there are three basic positions:

1. That animals have no moral standing and deserve no moral consideration and can, therefore, be treated as a means to an end,

[2]   Gruen, "The Moral Status of Animals," *Stanford Encyclopedia of Philosophy*.

2. That animals have full moral standing just as we (humans) do and that we, therefore, must give animals the same moral consideration we give to other humans,

3. That while animals do not have the same moral status as humans, since they can feel pain and can suffer, and since they have desires and can anticipate just as humans can, we are obligated to show them kindness and consideration, to minimize their pain and suffering when and where we can.

1. Those who advocate that animals have no moral standing argue simply that animals are not people, not humans. Humans, alone, who are rational and self-determined, who make moral choices, have moral status. This is an ancient position, dating back, not only to ancient Greece (Aristotle), but beyond, to the earliest days of ancient Hebrew thought in relation to humans being created in the image of God and thus being superior to animals. This position is rooted in the differences between humans and animals. Because animals are not humans they do not deserve the same  consideration as humans. For some who advocate this position in its most extreme form, animals, like the rest of non-human material reality, exist to be used as humans see fit: for entertainment, labor, sport, research, and so forth. For some, the position is simple speciesism, the idea that simply because we are humans we have a special status. However, not all who embrace this position would embrace simple speciesism. Some would suggest that humans deserve special consideration, not simply because they are humans, but because of what is entailed in humanness – rationality, morality, and so forth. For them, other species (other beings or entities) who share those traits, though not human, would also enjoy a moral status – and the responsibility that goes with it.

2. Those who advocate the opposite position, that animals have full moral status, point out, not the differences between humans and animals, but the similarities. They argue that animals can think and learn, can feel pain and suffer just as we can, are capable of enjoying pleasure just as we are; that they can be afraid, desire and anticipate just as we can. They are capable 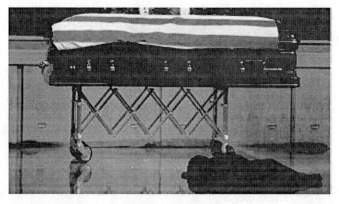 of gentleness and nurturing, of loyalty and devotion. Since animals are so much like us (even though they are different in other ways), and especially since they can be

hurt and can suffer, since they are *experiencing* beings (i.e., since they are capable of experiencing just as we are), animals have a moral status like our own. No one argues that animals make moral choices as we do. Animals do not ask, *what is the right thing to do*? They do not act in a certain manner *because it is the right thing to do* as humans do. Animals are not the kind of moral beings humans are. But because they are like us in so many ways, because they suffer just as we do, they have a moral standing that demands consideration. Thus, just as we do not cause needless (unjustified)[3] suffering for other humans, neither ought we to cause animals needless suffering.

"Animal Rights"

"Dog Waits for Deceased Man to Return Home"

The key differences between these positions (that animals have no moral standing and that animals have the same moral standing as humans) are 1) that one focuses on the differences between humans and animals and the other focuses on the similarities, and 2) that one position sees animals a resource to be used and the other sees animals as beings to be valued. One of the best-known proponents of animal rights, Tom Regan, explains what he considers to be the main problem.

> What's wrong – fundamentally wrong – with the way animals are treated isn't the details that vary from case to case. It's the whole system. The forlornness of the veal calf is pathetic, heart wrenching; the pulsing pain of the chimp with electrodes planted deep in her brain is repulsive; the slow, tortuous death of the raccoon caught in the leg-hold trap is agonizing. But what is wrong isn't the pain, isn't the suffering, isn't the deprivation. These compound what's wrong. Sometimes – often – they make it much, much worse. But they are not the fundamental wrong.

---

[3] The needless or unjustified suffering refers to the fact that it might be necessary to cause some suffering to animals (just as it is necessary for humans) if it is in their best interest or involves some greater good. An animal might need surgery, just as a human might, which may be a source of pain and suffering. It is caused, however, in a context of a greater good.

The fundamental wrong is the system that allows us to view animals as *our resources*, here for *us* – to be eaten, or surgically manipulated, or exploited for sport or money. Once we accept this view of animals – as our resources – the rest is as predictable as it is regrettable.[4]

Critics of this position argue that animals simply do not possess the features of humanness (rationality, morality, self-determination) and therefore cannot have full moral status and be protected by the rights that accompany full moral status. Regan and others, however, would argue that many "humans" do not possess those features and yet do enjoy the rights associated with full moral status. For instance, severely developmentally disabled people, a person with advanced dementia, and many young children could not be described as rational and able to make moral choices, yet they are afforded full moral status and are protected by the rights that accompany moral standing. Why, then, should that full moral status be withheld from animals? This is a good question. There are animals that have abilities that surpass those of severely developmentally disabled or demented people. Why should they be denied the rights given to humans who do not possess the abilities and traits the animals possess? To respond, *because those animals are not human*, is not a sufficient response. If humans are special it is because of what makes us human – the nature of our humanness. So if some "humans" do not possess those traits to the degree that some animals do, why should those humans be given a status that is denied to the animals?

"Tom Regan: Animal Rights – An Introduction 1/5"
"Tom Regan: Animal Rights – An Introduction 2/5"
"Tom Regan: Animal Rights – An Introduction 3/5"
"Tom Regan: Animal Rights – An Introduction 4/5"
"Tom Regan: Animal Rights – An Introduction 5/5"

In response to the kind of arguments animal rights advocates make, Carl Cohen argues that animals cannot possibly have rights because rights involve a claim one moral being claims in interaction with other moral beings. I have a right to be treated with dignity and respect. As a moral person who can ask moral questions (what is the right thing to do and why?) and who can act morally because I know the difference

---

4   Regan, "The Case for Animal Rights," in *Ethics: History, Theory, and Contemporary Issues*, 809.

between right and wrong, I have the right to expect certain kinds of behavior from other moral beings, and they have a right to expect certain kinds of behavior from me. *Rights exist only for rational, moral beings who can discern and demand a certain kind of behavior based on the recognition of moral principles.* As rational, moral beings, humans (as a kind of being) can understand the concepts of rights rooted in a moral reality. Because they can understand rights, they have rights. Animals are not rational, moral beings who can understand and demand rights. Thus, Cohen would argue, they have no rights.[5]

"Carl Cohen: Why Animals Do Not Have Rights 1/6"
"Carl Cohen: Why Animals Do Not Have Rights 2/6"
"Carl Cohen: Why Animals Do Not Have Rights 3/6"
"Carl Cohen: Why Animals Do Not Have Rights 4/6"
"Carl Cohen: Why Animals Do Not Have Rights 5/6"
"Carl Cohen: Why Animals Do Not Have Rights 6/6"

Animal rights advocates, as noted already, are quick to reply that not all humans are rational, moral beings. Neither the severely developmentally disabled, those suffering the effects of severe dementia, nor young children are capable of rationality and moral thinking and acting (one cannot act morally if one cannot think morally). Thus, according to Cohen's reasoning, there are several classes of humans who have no rights. Cohen's reply is that:

> This objection fails; it mistakenly treats an essential feature of humanity [rational morality] as though it were a screen for sorting humans. The capacity for moral judgment that distinguishes humans from animals is not a test to be administered to human beings one by one. Persons who are unable, because of some disability, to perform the full moral functions natural to human beings are certainly not for that reason ejected from the moral community.[6]

I think Cohen has made a good point here. I would add that comparing some normal animals (Chimpanzees or Gorillas, for instance) to abnormal

---

5   Cohen, "The Case for the Use of Animals in Biomedical Research," *Ethics: History, Theory, and Contemporary Issues,* 817-821.
6   Ibid.

humans (the developmentally disabled or demented) does not in any way prove or even suggest that animals and humans share the same moral standing.

3. Half way between these two extreme positions (that animals have no moral standing at all and that they have full moral standing just as humans do) is a mediated position, advocating that while animals do not have the same moral status as humans, they deserve to be treated with moral consideration. Why? Because they are like us in many ways, including their ability to enjoy and to suffer. Because they can suffer and because we understand how horrible suffering is, we are obligated to eliminate or at least minimize their suffering when and where we can. The only time causing suffering to animals can be justified is when there is a greater good involved, as in medical research. And even in cases of justified suffering, we are obligated to minimize the suffering as much as possible.

The strength of this position (as far as those who advocated it are concerned) is that humans retain their high status but animals still get moral consideration. The weakness of the position (as far as the animal rights advocates are concerned) is that it still allows for animal suffering when similar human suffering would not be tolerated. Animals are still denied full moral status. If animals deserve moral consideration how can causing them to suffer be justified? Also, the *greater good* argument, animal rights advocates point out, is questionable because there is a question as to whether or not the use of animals in medical research is necessary. Are there not other ways to do research and testing that do not involve the use of animals? Animal rights advocates insist that there are.[7] Opponents say, no, there are not.

"Alternatives to Animal Testing"

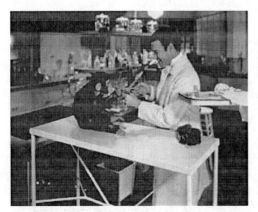
Some advocates of this mediated position argue that the best way to approach the problem is from a Virtue Ethics perspective.[8] The idea here is that if one is a virtuous person, kind, compassionate, courageous, and so forth, one will seek to minimize pain and suffering wherever it can be minimized. Whether or not animals have a moral status equal to humans, the virtuous person will not cause suffering and will seek to minimize suffering wherever it occurs. There may be something useful in this form of reasoning.

[7] Tom Regan's book, *The Case for Animal Rights*, includes a thorough presentation of all such arguments.

[8] Gruen, "The Moral Status of Animals," in *Stanford Encyclopedia of Philosophy*.

Of these three positions, this last one, the mediated position, is the one most people would find most satisfying (emotionally speaking) because it avoids the extremes of the other two positions. However, the apparent inconsistencies it embraces make it problematic as well. Also, it does not really address the issue of the moral standing of animals. Is there a way around this problem? Perhaps. Perhaps not. Perhaps thinking in terms of the Principle of Essential Humanness and Critical Ethical Eclecticism will be helpful.

The Morality or Immorality of Animal Suffering

Based on the Principle of Essential Humanness, CEE is deeply rooted in an appreciation of the intrinsic value of humanness. Humans have intrinsic value because of what being human entails: rationality, self-determination, and morality.. Attitudes and behaviors that recognize, honor or in some way enhance this value are moral; attitudes and behaviors that devalue and or diminish the value of humanness are immoral.

Once this foundation is in place, specific questions about specific concerns can be asked. Is causing or allowing animals to suffer moral? As noted earlier, asking this question raises the question of the moral status of animals. From a CEE perspective, animals do not share a moral status with humans. They are not moral beings. The fact that they can feel pain and suffer, desire and anticipate (features that make them like us in some significant ways) does not add up to moral equality with humans. Animals are not moral beings because they cannot think morally. They cannot ask moral questions such as, *what is just*, or *what is moral*, or *what makes an act moral or immoral*. To be able to think morally requires the ability to contemplate the abstract concepts associated with morality. Animals do not have that ability. They cannot think morally.[9] And if they cannot think morally they cannot act morally. The actions of animals are neither moral nor immoral; they are amoral. Animals are simply not moral beings. Therefore, they cannot have a moral status equal to that of humans who are moral beings. They do not, therefore, have intrinsic worth and value as moral beings do. Their value is instrumental. Their worth is derived as they fulfill their role as part of the larger cosmic reality.

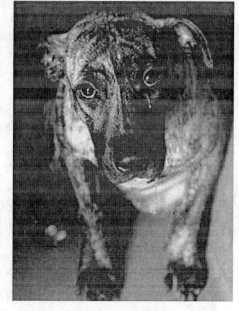

What, then, does this say about the relative morality or immorality of causing animal suffering? By itself it says nothing. The fact that animals do not share moral equality with humans does not suggest that it is or is not moral for humans to cause animal suffering. *The question of whether or not it is moral for humans to cause animal suffering has nothing to*

---

[9] Should the question be raised that neither do all humans have the ability for rational morality, my response would be similar to Cohen's.

do with the moral status of animals and everything to do with the moral status of humans. Because we are rationally moral, the responsibility for our behavior exists in relation to our rational morality and the value associated with it, not to the value of those with whom we interact, whether fully capable rationally moral adults or those who are not capable of rational morality – infants and children, the developmentally disabled and demented, or animals. The moral status of those with whom we interact is irrelevant. Who and what *we* are is what matters morally.

The eclectic perspective of CEE, Jesus' Golden Rule Ethic of Love, and Virtue Ethics provide some guidance in relation to how we ought to treat animals. Other thinking, feeling beings or creatures ought to be treated as we would like to be treated. The Golden Rule can be applied to animals as well as to people. And if we are kind, compassionate, respectful people, as virtue ethics encourages, we will treat other beings and creatures with kindness, respect, and compassion.

The problem with this approach, in the view of some, is that it is broad and general and does not appear to provide a specific or definitive answer regarding the morality of medical research or other causes of animal suffering. I may apply the Golden Rule and Virtue Ethics in my personal life and not cause animals to suffer, but others might not. Animals will still suffer. What is to be done about that? Probably very little.

Can any form of animal suffering be tolerated? In light of the good that comes of it in the field of medical research, the answer would appear to be, yes. Does the good that comes from the suffering of animals used in medical research justify the pain they endure? I believe it can if their suffering is minimized as far as possible. When our sons were babies and we took them to get vaccinated, we caused them pain. But in light of the greater good that was accomplished, the pain was justified. Greater good does justify suffering. Respect, compassion, and love for animals does not necessitate that we eliminate all pain. I believe it requires that we minimize it as much as possible. But to eliminate all animal suffering (as it relates to medical research) would be to increase human suffering because of the loss of medical advances that will reduce human suffering.

Is the complete elimination of all animal suffering the only moral response to the problem of animal suffering? I do not believe logical argument can demonstrate that. However, within the CEE framework, an individual moral response to animal suffering is: 1) not to cause or contribute to the unjustified suffering of an animal, 2) to oppose all instances of unjustified suffering, and 3) to advocate the highest standards for the humane treatment of those animals used in medical research.

Summary

Questions about the morality of animal suffering are complex. There are basically three positions regarding the morality of animal suffering: 1) that animals have no moral standing at all and may be utilized as we see fit, even if it involves inflicting pain on them; 2) that animals have a moral status equal to humans and cannot, therefore, be used as a means to our ends, especially where it involves causing them to suffer; 3) a mediated position that recognizes that while animals may not have a moral status equal to humans, we still have a  moral obligation to treat them with kindness and compassion, minimizing their suffering whenever and as fully as possible. Arguments advanced by advocates of these positions are complex and challenging to contemplate: do animals enjoy a moral status equal to that of humans, do they enjoy the rights of rationally moral beings, can suffering (human or animal) ever be justified, must all animal suffering be eliminated?

From a CEE perspective, animals do not enjoy a moral status equal to that of humans. However, that does not mean that animal suffering is acceptable. As rational moral beings, humans are obligated to act and interact in moral ways with all beings and creatures, regardless of the moral status of those beings or creatures. Their moral status is irrelevant; our moral status is what matters. Where suffering can be eliminated or minimized (without jeopardizing a greater good), it must be eliminated or minimized. The dictates of the Golden Rule and Virtue Ethics apply to our interactions with animals as surely as they do to our interactions with other humans.

Thought and Discussion Questions

1. Explain your thinking as it relates to traditional arguments about the nature of personhood and moral standing in relation to the moral standing of animals.

2. Explain what Rogers' means by his statement: *The question of whether or not it is moral for humans to cause animal suffering has nothing to do with the moral status of animals and everything to do with the moral status of humans.* Explain whether or not you agree and why.

3. Identify and explain the strengths and weaknesses of position one (that animals have no moral status at all).

4. Identify and explain the strengths and weaknesses of position two (that animals enjoy a moral status equal to that of humans).

5. Does CEE offer anything useful in the debate over animal suffering? Explain your answer.

Chapter 16
Capital Punishment

Introduction

According to the Death Penalty Information Center, 1,298 people were executed in America between 1976 and June 2012. The Federal government carried out 3 of those executions; the rest were carried out in 34 different states.[1] Were these executions moral or immoral? They were carried out as part of a larger criminal justice system that includes a component for punishing those who do not conform to the laws of society. Is that system of punishment in general moral or immoral?

Is it morally permissible for a society of people to include a system of punishment as part of their social structure? Is it morally permissible for a feature of that system of punishment to be execution? As we saw in Chapter Six, Hobbesian Social Contract Theory is inadequate as a stand-alone framework for moral thinking and acting. However, in this discussion of punishment, and especially capital punishment, it provides us with a framework for beginning.

Hobbes discussed humans living in a state of nature, a pre-social state where people, living as isolated individuals or in small family groups, had to compete for resources. They had to constantly live in a defensive mode, protecting and defending from others – aggressors who would take what they could. There was no law, no justice, no consideration, no cooperation, and certainly no morality. There was *get what you can by whatever means and hold on to it as long as you can*. It was, according to Hobbes, a brutal and ugly way to live. Somewhere along the way, Hobbes postulated, a few people began to see that if people lived together in a cooperative, interdependent community, giving up some of their freedoms (such as being able to take whatever one is strong enough to take), they would gain some important advantages. They would not have to worry constantly about every other person being an enemy who would oppress, steal or kill. Living interdependently would allow them to let their guard down, to relax a little, to enjoy life. For such a way of living to work, however, they would have to have some rules to live by. So, where there had been no rules to live by, they would create some. They would invent morality. Everyone would have to agree to abide by the rules if they wanted to be part of the new society. And for those who did not obey the rules, there would be consequences. Thus, not only was society conceived and brought forth, so were rules (social norms) and the concept of punishment.

[1] Death Penalty Information Center.

Hobbes believed that people invented morality, making morality a product of rationality instead of being co-existent with it. The difference between the two positions may appear insignificant, but it is not. The part of the story that helps us frame the conversation about punishment is that as people began living together in villages (the first societies),[2] the need for rules (not morality, but rules) and punishment for breaking the rules evolved into systems of crimes and punishment, with capital punishment being one of the forms of punishment. Was it right, was it moral, for those ancient people to establish a system of punishment, and was it right, moral, for one of the punishments to be some form of execution?

"Making History- First Organized Societies"

What is the Issue?

The issue, then, for contemporary society, grows out of humanity's ancient past. Is it right for a society of people to create and impose rules that include punishments of various kinds for when the rules are broken? And is it right that the punishment for some rule breaking be execution?

By observing how humans all over the world live, it appears the answer to the first question would be, yes. All societies have rules. Obviously, then, all groups of people feel that it is right and proper (not just necessary) for them to make rules for how to live in that society. And of course, if rules are to be meaningful, they must be enforced. All cultures have rules for living and systems of punishments associated with those rules. It is the way things are.

RULES
1. YOU CAN....
2. YOU CAN'T...
3. YOU CAN.....
4. YOU CAN'T

But because something *is* a certain way does not necessarily mean that it *ought* to be that way. Societies make rules and punish violators. But *should* they? Throughout the ages, all societies have practiced oppression and slavery at one time or another in one form or another. Did the practice of slavery make slavery moral? It did not. Just because people have always done something does not mean it is the right or moral thing to do. Tradition is not sufficient justification. So the question, *is it moral for societies to make rules and punish violators*, requires an answer rooted in something other than historical practices. Is punishment rationally defensible? I believe it is. Rules and punishment for breaking them follow logically from the concept of morality.

---

[2]   Historically we know that bands of hunter-gatherer groups, of between 10 to 50 people each, began to live, at least part of the time, in settled villages in the region of Sumer (ancient Mesopotamia) around 10,000 BCE.

1. Morality exists.
2. People ought to do the moral thing and ought not do the immoral thing.
3. People are self-determined, deciding whether they will behave morally or immorally.
4. For a society to be functional, there must be some agreement in that society as to that which is moral and immoral.
5. For the agreed upon morality to be meaningful, there must be a way to encourage conformity to it.
6. The ways to encourage moral conformity include: 1) teaching conformity during the socialization process, and 2) instituting a system of punishments for rule breaking.
7. Therefore, instituting a system of punishments for rule breaking is a legitimate (moral) part of a social moral system.

Even though there may be some ethicists who might prefer that this argument be structured differently, few would disagree with the conclusion: it is moral for a society of people to design, implement and manage a system of rules and punishment as part of their larger moral vision for themselves.

"The Story of Capital Punishment 1/6"
"The Story of Capital Punishment 2/6"
"The Story of Capital Punishment 3/6"
"The Story of Capital Punishment 4/6"
"The Story of Capital Punishment 5/6"
"The Story of Capital Punishment 6/6"

But what about capital punishment? Is it moral to execute people as a form of punishment for breaking specific rules or engaging in some forms of immoral behavior? Again, an overview of cultural practices throughout history would suggest that humanity, collectively, believes that execution is moral as a form of punishment for certain kinds of crimes. But once again, just because capital punishment *is* what humanity has practiced throughout the ages, does that mean that capital punishment is what humanity *ought* to have been practicing throughout the ages? Has it been *moral* for societies over the centuries to execute criminals? Is there rational moral justification for capital punishment?

What are the Arguments?

While all responsible people will agree that there is rational moral justification for punishment in general, not everyone agrees that there is moral justification for capital punishment. To consider the morality of capital punishment requires that we consider different approaches to punishment in general to see where and how execution might be rationally justified as a form of punishment.

Historically, there have been three approaches to, or three theoretical frameworks for, thinking about the role of punishment in society: the *utilitarian* approach, the *retributivist* approach, and the *compromise* approach.[3]

The utilitarian approach focuses on the balance between good and evil in a society. Happiness is good and therefore moral; unhappiness is bad and therefore immoral. Punishment, in whatever form it takes, will be judged moral or immoral based on how much happiness it produces. Rule breaking produces unhappiness and is therefore immoral. Punishment, which eliminates or at least minimizes crime, produces happiness for those who are negatively impacted by crime. Therefore, punishment, overall, is good because it generates more happiness than unhappiness.

Suppose, for instance, that there is a sudden increase in the number of home burglaries in a community. Thousands of people are upset because of the burglaries – either they have been robbed, might be robbed, or know someone who has been robbed. Everyone is unhappy. The police catch the criminal and he is convicted and put in jail. Now the people of the community are happy. The criminal is unhappy, but everyone else is happy; so, catching him and putting him in jail was the right (the moral) thing to do – because the morality of an action is dependent on the amount of relative happiness and unhappiness involved. The point of punishment for the Utilitarian is to make people (other than the one being punished) happy.

An additional point considered by utilitarian approaches is that criminals, while in prison, *may* be *rehabilitated* – especially if rehabilitation is one of the goals of the system and programs to facilitate it are in place. If that is the case, then even more happiness results for the criminals who are reformed and become productive citizens and for society, which experiences reduced recidivist crimes – that is, crimes occurring after unreformed criminals are released. The utilitarian approach may also generate concerns related to social challenges that might be the cause of crime – racism, poverty

---

[3]   Murtagh, "Punishment," in Internet Encyclopedia of Philosophy.

and other forms of inequality and injustice. The utilitarian approach is broad, encompassing much more than a specific punishment for a specific crime.

"Prison for Punishment, Not Rehabilitation"

"Reducing Recidivism"

One of the weaknesses of the utilitarian approach, theoretically speaking, is that it is possible that not punishing a wrongdoer might generate a great deal of happiness. The criminal, then, might go unpunished. Suppose there is a society where there is an individual who is advocating aggressively for social justice, complaining vigorously, getting everyone stirred up. Suppose also that most people of the society hate this individual because of the accusations he is making. Suppose also that someone assassinates this annoying person. Suppose, as well, that the majority of the society applauds the assassin because what is moral and immoral in a society based on utilitarian principles is determined by the amount of happiness generated, and because the people of this community are happy because of the killing the police are not working very hard to find and arrest the assassin. He did nothing immoral (in this utilitarian society) because what he did resulted in more happiness than unhappiness. Admittedly, this is only a theoretical example and may be remote, but it *is* a theoretical possibility where morality is determined by Bentham's Principle of Utility. In such a society, where punishment ought to be administered, it is not; where justice ought to carried out, it is not. Surely, this is a weakness. A strength, however, of the utilitarian approach to punishment is that it is concerned not only with forms of punishment, but about larger social issues related to crime in general.

The retributivist approach focuses on giving the criminal what he deserves – punishment for the wrong he did. The word *retributivist* involves the idea of *retribution,* or vengeance. Society is taking revenge for the wrong that was done. The criminal is getting what he deserves, his *just deserts*, for his wrongdoing. While society at large may be happy when criminals are punished and unhappy when they are not, society's level of satisfaction is not in focus in a retributive justice system. The point is punishment. Society could be unaware of the crime, unaware of the punishment, and thus have no feelings about it one way or the other. From a retributivist point of view, society's happiness or unhappiness is irrelevant because punishing the criminal must be done simply for the sake of punishing the wrong.

The weakness of the retributivist approach is that it is concerned only with retribution, only with carrying out social vengeance. Other matters, such as why a crime may have been committed or reforming the criminal are not matters of concern. The focus is very narrow: punish the wrongdoer. But the strength of the retributivist approach is that the wrongdoer does get punished.

The compromise approach focuses on combining the utilitarian and retributivist approaches, emphasizing the strengths of each – an interest in more than just retribution, yet an unwavering determination to see that justice is carried out.

These are the three paradigms most often utilized as avenues for the carrying out of justice. Regardless of which of these approaches a society might choose, the more important question (for our purposes in this chapter) is whether or not capital punishment is moral. What arguments can be offered for and against the morality of capital punishment?

Arguments for the Death Penalty

The first argument that usually comes to mind is the *deterrence argument*. The idea here is that people will be less likely to commit certain crimes (murder, treason, terrorism, hijacking a plane, the rape of underage victims, to name just a few) if they know the death penalty is associated with those crimes. The obvious question regarding the deterrence argument has to do with evidence. Is there any reliable scientific data that capital punishment
works as a deterrent? Some say yes; some say no. The problem that arises in supporting the argument for deterrence with data is that interpreting the data requires an element of prognostication. For example, some researchers have analyzed the data and concluded that each execution prevents between 3 and 32 additional murders. The range involved is obviously problematic. The typical margin of error for statistical data is + or – 2 or 3 points. A 29 point spread suggests sloppy analysis.[4] But the real problem is attempting to forecast what may or may not happen based on the possibility that

---

[4]   Van Den Haag quotes a more conservative estimate made by Ehrilch but falls prey to the same challenges related to prognostication ("In Defense of the Death Penalty," in *Ethics: History., Theory and Contemporary Issues*, 824-834.

some people will be convicted of a capital crime and executed. It is not easy to get a capital crime conviction and to execute a person in the United States. Bedau notes that according to a 1998 FBI report, "As things actually stand in American society today, a would-be murderer has one chance in three of not being arrested, and if arrested, one chance in three of not being convicted of a capital murder."[5] To argue that deterrence *is* (not *may be* but *is*) an effective deterrent requires a kind of prognostication that is not easily associated with sound, responsible scientific analysis.

"Deterrence and Incapacitation"

This, however, does not mean that there is no relevant data. According to the NAACP Legal Defense and Education Fund report, in April of 2012 there were 3,170 prisoners awaiting execution on death row.[6] Evidently, the threat of execution was not a deterrent for those people.

To know whether or not the threat of execution is an effective deterrent against capital crime, one would need to know why people commit capital crimes. Acts of terror are often capital crimes. Why do people commit acts of terror? Usually for ideological reasons. They are deeply committed to a cause, so much so that they are willing to die for it. Misguided as they might be, is the threat of execution if they are caught a deterrent? Evidently not. What about sex crimes committed against under-aged victims? Do the people who commit those kinds of crimes (a crime that involves a level of misguided and abnormal, but intense sexual drive) stop and ask themselves whether or not they want to risk the possibility of death in exchange for the gratification they will receive from committing the act they are considering? That sort of critical thinking analytical process is not part of the drive-reducing behavior of a sex offender. In fact, the kind of critical thinking required for the death penalty to act as a deterrent is not part of the "thinking" involved in most crimes that carry the death penalty. People who commit those kinds of crimes do not pause to analyze the potential consequences. Even in crimes that involve what is described as *pre-meditated* murder (a murder that was not a crime of passion but was planned out), a sound rational analysis of potential consequences is not part of the planning process. Those who believe that thoughtful critical analysis of the potential consequences precedes the committing of capital crimes are mistaken.

But perhaps the most crucial factor is that if capital punishment serves as a deterrent to capital crimes one would expect that states that have capital punishment would have lower rates of capital crimes than states that do not have capital punishment. But that is not the case. Capital crime rates are remarkably similar in states that practice that

5   Bedau, "Capital Punishment," in *The Oxford Handbook of Practical Ethics*, 712.
6   Death Penalty Information Center.

practice execution and those that do not. According to the *Death Penalty Information Center,* murder rates are consistently lower in states that do not have the death penalty.

The idea that capital punishment serves as an effective deterrent against capital crimes does not appear to have adequate support.

Another argument for the death penalty has to do with *punishment that fits the crime.* In the literature dedicated to considerations of punishment and capital punishment, this idea is often referred to as *deserts* – as in one getting his *just deserts,* getting what he deserves. Very serious crimes need to result in very serious consequences. Murder is such a horrible act that it requires an equally horrible punishment, a *like-kind* punishment – the punishment for murder ought to be death. The principle behind this idea is ancient. The idea of an *eye for an eye and a tooth for a tooth* (like-kind punishment) was part of the ancient Hebrew law (the Mosaic Covenant of the Old Testament). While there is a certain logic to the idea that most people would agree with, it has its challenges. The rape of a child carries the death penalty in many states. But death for rape is not a like-kind punishment. Espionage also carries the death penalty in many countries. Yet executing a spy or a traitor is not a like-kind punishment. Therefore, the argument is not sound for it lacks consistency. One cannot argue that the death penalty is moral because it is moral to take the life of one who has taken the life of another when we also take the lives of those who have not taken a life. The lack of consistency renders the argument unsound.

A third argument in favor of the death penalty has to do with the forfeiture of rights. Those who commit capital crimes, the argument goes, have forfeited their right to life. The challenge of any such argument would be to explain how a "right" can be forfeited. This, of course, has to do with how one defines a right. If a right is that to which one is entitled because of his humanness, then as long as one is a human, the rights associated with humanness cannot be forfeited or revoked. Philosophers have spoken about certain rights that are *unalienable* rights, as in our Declaration of Independence. What are *unalienable* or *inalienable* rights? They are rights that cannot be taken away. What would make a right unalienable? Its association with humanness. If there are certain things that are part of being human, rights that belong to us simply because we are human beings, then, as long as we are human, those rights ought not to be denied us. And to do so is immoral. What rights would those be? Whatever else might be on the list, life certainly would be on the list. One of the most basic rights that humans have because of our humanness is the right to life. No one has the right to deprive another of that right – except perhaps in the case of self-defense. I have a right to life and no one has the right to take it from me. If they try, I have the right to defend myself to whatever extent is necessary, including taking their life to preserve my own. We believe this. We believe the right to life is so basic that we allow for self-defense to the point of killing an attacker. The right to life is that basic and that important. Depriving another person of his right to life is one of the most serious violations imaginable. We respond by saying that the murderer has forfeited his right to life. But can a right that grows out of the nature of one's being be forfeited? Even the murderer does not stop being human. If one cannot forfeit his

humanness, how can he forfeit the rights associated with his humanness? But suppose one could make the argument that the act of murder did involve the forfeiture of one's humanness and the rights associated with it. What about the other capital crimes that do not involve murder – espionage, treason, child rape and so forth? As heinous as those crimes are, how does committing those crimes lead to a forfeiture of one's humanness and the rights associated with it? The spy who is caught spying is still a human.

Part of the problem is that we confuse rights and privileges. Privileges can be forfeited or revoked; rights cannot. Having a driver's license is a privilege that can be revoked; having a driver's license is not a right. The right to life, some would argue, is a right that cannot be forfeited or revoked. Those who argue that in committing murder the murderer forfeits his right to life will need to present an argument that explains how someone can forfeit that which is part of his nature.

These three arguments – deterrence, punishment that fits the crime, and the forfeiture of rights – are the most important and influential arguments offered in support of capital punishment. They are not conclusive. Each has some serious weaknesses associated with it. None of them prove that the death penalty is a moral form of punishment.

Arguments against the Death Penalty

If a sound argument for the death penalty cannot be made, can a sound argument against it be made? Perhaps.

Some have argued that utilizing the death penalty is illegal. One of the earliest arguments against the death penalty was made by Cesare Beccaria in his 1764 work entitled *On Crimes and Punishments*.[7] In that work he argued that no rational person would want to live in a society that made use of the death penalty. Why not? Because in that kind of a society every person might himself be a victim of the system. Besides, since a government can only do what the people empower it to do, no government would have the right to execute its citizens, for rational self-interested people would never permit it to do so. The weakness of Beccaria's argument ought to be obvious. Rational people do live in societies that make use of the death penalty. And rational people empower their governments to make use of it.

However, because people do those things does not mean that they ought to do those things. A thing is not moral because people do it.

"Cesare Beccaria"

The United States Supreme Court has ruled that the death penalty is legal (Furman v. Georgia 1972 and Gregg v. Georgia 1976). Of course, legality is not the issue. A thing can be legal but immoral. A thing can be moral but illegal. The ethical dilemma associated with the death penalty is not its legality, but its morality. Simply because the court has said it is legal and simply because we make use of it in our legal system does not make it moral. Claiming that it is illegal does not make it illegal, and it certainly does not make it immoral. The claim that the death penalty is not legal is not a sound argument against the morality of the death penalty.

Another argument against the death penalty is that it is immoral because it violates the criminal's right to life. Bedau observes that this argument would be plausible if it could be demonstrated that the right to life is absolute, that is, cannot be forfeited or revoked.[8] As I noted in the last section, such arguments hinge on the definition of a right. If a right is a claim one can make because it is part of the nature of humanness, how can it not be absolute? If humanness has certain rights associated with it, those rights remain intact as long as humanness remains intact. If someone wants to argue otherwise, they will be obliged to demonstrate how the basic rights claimed by humans (human *rights*, not privileges) can be *human* rights but somehow dissociated from one's humanness. That will be difficult to do because, logically, as long as one is human, one

---

[7]   Bedau, "Capital Punishment," in *The Oxford Handbook of Practical Ethics*, 720.
[8]   Bedau, 721.

has the rights that are associated with being human. It appears to me that this argument is sound and demonstrates the immorality of the death penalty.

A third argument for abandoning the death penalty is that it is impossible to administer it without making mistakes. We try to eliminate the mistakes. What could be worse than executing an innocent person? That's why it is so difficult to get a capital conviction and why there are so many appeals and reviews – to be sure an innocent person is not being executed. Yet it is highly unlikely that only guilty people have been executed. Innocent people go to prison all the time. Only recently has DNA testing been able to demonstrate the innocence of wrongly convicted people who have been in prison. Without a doubt, some of the people who have been executed were innocent. The fact that mistakes are made is, for many people, a good reason for abandoning the death penalty. However, the fact that mistakes are made in the application of the death penalty does not demonstrate the immorality of the death penalty.

"Dennis Maher, Exonerated in Massachusetts"

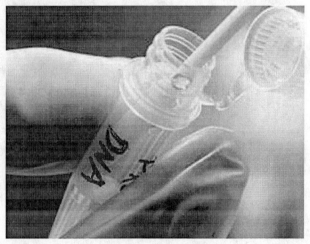

Yet another argument for abolishing the death penalty is that executing people is not appropriate behavior for a civilized society. The idea is intriguing, but would be difficult to prove. What is and is not appropriate for a "civilized" society depends on: 1) the definition of a civilized society and, 2) what is appropriate behavior in such societies. How one defines a "civilized" society today is likely to be very different from how a civilized society will be defined 5,000 years from now. If defining a civilized society is difficult, than determining what is appropriate behavior in a civilized society is just as challenging. But more to the point, since morality is absolute and not relative, what is moral and immoral does not change from time to time. That which is immoral was immoral 5,000 years ago and will still be immoral 5,000 from now. Morality does not change with time; it does not evolve as civilization evolves.

These are the major argument for the abolition of the death penalty. Only one of them, the argument that executing criminals violates their basic human right to life, appears to be a sound argument. But the morality or immorality of the death penalty has not yet been clearly established one way or the other. Perhaps evaluating it from the perspective of CEE and the Principle of Essential Humanness will help us will allow us to do that.

The Morality or Immorality of Capital Punishment

According to CEE and the Principle of Essential Humanness, if humanness has intrinsic value and if that intrinsic value generates rights that grow out of and are thus part of what it means to be human, that reality must be factored into a consideration of what is and is not moral as far as punishment is concerned. So, from that perspective we see that *morality involves recognizing the intrinsic value of humanness (one's own and that of others), along with actions, reactions, and interactions that reflect an appreciation of human value. Immorality involves a failure to recognize the intrinsic value of humanness (one's own and that of others), along with a subsequent failure to act, react and interact in ways that reflect an appreciation of human value. Thus, an act is moral if it recognizes and or enhances human value, and is immoral if it fails to recognize or in some way diminishes the value of humanness.*

Once this premise is accepted, determining the morality or immorality of the death penalty is relatively simple. Does executing a person recognize or enhance his or her humanness, or does it diminish or devalue his or her humanness? It might be objected that framing the question in this way calls into question, not just capital punishment, but punishment in any form. I disagree. Punishment itself does not devalue or diminish

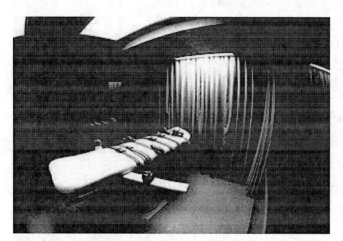

one's humanness, especially if the punishment is carried out from the perspective of reform and rehabilitation. If the goal of punishment is to help the person become a better person, his or her humanness is not diminished by punishment, but enhanced. Execution, however, does not enhance one's humanness in any way. It suggests that life is not intrinsically valuable and thus may be ended prematurely because a certain kind of a crime has been committed.

If humanness has intrinsic value, and if rights grow out of that value, then those rights are unalienable. Those rights cannot be revoked by others, neither can they be forfeited by the individual himself. If a person cannot stop being human he cannot dissociate himself from the rights that are part of being human. Neither can anyone else. Human rights are inviolable, and to deny anyone his or her basic rights, such as the right to life, is immoral, regardless of how badly one has behaved as a human being. Someone may argue that a murder has deprived a person of his right to life; thus, the state has the right to deprive the murderer of his right to life. How so? If it was wrong for an individual to deprive another person of his right to life, how can it be right for the state to deprive a person of his right to life? If depriving a person of life is wrong because life is intrinsically valuable, then life is valuable in every case and may not be taken away. What is it about the state being the state that makes its action moral when the same action on the part of an individual is immoral? Morality is absolute. An act that is immoral for an individual is also immoral for the state, for the state is nothing more than a collection of individuals who empower others (government leaders) to act on their behalf.[9]

The question, then, can be asked, what is it about "punishing" that makes taking a life (as a form of punishment) moral? Calling it execution instead of murder does not make it moral. As Kant has pointed out, motive matters in moral considerations. But how does the motive of punishment make execution moral? If life has intrinsic value, then in takes more than the motive of punishment to make depriving a person of his right to life a moral action.

There doesn't appear to be any way around the fact that execution is depriving a person of his unalienable right to life and that depriving a person of that right is immoral.

How, then, are we to punish the most heinous crimes humans commit? By putting them in prison and keeping them there. Life in prison without parole is severe punishment for the criminal, and provides protection for society. It is quite severe. How many of us would choose to live in a small confined space (six foot by nine foot) with limited contact with other people for the rest of our lives? It is not a very pleasant prospect.
Factor in having to live with the memory of the actions that put one in that situation and the severity factor is increased even more. It is simply not necessary to kill people as a form of punishment. If life is to be valued, it must be valued at all levels – at the beginning, the middle, and the end.

Additionally, studies have shown that it is more expensive to execute a criminal than to keep him in prison for life. In 1995 the cost of life imprisonment was about $800,000, but the cost of an execution (depending on how many appeals there are in the case) will be between 2 and 5 million dollars.[10] Of course the amounts today will be higher, but

---

[9]   I have already noted that an individual killing another in an act of self-defense would not be immoral because the person defending himself is simply trying to protect that which has intrinsic value. Taking a life in the process of self-defense is not immoral. The only argument that one might make in defense of state sanctioned capital punishment is that the state is engaging in a form of self-defense – defending itself from murderers. However, it would be very hard to make that argument, for there are other ways for the state to "protect" itself rather than executing criminals. At the time of execution, the criminal is already incarcerated and incapacitated. The state is already protected and can continue to protect itself by keeping the criminal incarcerated and attempting to reform and rehabilitate him.

[10]   Mackinnon, 315.

the cost difference between the two options, life in prison or execution, will be approximately the same.

"Cost of Death Penalty: Life in Jail Cheaper"

From the perspective of CEE and the Principle of Essential Humanness, it appears that the death penalty is not moral and should, therefore, be abolished. The states that have already done so have not experienced an increase in the rate of capital crimes committed. There would be nothing lost and a great deal gained in abolishing the death penalty.

Summary

It is impossible to discuss capital punishment without discussing the principle of punishment in general. As societies began to emerged 12,000 years ago, it became apparent that not only did those new societies need rules for how to live effectively in an interactive context, but that they also needed some way to enforce the rules and punish rule breakers. Over the centuries, three ways of thinking about punishment evolved: the utilitarian approach, the retributivist approach and the compromise approach. The utilitarian approach to punishment judges the morality of an act (including punishment) on the basis of how much happiness it produces. The retributivist approach to punishment focuses on giving the  criminal his just deserts, giving him what he deserves for what he did. It is a system of retribution, of vengeance. The compromise approach seeks to combine the strengths of each of those systems to create a more balanced approach to punishment than either one alone can offer.

Reflecting on a society's need to maintain control and conformity to social norms, it appears that some sort of a system of punishment is appropriate and moral – depending on the system and specific punishments involved. However, when one turns specifically to the issue of capital punishment as an element of a morally acceptable system of punishment, issues arise regarding the morality of the death penalty.

The problem with the death penalty seems to be that it denies the criminal his basic right to life. Since humanness has intrinsic value, humans can lay claim to rights that they possess, rights that grow out of the value of humanness. All humans have these rights (we can call them human rights) and they are unalienable. They cannot be forfeited by the rights holder, and cannot be revoked by others. To revoke irrevocable rights is immoral. The death penalty is a revocation of a person's right to life. Thus, the death penalty is immoral.

Thought and Discussion Questions

1. Discuss your insights regarding a society's need for a system of punishment.

2. What one argument do you believe is the strongest for demonstrating that capital punishment is moral? Explain why.

3. What one argument do you believe is the strongest for demonstrating that capital punishment is immoral? Explain why.

4. Discuss your thinking in regards to Rogers' claim that capital punishment is immoral because it diminishes the value of humanness.

5. Explain your thinking regarding the morality or immorality of the death penalty. Be sure you offer an argument (not just an opinion) for why you believe what you believe.

Chapter 17
Embryonic Stem Cell Research

Introduction

Cells are the building blocks of life. There are cells that build eyes, cells that build ears, cells that build livers, and so forth – specialized cells. Embryonic stem cells are cells that exist in a non-specialized state for a brief period of time – 3 to 5 days after fertilization.[1] Before these cells become specialized, becoming cells that will work with other specialized cells to build a stomach, a spleen, or whatever, they are called *undifferentiated* cells. Undifferentiated cells are

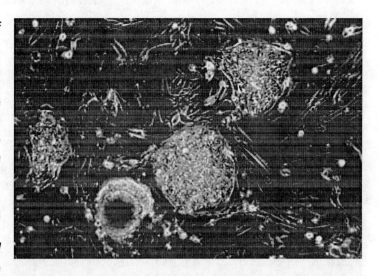

pluripotent, meaning that they have the potential to become any kind of a cell: an eye cell, a vocal cord cell, a tooth cell, and so forth. These undifferentiated pluripotent embryonic stem cells are important in the field of *regenerative medicine* because they can become any kind of a cell they need to become. Why is this important? Suppose that there are many people who need a new liver. Suppose there aren't enough livers donated (from accident victims, for instance) and patients are dying because there aren't enough livers for all of them to get transplants. But suppose researchers could grow livers in a laboratory. Suppose they could grow eyes, pancreases, heart valves, and other body parts that would be available for transplant wherever needed. That would be very helpful. Embryonic stem cells can be used to grow new organs or help repair damaged or failing organs, or to fight diseases that damage cells.

"Regenerative Medicine"

Obviously, embryonic stem cells are important for medical research. The problem is that they are available only in embryos 3 to 5 days old and that taking the stem cells out of a living, growing embryo kills it.

---

[1] This is a very basic explanation of embryonic stem cells and is not meant to be a thorough scientific explanation.

What is the Issue?

The moral issue related to embryonic stem cell research is essentially the same as the moral issue related to abortion: is it moral to "kill" the living, developing human during its embryonic or fetal stage of development? Put simply, the question is, is the embryo a living human being? Some will frame the question as it relates to personhood. When does the developing embryo become a living person who has a right to life? Is an embryo a living person? However, as we discovered in our discussion regarding abortion, the "personhood" argument is problematic. If the embryo is not a living human being, harvesting the cells within it is not a moral issue. But if the embryo is a living human being, the harvesting of stem cells, which destroys the embryo, is killing a human being – an obvious moral concern.

What are the Arguments?

The arguments related to embryos in stem cell research are the same basic arguments presented in relation to abortion. Is the embryo a living person? Framing the question in relation to personhood requires that we define a person. Normally a person, that is, one having the qualities or traits of personhood, is described as one who is rational, self-determined and moral. Animals think but cannot engage in higher-level abstract conceptualization, that is, they are not rational. Neither do animals make moral choices. Rationality, self-determination and morality are some of the features that make us human, that make us fully formed human persons.

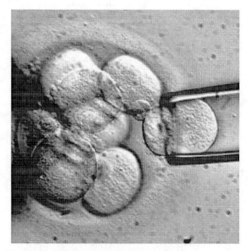

But if personhood consists of the exhibition of these traits, then lots of people that we normally define as human beings do not qualify as persons: not only embryos and fetuses, but new born infants and children, developmentally disabled people and people with dementia. If one is only a person when he or she can exhibit the traits of rationality, self-determination and morality, and if only persons are fully human and have human rights such as the right to life, then those who are not persons and do not have the right to life can be killed without issues of morality being raised. With this definition of a person, babies are not people. The child is not a person. The Alzheimer's patient is no longer a person. They have no human rights and can be treated accordingly. This is the clear implication of the personhood argument as it is normally presented in discussions involving either abortion or embryonic stem cell research.

Obviously, it is not a very good argument. Is anyone willing to suggest that a three-month old baby or a five-year old child does not have basic human rights even though they have not achieved the personhood of the fully functional adult? Are senior citizens suffering from Alzheimer's no longer people with rights? Many are willing to suggest that the unborn child who lacks the traits of adult personhood is not a person and has no rights. This is quite inconsistent and illogical. The argument that says that it is morally permissible to kill an embryo because the embryo has not achieved personhood is a flawed argument.

Let us, however, assume for the moment that the personhood argument, as it is normally presented, has merit and that the embryo is not a person with rights. When will it become one? Some suggestions include: when it has measurable brain activity (usually between 6 and 8 weeks), when it has a heartbeat, when it is viable (that is, when it can be sustained outside the womb), or when it is born. But notice, none of these criteria has any relation to the features that we normally associate with personhood in the personhood argument. The problem with determining when a living human being is present, if it is not present beginning at conception, is that whatever criteria are proposed, in addition to having no relation to the traits normally thought to define personhood, are entirely arbitrary. The entire enterprise of trying to determine when a non-person becomes a person involves a flawed concept and is not going to produce any kind of consensus.

Most of those who specialize in embryology do not embrace the potential person position. As noted in Chapter Fourteen, George and Gomez-Lobo say:

> A human embryo (like a human being in the fetal, infant, child, or adolescent stage) is not properly classified as a "prehuman" organism with the mere potential to become a human being. No human embryologist or textbook in human embryology known to us presents, accepts, or remotely contemplates such a view. The testimony of all leading embryology textbooks is that a human embryo *is – already* and not merely potentially – a human being. His or her potential, assuming a sufficient measure of good health and a suitable environment, is to develop by an internally directed process of growth through the further stages of maturity on the continuum that is his or her life.[2]

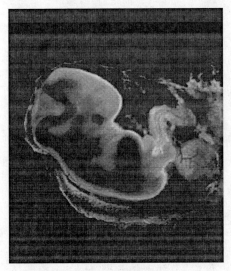

Subtly of language is important in philosophical discussions. Consider, for instance, the difference in asking if the embryo is a person and asking if it is human. If the parents are human, then the offspring is human. What else would it be? It is not a monkey or a horse. It is a human. And humans have rights. Humans cannot be killed because it suits someone else's purposes. As soon as we begin to discuss the embryo as a human, the discussion goes in a very different direction. We saw how this worked in relation to the abortion issue. That which makes humans valuable is the kind of being a human is – a being that is rational, self-determined, and moral, a being that values and is therefore valuable. But it is not just that a human can, at a specific moment in time, think

---

[2] George and Gomez-Lobo, *Human Cloning ad Human Dignity*, 258-266.

rationally or make a moral choice – the kinds of things fully functional adults can do. Humanness itself, because it involves valuing and the potential for good, is inherently valuable. The potential for rational morality is of supreme value. This is what we see in the three-year old child that makes that child more valuable than a three-year old German Shepherd – the promise of rational morality, the potential for full humanness to manifest itself.

"The Ethical Questions of Stem Cell Research"

As I noted in Chapter Fourteen, this may sound like the potential person argument, but it is not (even though I just used the phrase, *the potential for full humanness*). Humanity has an innate value even when the potential has not yet been achieved – even if it is never achieved. What if the three-year old died in an accident? Was that three-year old not a human because his full rational and moral potential was not

achieved? Certainly not. A living thing is either human or not human. There is no in between. If it is not human it cannot become human. So says the law of the excluded middle. Humanness, which a living thing has or does not have and cannot acquire, has intrinsic value that must be recognized and appreciated. Discussing an embryo's humanity instead of its personhood may be a subtle distinction, but it is, I believe, an important one.

The morality of harvesting embryonic stem cells turns on the embryo's status. If the embryo is a living human, killing it to harvest its stem cells is immoral. If it is not a living human, then harvesting the stem cells in it is not immoral. The arguments that an embryo is not a living human are not conclusive and not convincing. What will we see if we approach the subject from the perspective of CEE and the Principle of Essential Humanness?

The Morality or Immorality of Embryonic Stem Cell Research

The foundational idea of CEE is that humanness has intrinsic value that must be acknowledged and respected. To value and enhance humanness is moral, to devalue and diminish humanness is immoral. This idea by itself does not help us with the question about the humanness of an embryo. Whether or not the embryo is a living human must be answered in a separate argument, which has been alluded to in the section above. Here I will state the argument in a more specific fashion.

1. When a human sperm fertilizes a human egg, the resulting zygote (which becomes an embryo) is human.
2. A human is not only human if it reaches its full potential as a mature adult, but comes into existence as a human. A thing is or is not human. A thing cannot become human.
3. A human embryo is a human.
4. Humanness has intrinsic value, not because of specific skills a mature human has, but because of the nature of humanness – which includes rational and moral valuing and the potential for good freely chosen.
5. Thus, a human embryo has intrinsic value.
6. To value and enhance humanness is moral. To devalue and diminish humanness is immoral.
7. To kill a human embryo is to devalue and diminish its humanness.
8. Therefore, to kill a human embryo is immoral.[3]

If one accepts the basic premise underlying CEE, the Principle of Essential Humanness, that humanness has inherent value, then killing a human embryo cannot be a moral action.

But what about the good that continued embryonic stem cell research will accomplish? Surely the good that can be accomplished counts for something. A utilitarian approach would weigh the amount of unhappiness experienced by the dying embryos (which is probably none because they are unable to experience anything at that stage of development) against the amount of happiness experienced by the people and their loved ones who benefit from the medical advances resulting from stem cell research. As we have seen, however, in Chapter Eight, the underlying premises of Utilitarianism (as a formal system) are questionable. To kill one group of humans in order to provide benefits to another group of humans is simply unacceptable.

So, are the potential benefits of research to be lost? Fortunately, no. Ongoing research has revealed that there are other kinds of cells (cells that can be utilized without embryos being killed) that can be used, which offer the same kinds of results as embryonic stem cells. The following is an article (published 2010) by the American Council on Science and Health.

While an appeals court has lifted a federal judge's previously imposed injunction disallowing federally funded embryonic stem cell research to continue, scientists are making new breakthroughs in research that circumvent the use of embryonic stem cells, a highly charged moral and political field of medical research. The first batch of

---

[3] This same argument can be made in regards to abortion.

good news comes from a team led by Dr. Derrick J. Rossi of the Children's Hospital Boston. His group has artificially reproduced naturally occurring biological signals that can convert ordinary skin cells into cells that act almost identically to embryonic stem cells, or pluripotent cells capable of differentiating into specific tissues used for transplantation or the treatment of various diseases.

ACSH's Dr. Gilbert Ross believes the new research, published in the journal *Cell Stem Cell*, "represents hopeful progress in the use of stem cell technology." He adds, "With targeted manipulations, this and similar technologies will one day be used to replenish and replace diseased organs and tissues – amongst many other uses – in diseased individuals."

In another study published in this month's *Stem Cells and Development*, scientists investigated the therapeutic efficacy of stem cells found in menstrual blood (MenSCs) for the treatment of brain damage caused by stroke and other central nervous system disorders. It has been shown that menstrual blood is a renewable stem cell source that also offers a non-controversial alternative to the use of embryonic stem cells. According to study investigator Dr. Cesar Borlongan, a neurologist at the University of South Florida, the retrieval of MenSCs "offers greater ease, and with a wider window of opportunity for harvest than other adult stem cells."

"These new breakthroughs are that much better because they both bypass the concern of using embryonic stem cells – a subject fraught with controversy over some people's belief that obtaining stem cells from embryos is morally equivalent to taking a human life," says Dr. Ross.[4]

A detailed report prepared by the Witherspoon Council on Ethics and the Integrity of Science, discusses:

...[T]wo of the most prominent methods suggested for obtaining pluripotent stem cells without extracting them from embryos. The first approach is called *altered nuclear transfer* (ANT), or, sometimes, altered nuclear transfer with oocyte-assisted reprogramming (ANT-OAR). The second approach, developed independently by Shinya Yamanaka in Japan and James Thomson in Wisconsin, is called somatic cell dedifferentiation, but is typically referred to by the name of its product, *induced pluripotent stem cells* (iPS cells).[5]

[4] "Two Alternatives to Embryonic Stem Cell Research," American Council on Science and Health.

[5] "Appendix A: The Science of Embryonic Stem Cell Research," The Witherspoon Council on Ethics and the Integrity of Science, *The New Atlantis*.

The rest of the article goes on to discuss these alternatives and the additional research that needs to be done. But the point is that embryos do not need to be destroyed for medical research to continue. There are alternatives.

"What Are Induced Pluripotent Stem Cells?"

Summary

The moral concern related to embryonic stem cell research is the same as that of the abortion issue: the morality of destroying an embryo or fetus. If the embryos destroyed in the process of harvesting stem cells are living human beings, then the process is immoral. If the embryos are not living human beings, the process that destroys them is not immoral. The challenge is to determine whether or not an embryo is a living human being.

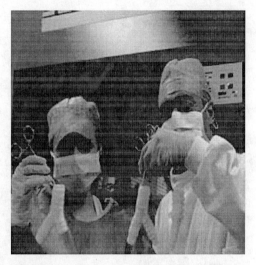

Those who argue that the embryo is not a living human argue that it cannot be a person since it displays none of the crucial features normally associated with human life, features that are uniquely human: rationality, self-determination, morality, and so forth. Many will respond, arguing that the embryo has those features in potential, and that the potential person deserves the status of a person. The response to this is to ask, does the acorn deserve the status of an oak tree? Most people would say, no.

This entire line of argument, on both sides, is problematic because it defines personhood and the rights associated with it (such as the right to life) by focusing on the traits and skills manifested by mature, healthy humans. It selects a specific range on the human developmental continuum and says the things associated with that part of human existence are the only things that matter. Using this reasoning, embryos are not persons with rights. And if we are going to be logically consistent, neither are babies, children, the developmentally disabled, or those with dementia. And accordingly, if destroying embryos is not immoral, neither is destroying babies, children, the developmentally disabled, and the demented.

A better approach is to think in terms of humanness. Human parents produce human embryos. A human is a human, and humanness, because of what it entails, has intrinsic value. That which is human must be valued. A living thing is either human or not human. A living nonhuman thing cannot become a living human. A thing is human when it begins to exist, or it is not. It cannot become a human. Human embryos are human and as such have the same intrinsic value as any other human. It matters not what skills the human has developed or lost, a living human is a living human. Embryo's are living and are human. Destroying an embryo is killing a living human. Therefore, it is immoral to kill an embryo.

However, some say that not harvesting embryonic stem cells will hinder medical research. Probably not. Medical researchers have already found several alternative sources for pluripotent stem cells. These alternative sources are viable and do not require that embryos die.

Thought and Discussion Questions

1. Discuss the similarities and the differences, as you see them, between the issues of embryonic stem cell research and abortion.

2. Explain the argument of personhood (what personhood consists of) and of the argument regarding potentiality. What are the strengths and weaknesses of each?

3. Describe Rogers' alternative to the personhood-potentiality argument. Identify the strengths and weaknesses.

4. Discuss your understanding of alternatives to embryonic stem cell research. How do these alternative factors impact the process of harvesting embryonic stem cells?

5. What is your position on embryonic stem cell research? Support your position with arguments.

Chapter 18
Environmental Pollution

Introduction

The morality of environmental pollution is a topic that falls under the broader category of the philosophical discipline known as *Environmental Ethics*. Environmental Ethics is perhaps the newest sub-discipline in philosophy, developing in the 1970s as a result of the heightened environmental awareness of the late 1960s. Environmental Ethics studies the moral relationship humans sustain to the environment, including future generations of humans, animals, the air, water, trees and plants and so forth. Cochran notes that "the two fundamental questions that environmental ethics must address are: what duties do humans have with respect to the environment, and, why?"[1] In order to think critically about the first question, what moral obligations do humans have regarding the environment, we have to first think about the second question, if and why humans have a moral obligation to the environment? Thinking about that question will lead to a consideration of the value and possible moral status of the environment[2] in general, or of various aspects of it such as the moral standing of animals. The place to begin, therefore, so we can eventually arrive at our specific question regarding the morality of environmental pollution, is with the value and moral standing of the environment, as a whole or of an individual aspect of it.

"Environmental Ethics"

Does the environment have value? Most people would say, yes. We need food to eat, water to drink, air to breath. These things are features of the environment and have value. The environment, then, has value. But what kind of value? If a thing has value in and of itself, a value that is not derived from use, that thing has *intrinsic value*. I have argued that humans have this kind of intrinsic value. The Principle of Essential Humanness says that rational, moral beings like humans have intrinsic value – we are valuable because of what is entailed in being human. However, if a thing has derived value, a value that grows out of that thing's usefulness (an apple has value because it can be eaten, shoes have

---

[1] Cochran, "Environmental Ethics," in *Internet Encyclopedia of Philosophy*.
[2] Brennan and Lo, "Environmental Ethics," in *Stanford Encyclopedia of Philosophy*.

value because they protect one's feet), then that thing has *instrumental value*. Its value is derived from its usefulness. If the environment, then, has value, what kind of value does it have – intrinsic or instrumental?

Some philosophers have argued that anything that has a goal, that is, that is teleological in nature (goal-oriented with a purpose to accomplish) has intrinsic value.[3] This position appears problematic, however. An apple has a goal, to ripen, but it is not a conscious goal of a thinking being like goals humans might set for themselves. The apple did not set for itself the goal of becoming ripe. Does the goal someone else or something else set for the apple provide the apple with intrinsic value? Or is the apple's value still in its usefulness as food? What if it had no usefulness at all, to other plants, to animals, or to humans? Would its nature to ripen make it inherently valuable if it had no use? I think not. An apple does not have intrinsic value, but has only instrumental value.

Other philosophers have argued that animals have intrinsic value and therefore ought to be given moral status like humans. Tom Regan and Peter Singer advocate this, though each has a slightly different perspective, Singer working out of a Utilitarian framework and Regan out of a Deontological paradigm.[4] For Singer, because animals are sentient and can suffer, they have moral standing. For Regan, because animals can anticipate and desire and want to avoid suffering, they have moral  status. Without a doubt, animals deserve consideration. We can even say that when humans cause animals to suffer (where there is no greater good to be realized) it is wrong. But why is it wrong? Regan and Singer would say that it is wrong because animals have moral standing, that they are moral creatures. I would say that it is not because animals are moral creatures, but because we are moral beings. It is wrong to hurt animals needlessly because animals can suffer and moral beings (like humans) ought not cause needless suffering. I would say that animals do not have intrinsic value, but have instrumental value. Their value is in the purpose they serve as part of a larger cosmic system or reality. If apples and animals have instrumental (rather than intrinsic) value, I think it is safe to say that if we examined each aspect of the non-rational, non-self-determined, non-moral cosmos, that is to say, the non-human material reality, we would see that the environment in general has instrumental rather than intrinsic value.

If the inanimate environment does not have intrinsic value and if the animate, but non-human aspect of the environment (animals), do not have intrinsic value, what does have intrinsic value? I would say that only humans have intrinsic value. Why? Because humans are rational, self-determined, and moral. These are features unique to humans

---

[3]   Cochrane (Environmental Ethics) notes that Paul Taylor advocates this position.
[4]   Brennan, "Environmental Ethics."

and they make humanness intrinsically valuable. A being who can engage in abstract conceptualization, contemplate concepts such as the nature of reality, truth, morality, goodness and justice, and who can choose to be good has intrinsic value, inherent worth.[5] These features are characteristic of humanness and make humanness intrinsically valuable.

This view of what is intrinsically valuable is referred to as *anthropocentric*, meaning human-centeredness. An *anthropocentric environmental view* is one that says, in effect, only humans have intrinsic value and the environment, inanimate or animate, has only instrumental value. Specifically, the environment has value only as it is useful in some way, especially to humans.[6]

An anthropocentric environmental view is not very popular today. It is more politically correct (at least for environmental ethicists) to espouse a non-anthropocentric view. Such a view might be might be called: 1) a *sentient-centric* view, that animals that are aware and can suffer and enjoy, deserve moral consideration; 2) a *biocentric* view, that all-living things deserve moral consideration; or 3) an *ecocentric* view, that specific ecosystems or our entire ecosystem deserves moral consideration. It is important to remember that in saying all living things or our entire ecosystem deserves moral consideration, advocates of these positions are claiming that it is immoral to behave in ways that devalue the intrinsic value of the thing under consideration. For instance, a strict (or strong) biocentric view would advocate that it is immoral to fail to recognize the "rights" of a species of animal (a kind of a bird or squirrel, for instance) that might be endangered by the building of a new refinery or power plant in a given location. A strong ecocentric position would say that it is wrong not to respect a river's "right" to flow as it does or a mountain's "right" to stand where it does. To divert the river or build a dam would be immoral because it violates the river's rights. To cut through the mountain to build a road would be immoral because it violates the mountain's rights.

"Preservation Ethic"

---

[5] As noted in previous chapters, I include all humans in this category, those humans who have, because of maturity, acquired the skills associated with rationality and self-determination, and those who, because of some physical or mental challenge, have lost or never developed those traits. The intrinsic value of an individual human exists because he or she is human, not because he or she has acquired the skills or traits of a healthy, mature human.

[6] Sheader-Frechette, "Environmental Ethics," in *The Oxford Handbook of Practical Ethics*, 189-190.

"Resource Conservation Ethic"

"Land Ethic"

"Sustainability"

The first task, then, of environmental ethics is to select a paradigm from which to proceed: *anthropocentric* or *non-anthropocentric*. If non-anthropocentric, which form: sentient-centric, biocentric, or ecocentric? But it is not enough to simply select one (and the ones I have mentioned are only a few). One must be able to defend one's selection, to present arguments demonstrating that position's correctness. As I have defined humanness in this presentation, it is obvious that I would embrace an anthropocentric position as the one that can be logically demonstrated as sound and viable.

Those who have been critical of the anthropocentric position have argued that working out of an anthropocentric framework would mean that if one wanted to kill an animal (a dog or cat, for instance) just because one wanted to do so would not be immoral, because according to the anthropocentric position only humans have a moral standing. Killing an animal, therefore (for whatever reason), is acceptable and does not violate the animal's moral standing because the animal does not have a moral standing.  Killing a dog is no different than spraying weed killer on a dandelion in your yard.

This appears to be something of an exaggeration, to say the least. I would hope that those who advocate an anthropocentric paradigm would not advocate the morality of killing sentient animals simply because they are not humans. I would hope that because humans are moral beings that the very idea of causing needless suffering would be repugnant, whether human or animal suffering. If a thing can suffer it deserves not to suffer; it deserves consideration and compassion – not because of its moral standing, but because of ours. Anyone who embraces the Principle of Essential Humanness and Jesus' Golden Rule Ethic of Love along with Virtue Ethics would not engage in the degenerate behavior of causing needless suffering. People who value humanness, their own and that of others, will have a general appreciation and respect for all life.

What is the Issue?

Having provided this general overview of environmental ethics, we can move on to the specific concern of this chapter: the morality of environmental pollution. Specifically, 1) is environmental pollution a moral concern, and 2) if it is, how would one determine the morality of environmental pollution? Perhaps pollution is neither moral nor immoral; perhaps it is amoral, that is, not a moral issue at all. There are some things, after all, that are morally neutral, neither good nor bad. Is pollution one of them?

To answer the first question we have to answer the second question. I suspect the simplest way to determine if something is a moral issue is to ask if it is something that is thought of as either good or bad. Some things are neither. One's choice of salad dressing, for instance, is morally neutral. Some things, though, are definitely good, like kindness; and some are definitely bad, like murder. Kindness and murder are moral issues. If we are not sure whether or not a thing is a moral issue we might begin by asking, is it, generally speaking, considered good or bad? If it is considered bad, why is it? Is it harmful in some way? I would suggest that anything that is harmful, anything that causes pain or suffering or results in injustice is a moral issue. Whether or not a thing (even if it causes pain or suffering) is moral or immoral might depend on other factors, such as its relationship to a possible greater good.

Having answered the second question, we can now answer the first question, is environmental pollution a moral concern? Virtually everyone who understands the effects of what we identify as pollution says it is a bad thing, a dangerous thing that causes serious problems on many different levels. Pollution is harmful; it causes suffering. Therefore pollution is a moral concern.

"Heavy Smog, Called "Fog" Covers Beijing"

How serious a concern is environmental pollution? It is very serious. The May 4, 2007 edition of the New York Times, carried a story by Elizabeth Rosenthal about an English farmer, Roger Middleditch. A 50-foot-wide strip of his sugar beet field fell into the North Sea. Why? Because of coastal erosion due to climate change. The article goes on to mention, "A report this year from the Intergovernmental Panel on Climate Change estimates that rising seas will force 60 million people away from their coastal homes and jobs by the year 2080."[7]

"What is Coastal Erosion"

Climate change is one of the most serious challenges facing our planet today. Because of the amount of pollutants that humans release into the air each day, our atmosphere is heating up at an alarming rate. There is now more carbon dioxide in the atmosphere than there has been for thousands of years. One of the main, if not the main, sources of the pollution causing this is the burning of fossil fuel in cars, planes, trains, and power plants (we burn fossil fuels to generate electricity). The greenhouse gases that are produced by fossil fuels create global warming that is causing the polar ice caps to melt, causing sea levels to rise. The warmer ocean water caused by the warmer climate also causes changes in air currents, the flows of warm and cool air, resulting in changes in weather patterns – specifically, more and more severe tornadoes and hurricanes. This alone adds up to a global disaster. But it gets worse, pollution also impacts the health of individuals. According to the World Health Organization (WHO), 1.3 million people worldwide living in urban contexts die each year from what is referred to as urban outdoor air pollution.[8] High levels of air pollution can cause or contribute to health problems such as asthma, COPD (Chronic Obstructive Pulmonary Disease), and Cystic Fibrosis. Additionally, people who suffer from chronic health conditions such as heart disease and diabetes have a higher risk of complications and death when living in regions with higher levels of air pollution.[9]

---

[7]   Rosenthal, "As Climate Changes, Bits of England's Coast Crumble," *New York Times*.
[8]   WHO, "Air Quality and Health," Fact Sheet N313, September 2011.
[9]   LaMarco, "Diseases Caused by Air Pollution," Bright Hub, March 2010.

"Al Gore: New Thinking on the Climate Crisis"

All of this is only in relation to one kind of pollution: air pollution caused mostly by burning fossil fuels. Our water is also being polluted. The Environmental Protection Agency issued the following report:

* About 44% of assessed stream miles, 64% of assessed lake acres, and 30% of assessed bay and estuarine square miles are not clean enough to support uses such as fishing and swimming.

* Leading pollutants in our nation's waters include bacteria, mercury, nutrients such as phosphorus and nitrogen, and low levels of dissolved oxygen, which are often caused by the decomposition of organic material.

* Leading sources of pollution in our nation's waters include air deposition, agricultural runoff, and hydrologic modifications such as water diversions and channelization of streams.

* A recent study of the nation's streams found that only 28% have healthy biological communities compared to best possible conditions in their region[10]

"The Devastating Effects of Water Pollution"

Pollution exists and pollution is bad, that is, it produces bad results. But is pollution immoral? Is all pollution immoral? Can it be that there are some levels of pollution that are acceptable, and therefore, not immoral? These are the issues that need to be addressed.

[10] The National Water Quality Inventory Report to Congress (305(b) report).

What are the Arguments?

As noted earlier, the main perspectives and arguments in environmental ethics can be divided into two groups, anthropocentric and non-anthropocentric, with the non-anthropocentric group being further divided into a number of smaller groups.

The anthropocentric perspective is that issues concerning environmental morality must be rooted in a focus on human needs and goals. As the most highly developed species on the planet, humans have the right and responsibility to utilize and manage resources for our purposes. How can life and living conditions be improved for all people? What do we need to accomplish? What do we need to accomplish it? How ought we to manage our resources in order to accomplish it? The orientation of this approach is centered or rooted in a human perspective. Humans are what matter – mostly. Very few ethicists, if any, who advocate an anthropocentric perspective would say humans are all that matters. They would say that humans matter most. Thus, ethically or morally, what is right has to do primarily with human needs and goals. Why? Here's the argument. Humans matter most 1) because humans are capable of a level of rationality that is so far above every other thinking animal on the planet that the difference can't effectively be measured, and 2) because we are also self-determined and moral, two more features unique to humans. These fundamental differences between us and everything else on the planet put us in a unique position, granting us unique privileges and binding on us serious responsibilities. We are in charge. We must decide what is to be done, when, and how. Hopefully, we will do so intelligently and responsibly.

The non-anthropocentric perspective is that issues concerning environmental morality must be rooted in a focus that includes much more than human needs and goals. Depending on the exact non-anthropocentric paradigm involved, any number of other foci might come into play. For instance, some will claim that all sentient animals must be given the same consideration as humans in how they are treated as to the "rights" that are afforded them. Suppose, for example, that some new mineral is discovered under the ground in Southern California. Suppose it has enormous energy in it and that mining it would solve all our energy problems for the next 50,000 years. However, 25 million people inhabit Southern

California and whoever wanted to mine this new mineral would not be allowed to simply start tearing up the infrastructure of Southern California, making it uninhabitable, driving the people out, in their attempts to mine the valuable new mineral. People live there. They have rights. No one can simply make their home uninhabitable. Doing such a thing would be immoral. Those who advocate animal rights say that we do that sort of thing all the time to animals when we destroy animal habitats in order to cut timber or drill for oil and mine coal or copper or some other substance. They argue that if it is immoral to do that to humans, it is also immoral to do it to animals. Why? Because causing animals who can suffer to suffer is immoral. Because sentient animals can suffer, they have the same moral status as humans who can suffer. So if treating a human a certain way is immoral, treating an animal that same way is also immoral.

There are other non-anthropocentric positions that extend rights not just to animals, but to inanimate objects such as trees, rivers, mountains, and so forth. Thus, damming up a river would be immoral because the dam interferes with the river's right to flow where it will. Human rights do not carry more weight than the river's right. Cutting down a tree violates its right to exist. Cutting away all or part of a mountain or tunneling through it to created a road or a train track is immoral because such actions violate the mountain's right to exist unharmed or unhindered. In what sense? In the sense that everything on the planet has an equal standing as a feature of an ecosystem, of an interdependent holistic system that must be respected and valued as a whole system if it is to function properly.

Which of these positions (anthropocentric or non-anthropocentric) makes the most sense as a paradigm from which to think about environmental ethics is for you to determine. What I want to do now is consider the specific topic of environmental pollution based on the Principle of Essential Humanness and Critical Ethical Eclecticism.

The Morality or Immorality of Environmental Pollution

Once again, the cornerstone of CEE is the Principle of Essential Humanness and its view that *morality involves recognizing the intrinsic value of humanness (one's own and that of others), along with actions, reactions, and interactions that reflect an appreciation of human value. Immorality involves a failure to recognize the intrinsic value of humanness (one's own and that of others), along with a subsequent failure to act, react and interact in ways that reflect an appreciation of human value. Thus, an act is moral if it recognizes and or enhances human value, and is immoral if it fails to recognize or in some way diminishes the value of humanness.*

With this as a place to begin we can ask about the morality of environmental pollution. Does polluting the environment demonstrate an appreciation for the value of humanness? If polluting the environment is bad for the health of individuals and if it threatens the balance necessary for the healthy functioning of the environment, making the world a less friendly place to live in than it would otherwise be, how can polluting the environment be anything other than immoral?

But is *all* pollution immoral? Some levels of "pollution" are normal, cannot be avoided, and are not harmful. That kind of pollution would not be immoral. For instance, one of the pollutants in the atmosphere that is causing the greenhouse effect (global warming) is methane. Yet methane is produced by humans and animals. In quantities that the atmosphere can handle, methane is not a problematic pollutant; however, it is when produced in massive quantities. All living things produce waste. Again, in manageable quantities human and animal waste does not rise to the level of problematic pollution. But in massive quantities that the atmosphere cannot manage, waste becomes problematic. Thus, whether or not "pollution" is a moral problem depends on the amount under consideration. When there is enough pollution in the air to deplete the ozone layer[11] and allow the sun's radiation to reach dangerous levels, then we are dealing with a level of pollution that has moral implications. In other words, activity that generates amounts of pollution that are dangerous and/or harmful to humans, animals, or the environment in general is immoral activity.

"Methane Bubbling from Arctic Ice"

For example, I have noted that too much methane in the atmosphere contributes to the greenhouse effect, to global warming. There are other gasses that are problematic as well. Human activity in various forms is what causes the increase in these gasses. The burning of fossil fuels is one of these behaviors, but only one. The large number of farm animals (such as sheep and cows) that we utilize, generate increased levels of methane in the atmosphere. The generation of methane is part of the normal biological process. But

---

[11] The ozone layer is a layer of a special kind of oxygen (oxygen that has one additional oxygen atom) that surrounds the earth and blocks the ultraviolet radiation of the sun. As the ozone layer is depleted by an imbalance of gasses in the atmosphere (such as high levels of methane) the sun's ultraviolet rays are not blocked, but reach the earth causing serious health problems for humans and animals.

those who raise cattle, for instance, add higher levels of nitrogen to their cattle feed. The increased amount of nitrogen in their food makes the cattle feel full so that they eat less. This reduces feed costs and increases profit margins. But the nitrogen in the food feeds not only the cattle but also the microorganisms that grow in their stomachs. These well-fed microorganisms then increase the production of methane. Huge herds of cattle and sheep produce a lot of methane. The thousands of herds of sheep and cattle that are needed to meet our needs produce massive amounts of methane – more than they otherwise would because of the nitrogen added to their food. The added nitrogen is good for the profit margin, but bad for the atmosphere. Could it be that some nitrogen is helpful but too much harmful? If too much nitrogen in cattle feed generates results that are harmful to the environment, then what conclusion does that lead us to regarding the morality of adding too much nitrogen to cattle feed? It does not take a genius to figure this out.

"Knowing Your Nitrogen Footprint"

This application of CEE is rooted in a consequentialist[12] perspective. The consequences for our planet and all the life forms that live on it must be taken into consideration as we evaluate the morality of our actions. And it must not only involve the consequences for the present population, but future populations as well. Some philosophers have argued that we have no moral obligation to future generations to see to it that they have the essentials they need not only for survival but to thrive and be happy. What is their argument? Their argument is that future generations who do not yet exist are not part of a morally reciprocal community and do not participate in the give and take of a moral community where rights and obligations are acknowledged and exchanged. Moral rights and obligations can only be claimed and exchanged by participants of a moral community. Since future generations are not part of the existing moral community, they have  no rights and we have no obligations to them. I see the logic of the argument, but disagree that only present participants of a moral community have rights and obligations. I would argue that the knowledge that one generation will pass away and be replaced by another obligates the present generation to do what they can to secure the needs of future generations. After all, a baby is not yet a participating member of a

---

[12] I am not making use of Utilitarianism but of simple consequentialism, which says that the consequences of an act must be considered in an evaluation of the morality of the act.

moral community. Does that mean that we have no obligations to babies to provide them with clean air and water? They may not yet be participants in a reciprocal moral community, but they will be. So will future generations. Because we are rational beings with the ability to anticipate the future, and because our present actions impact that future, we have a responsibility to secure that future to the best of our ability. We have a moral obligation not to behave in ways that jeopardize the future.

I want my children, who are part of the moral community, to have clean air to breath, clean water to drink, and to be able to go outdoors and enjoy the sunshine without being bombarded with dangerous levels of ultraviolet rays. I also want this for my grandchildren, my great grandchildren and for as many generations as there will be. If our behavior depletes resources, making the world an unfriendly or even a dangerous place to live, we are selfishly devaluing the humanness of future generations. Any behavior that does that without some mitigating circumstances that justify the behavior, whether it impacts present or future populations, is morally questionable.

Summary

Environmental ethics is a new branch of philosophical inquiry and involves questions about the morality of how we interact with our environment. There are two fundamental ways of approaching the questions involved: from an anthropocentric perspective or a non-anthropocentric perspective. The anthropocentric perspective is human centered, suggesting that humans are primary, the most significant beings on the planet. The rest of the planet, animate creatures and inanimate objects, are here for humans to utilize and manage in the meeting of our needs and the accomplishing of our goals. The non-anthropocentric perspective can be broken into additional subgroups that focus their attention on different aspects of the world: those who advocate that sentient animals have the same moral standing as humans and must be given the same considerations as humans, and those who advocate that even inanimate objects such as rivers, trees, and mountains,  also have a moral status and must be given consideration equal to that of humans. I have espoused an anthropocentric perspective, but argued that it must be a humble, compassionate form of anthropocentrism.

In considering the specific question of environmental pollution, I have said that pollution that is harmful to humans, animals, and the environment in general is problematic. Actions that cause harmful effects are immoral. The amounts of harmful gasses we are pumping into the atmosphere is damaging the ozone layer and causing global warming, problems that lead to all sorts of additional dangers. Behavior that harms humans (without justifiable mitigating circumstances) is immoral.

Thought and Discussion Questions

1. Explain your thinking regarding anthropocentric versus non-anthropocentric perspectives on environmental ethics. Identify your position and explain why you prefer that paradigm.

2. Explain what you think Rogers means when he refers to a humble, compassionate anthropocentrism.

3. Discuss and explain your agreement or disagreement with the idea that behavior that generates harmful environmental effects is immoral.

4. If behavior that generates harmful environment effects is immoral, what would you propose we do about it? Select a polluting behavior and explain your plan of action in relation to that behavior.

5. Discuss how CEE as a framework for moral thinking and acting helps (if it helps) one think more clearly about environmental pollution.

Chapter 19
Euthanasia

Introduction

The English word *euthanasia* comes from a Greek word that means *a good death*. The practice of euthanasia was one of three ancient practices (infanticide and ritual suicide being the other two) associated with the termination of life. Euthanasia, sometimes referred to as *mercy killing*, involves one person ending the life of another person, at the request of that person, to alleviate that person's suffering. For example, Fred has cancer and will die soon. But before he does he will experience greater and greater levels

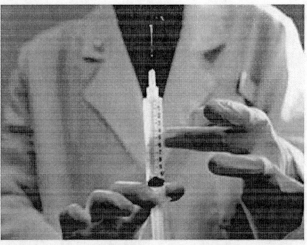

of pain and will suffer significantly. His family will also suffer because they will have to witness his suffering. Fred does not want that. He's going to die anyway. Nothing can change that. So why should he continue to live (for two or three additional months) when doing so will only involve increasing levels of suffering for himself and his family? Why not die now, before the suffering becomes too intense? Why not say good-bye to his family and go to sleep, dying with dignity, sparing everyone the horrors that are approaching?

Fred is asking a good question. Why not take control of the situation and end his life before it becomes horribly painful, physically and emotionally, for everyone concerned? Why not have *a good death* instead of a horrible one? This is the concern, a very significant moral concern, associated with euthanasia.

What is the Issue?

Questions surrounding the practice of euthanasia are complex. As our Western worldview developed, influenced not only by Greek philosophy but also by Judeo-Christian perspectives, life came to be viewed as sacred. One does not murder other people, neither does one end one's own life. To do so is simply unacceptable. It is immoral. But is it really? Is it immoral to end one's life prematurely, or request that it be ended by another, when one is faced with a rapidly approaching horribly painful death? Why is a random natural death moral and a timed self-termination immoral? The answer is usually that only God has the power of life and death. Well, that's obviously not correct. People kill other people all the time. People (and even animals) obviously have the power to end life. Perhaps what is meant is that only God has the moral right to determine when one lives and when one dies. Perhaps. But perhaps not. That is one of the arguments that will have to be considered. But before considering the arguments for and against euthanasia there are other aspects of the issue that need to be introduced and discussed.

The morality of euthanasia is a complex issue. It involves: 1) a dispute about whether or not an individual has the right to determine the time and circumstances of his or her own death, and 2) questions about the details of how, by whose hand and under what circumstances, the intentional termination of a life might be brought about. Before we consider the arguments related to question 1, we need to clarify the issues related to question 2.

Euthanasia takes two basic forms: *active* and *passive* euthanasia. *Passive euthanasia* involves withholding or withdrawing life-saving or life-sustaining treatment. There might be a horrible automobile accident, for instance, in which Emily is terribly injured. Her respiratory and circulatory systems are seriously damaged and she will almost certainly die unless she is hooked up to machines that will breathe for her and keep her blood circulating.  Anticipating the possibility of such a tragedy, Emily has included a document in her will that says if she is seriously injured and will die without extreme measures being taken, such as being hooked up to life-sustaining machines, she does not want to be hooked up and kept alive, but wants to be allowed to die. Her desire is to let nature take its course. If she dies, she dies. Not knowing this, however, the doctors in the emergency room hook her up to the machines and keep her alive. Her family, through, brings the document to the hospital and shows it to the doctors, who then disconnect the machines. Emily dies. This is an example of passive euthanasia.

Our society has, for a long time now, acknowledged an individual's right to decide whether or not life-saving treatment will be withheld or withdrawn so that he or she is *allowed* to die *naturally*. The situation is more complicated if the individual does not have a legal document prepared in advance providing doctors with instructions. In such cases, if the sick or injured individual is unable to give *informed consent*, spouses or other relatives must decide whether or not to withhold or withdraw treatment. The decision can be agonizing. Disputes between family members (some wanting to withdraw treatment and others wanting to continue it) occur often, making a difficult situation even more painful and frustrating.

Active euthanasia involves using death-causing means of some kind to intentionally bring about the death of an individual who is suffering. Active euthanasia often involves a sick person, like Fred in my example above, who is terminally ill and going to die in a short time. Before death comes, however, Fred is going to experience increasing amounts of pain and suffering. Wanting to avoid the suffering and spare his family the trauma of the experience, Fred requests that his doctor give him something (a drug of some sort) that will end his life at a time of his choosing. This is where we run into a problem. While we recognize the individual's right to determine whether or not treatment will be given to sustain life after an accident or as one's condition deteriorates or an illness progresses, thereby allowing nature to take its course, allowing death to occur without interference, we do not recognize the individual's right to request to die. We do not allow individuals to determine when they will die by requesting they be given something that will cause their death. Why not? Why is withholding treatment and allowing death to occur considered moral and causing death at an individual's request in order to avoid suffering considered immoral?

"Types of Euthanasia"

Active euthanasia is categorized as *voluntary euthanasia*. The individual (Fred in my example) is asking his doctor to give him something to cause his death. Fred is volunteering to die. But there can be other situations that arise. Suppose in our other scenario described above, where Emily has been involved in a horrible accident and has been connected to life-sustaining machines, that no legal document with her wishes for how to proceed in such cases has been prepared. Suppose also that Emily is married, and her husband Ben knows (because of statements she has made over the years) that she would not want to be kept alive by being hooked up to machines. However, Emily is in a coma and cannot give instructions; she cannot volunteer to die. Ben must make the decision for her. He can decide and instruct the doctors to withdraw treatment. When they do, Emily dies. This is kind of euthanasia is called *non-voluntary euthanasia*.

A third form of euthanasia is *involuntary euthanasia*. "Euthanasia is involuntary when it is performed on a person who would have been able to give or withhold consent to her own death, but has not given consent – either because she was not asked, or because she was asked but withheld consent, wanting to go on living."[1] The difference between involuntary euthanasia and murder would be the intention or motive of the one doing the killing. The killing in involuntary euthanasia is done to keep the individual from suffering, even though the person does not ask or give consent. In the 1992 version of movie *The Last of the Mohicans*, a British officer is about to be burned alive by the Indians who captured him. From far outside the village, Daniel Day-Lewis' character,

---

[1]   Kuhse, "Euthanasia," in *A Companion to Ethics*, 295.

Hawkeye, shoots the officer in the head to keep him from suffering the pain of being burned alive. That is an example of involuntary euthanasia. In our culture it would most likely occur in the context of a doctor knowing a terminally ill patient was going to suffer a great deal before he or she died, and even though the patient has not asked to die and might not consent to such if the doctor suggested it, the doctor goes ahead and terminates the patient's life on his own. His motive may be to save the patient from suffering, but his actions would be considered murderous.

"The Last of the Mohicans"

Let us assume, then, for the sake of our discussion, that involuntary euthanasia, because of the possibility of abuse (people being killed who don't want to die), is unacceptable. In all but the most special circumstances it is immoral because someone who has not expressed a wish to die is being killed. Let us also consider that non-voluntary (passive) euthanasia is acceptable in that treatment is withheld or withdrawn and people are allowed to die. Generally speaking this is considered moral because death is considered to occur *naturally*.[2]

That leaves us, then, with active, voluntary euthanasia. Many consider it immoral to end a person's life prematurely even if that person has requested it to avoid the inevitable suffering that is approaching. But just because many believe it to be immoral does not mean that it is immoral. And that some people believe that active euthanasia is moral does not make it moral. To determine the mortality or immorality of active euthanasia we will need to analyze the arguments.

---

[2] It must be noted, however, that in a more detailed discussion we would consider whether or not there is, in fact, a difference between the *active* killing and the *passive* withholding that causes death. In each case a death was caused. Is not what we call passive actually an active withholding that causes death? If an intentional action causes death, why does it matter whether it is intentionally giving a drug that causes death or intentionally withholding a treatment that could save or sustain life? A considerable argument can be made that there is not much difference between what we call active and passive euthanasia. However, we will skip this argument and continue on our way assuming that passive euthanasia is morally acceptable and active euthanasia is not.

What are the Arguments?[3]

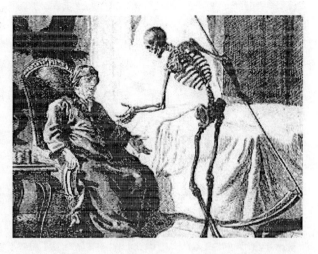

There are two arguments in favor of (for the morality of) active euthanasia. One is *the argument from autonomy*. Human beings are self-determined and make choices about life. Even though circumstances shape and impact us throughout life, in most situations we decide how to act, react, and interact. To a large degree, we are in charge of our lives. Death is a part of life. Unless an accident or some other kind of tragic event occurs, ending our lives unexpectedly, we ought also to be able to make decisions about our own death – how and when. If a rational, informed person, facing a death that will come only after a great deal of suffering, requests to die before the suffering increases (or in the midst of it), a doctor ought to be allowed to assist that person in terminating his or her life.

"The Debate that Never Dies – Euthanasia and Ethics"

The objection that is often raised to this argument is that patients suffering from terminal illness are often depressed (perhaps significantly so) and cannot make a truly rational choice. However, a response to this objection could be that while this *may* be true some of the time. It is certainly not true all of the time. Also, a doctor, working in conjunction with a psychologist or psychiatrist, could determine whether or not a patient is depressed and incapable of a rational decision. If the patient isn't capable of a rational decision, then the request for assistance in dying should not be honored. But for those who can make a rational choice, why should their request be denied?

To this some might reply that even if a person can make a rational choice, making a rational choice does not make an immoral act moral. This response, however, simply assumes that intentionally ending one's life in the face of severe suffering is immoral. That position has not yet been proven.

---

[3]   The arguments I will offer in this section are based on the overview of arguments for and against euthanasia presented by Battin in her presentation, "Euthanasia and Physician-assisted Suicide," in *The Oxford Handbook of Practical Ethics*.

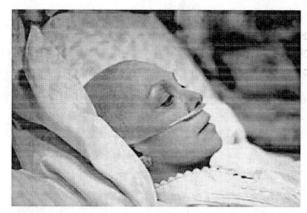

A second argument in favor of (for the morality of) active euthanasia is *the argument from relief from pain and suffering*. The argument is quite simple: why should a person be forced to endure increasing amounts of pain and suffering connected with a terminal illness? If death is coming only after intense and perhaps increasing suffering, and if the pain and suffering cannot be relieved in any other way, and if the patient requests to die, why make the person endure the pain? The doctor should be allowed to grant the person's request.[4]

A response to this argument might be that with the drugs and techniques presently available, most pain can be managed, making it unnecessary for a patient to die as a form of pain management. However, even though most pain can be managed to some degree, not all pain can be managed. Sometimes the pain is so severe that the only relief is to pump the patient so full of drugs (such as morphine) that he or she is, or is nearly, unconscious. Technically the patient may be alive, but for all intents and purposes he or she has no quality of life left. At that point everyone is simply waiting for the inevitable. What is the point?

There are three arguments often made against active euthanasia. The first is usually that *killing is wrong*. Hence, in the Ten Commandments of the Mosaic Covenant we have the commandment, *You shall not kill*. The problem with this argument is that it is based on a misunderstanding of the commandment due to an old and inaccurate translation. A number of Hebrew language scholars have noted that the word translated kill ought to be translated *murder*. The prohibition is against murder, not killing. The Old Testament is full of killing of all kinds, including killing as capital punishment for certain sins. It would make no sense for God to issue a prohibition on killing and then turn around and instruct people to kill. The prohibition is on murder. Thus, killing, as in accidental killing, self-defense, war-time or police actions, and executions were not part of what God legislated against in the Mosaic Covenant. Clearly, the prohibition on murder would not apply to active, voluntary euthanasia.

"Euthanasia: A Good Death? 1/8"
"Euthanasia: A Good Death? 2/8"
"Euthanasia: A Good Death? 3/8"
"Euthanasia: A Good Death? 4/8"

[4] This assumes, of course, that appropriate safeguards are in place so the possibility of mistakes and/or abuses are minimized as much as possible.

A second argument advocating the immorality of active euthanasia is an argument having to do with *the integrity of the medical profession*. Doctors, the argument asserts, are to *do no harm*. They take an oath to this effect. Killing a patient is to do harm. Thus, doctors ought not to kill patients. Doctors do, in fact, take an oath to do no harm. But how is honoring a patient's request to die mercifully to end suffering that will result in death anyway doing harm? But even if the Hippocratic Oath forbade doctors from performing euthanasia (and it does not), that, by itself, does not make the practice immoral. Neither does their being able to perform active euthanasia make it moral. What doctors can or can't do is irrelevant as far as the morality or immorality of the process is concerned.

A third argument against active euthanasia is *the potential for abuse* argument. Here the argument is that if we allow doctors to end patient's lives when they request it, there could be cases when doctors take it upon themselves to end a patient's life without the patient having requested it. This is especially possible where a patient is already suffering in pain and on medication and may not be entirely lucid but is suffering. A "compassionate" doctor might feel that he is doing the right thing by ending a patient's life to relieve his or her suffering. Thus, people who have not requested death might be killed.

"Euthanasia: 'Evolution' or 'Slippery Slope'?"

Such a scenario is possible. But it is just as possible now when active euthanasia is not legal as it might be if the practice were to be legalized. Rogue doctors who act on their own will always be possible regardless of the law. However, just because abuses in relation to euthanasia are possible, does not make euthanasia itself either moral or immoral.

Another argument against active euthanasia is that it is immoral because only God has the right to decide when someone dies.[5] The problem with this argument is that it is based on an assumption that is not supported in the Hebrew or Christian Scriptures. There is no passage in the Bible that says only God has the right to make decisions regarding life and death. In creating people with free will, God has clearly given people the power to decide regarding life and death. When a couple decides to reproduce it is their choice of timing that results in a new life being created. God has set up the process to work naturally and it is the couple's timing (their choice) that generates a new life.[6] Also, in regards to death, God has given humans the right to decide who dies and when. Consider capital punishment. If it is moral, it is so because God has given humans the right to make such choices. Consider also passive euthanasia. The withholding of treatment is an intentional decision that results in death. If passive euthanasia is moral (and we believe it is), then it is so because God has given people the right to decide whether or not a person lives or dies. The argument that only God has the right to make decisions regarding life and death is simply not a sound argument.

Aside from this last argument, which is certainly not a sound argument, you must decide for yourself if any of the arguments outlined above are convincing. They may or may not be. At this point, then, we need to consider euthanasia from the perspective of the Principle of Essential Humanness and CEE.

The Morality or Immorality of Euthanasia

The Principle of Essential Humanness is based on the value of humanness. The morality or immorality of a behavior is based on whether it enhances or diminishes one's humanness. The question we must ask, then, is: *does active euthanasia enhance or diminish humanness?*

While it might be tempting to argue that since active euthanasia ends life prematurely, it diminishes the value of life and, therefore, of humanness, I'm not sure that this is sound reasoning. While suffering itself may not be inherently evil because good things can come of it (lessons can be learned), if it is pointless suffering as end of life suffering often is (the one who suffers and then dies learns no valuable lessons that can be applied in any useful way), the suffering

---

5   This argument is not discussed by Bittin in her overview.
6   For those who believe that God is involved in the reproduction process, working in combination with the couple, the couple providing the body and God providing the spirit or soul, it is still the couple's choice of timing that generates the new life, not God's. God has given humans the right to make that choice.

diminishes the quality of one's humanness; thereby, diminishing humanness in general. Pointless suffering is valueless suffering. If a thing has no value, it cannot be good. I think it would be very difficult to argue successfully that it is immoral to eliminate something that is not good.

But I believe a positive argument can be made.

1. If humanness, one's own and that of others, ought to be valued, then the elimination of that which devalues or diminishes humanness ought to be a priority.
2. Pointless suffering diminishes the value of humanness.
3. End of life suffering (intense suffering that culminates in death) is pointless suffering.
4. Therefore, pointless suffering ought to be eliminated to whatever degree possible.
5. If a patient facing intense suffering that will culminate in death wishes to by-pass the pointless suffering and proceed directly to death, those who value the patient's humanness and their own ought to assist the patient in achieving his or her goal.

If this is a sound argument, then (assuming appropriate safeguards are in place so that mistakes and abuses are minimized) active euthanasia is moral.

Summary

The English word euthanasia comes from a Greek word that means *a good death*. The practice of euthanasia was one of three ancient practices (infanticide and ritual suicide being the other two) associated with the termination of life.Euthanasia, sometimes referred to as *mercy killing*, involves one person ending the life of another person, at the request of that person, to alleviate that person's suffering.

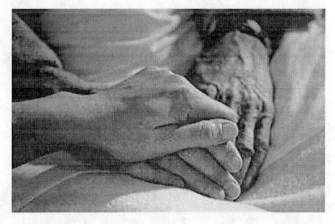

Questions surrounding the practice of euthanasia are complex. As our Western worldview developed, influenced not only by Greek philosophy but also by Judeo-Christian perspectives, life came to be viewed as sacred. One does not murder other people, neither does one end one's own life. To do so is simply unacceptable. It is immoral. But is it really? Is it immoral to end one's life prematurely, or request that it be ended by another when one is faced with a rapidly approaching horribly painful death?

Euthanasia takes two basic forms: *active* and *passive* euthanasia. *Passive euthanasia* involves withholding or withdrawing life-saving or life-sustaining treatment. *Active euthanasia* involves using death-causing means of some kind to intentionally bring about the death of an individual who is suffering. The arguments most often put forward *for the morality* of active euthanasia are the argument from autonomy and the argument from the relief from pain and suffering. Arguments *for the immorality* of active euthanasia that are often put forward are: that killing is wrong, the integrity of the medical profession does not allow for killing, and that potential abuses might occur.

CEE approaches the issue from the perspective of the value of humanness. Does pointless suffering devalue humanness. Yes. Is it moral to relieve pointless suffering that will culminate in death by bypassing the suffering and going straight to death? I believe it is.

Thought and Discussion Questions

1. Provide your own evaluation of the arguments that active euthanasia is moral.

2. Provide your own evaluation of the arguments that active euthanasia is immoral.

3. Explain Rogers' argument regarding the mistranslation of the Commandment, You Shall Not Kill – that it ought to be You Shall Not *Murder*. What difference does it make and how does it impact the argument regarding active euthanasia?

4. Evaluate Rogers' comments about whether or not only God has the right to make choices about life and death.

5. Evaluate Rogers' 5-point CEE argument that active euthanasia is moral.

Chapter 20
Human Reproductive Cloning

Introduction

Human cloning. It can be an intriguing or frightening idea, depending on your point of view and background in science. Most of what most people know about human cloning comes from movies and other forms of media, and most of what the media puts out about cloning is inaccurate. Movies where people are being cloned and replicas of them used for various purposes are as far from scientific reality as they can possibly be – not unlike the movies that feature talking dogs and cats who are international spies with black belts in Karate.

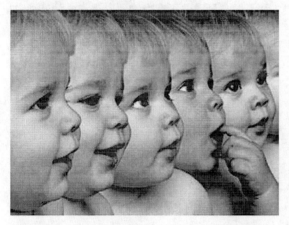

The first things that need to be done in a discussion of human cloning is 1) to separate fact from fiction so that we know what human cloning is (that's the easy part) and then 2) to ask whether or not the issue has moral implications. If human cloning is a moral issue, is cloning a human moral or immoral? The interesting thing about most discussions related to the ethics of human cloning is that they have little to say about the ethics or the morality of the process. There are those who are in favor of human cloning but who do not usually discuss the process in terms of it being a moral process. For the most part, their discussions amount to a commercial for human cloning because of all the wonderful things that will come of it. Then there are those who believe human cloning ought to be banned. Their discussions, for the most part, involve speculation about the horrors of genetic manipulation. Among those who oppose the practice, there are some who actually argue that it is immoral – or at least that appears to be what they are attempting to do. Most, however, appear unable to articulate a sound argument to that effect. Why is this the case? Probably because human cloning is such a complex and challenging issue. The technology appears to give us god-like powers. Does it? And if it does, ought we to use them? Should humans be creating humans in laboratories – at least in the early stages of the process? Is that moral? Do we have the wisdom to do that sort of thing without generating horrible consequences?

These are the questions related to human cloning. And one of the questions is: *is human cloning a moral issue*? Should the issue of morality even come into the discussion? Of course it should. If morality has to do with humanness, and if human cloning has to do with the generation of humans, then the practice obviously has to be assessed to determine whether or not it is moral.

To begin to answer some of these questions we need to understand what is involved in the human cloning process. Human cloning is a process that begins at the cellular level. The goal is to create a genetically identical copy of a human being. The process occurs naturally when a single fertilized egg becomes a zygote that, within the first few days, splits in two

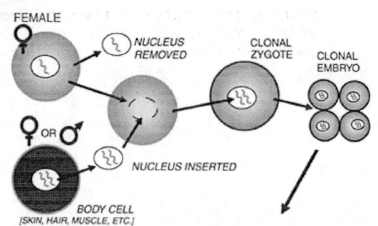

creating identical twins. Each twin has identical genetic material. Thus, they are identical twins (rather than fraternal twins whose genetic material is only 50% similar). Identical twins are clones of each other, genetic replicas – which is why they are the same sex and look so much alike. Human cloning can occur naturally. No one questions the morality of natural human cloning. Questions begin to be raised, however, when scientists get involved and attempt to intentionally generate a clone.

There are two kinds of cloning: *therapeutic* and *reproductive*. The following is a simple explanation of therapeutic cloning:

> Therapeutic cloning is another phrase for a procedure known as somatic cell nuclear transfer (SCNT). In this procedure, a researcher extracts the nucleus from an egg. The nucleus holds the genetic material for a human or laboratory animal. Scientists then take a somatic cell, which is any body cell other than an egg or sperm, and also extract the nucleus from this cell. In practical human applications, the somatic cell would be taken from a patient who requires a stem cell transplant to treat a health condition or disease.

> The nucleus that is extracted from the somatic cell in the patient is then inserted into the egg, which had its nucleus previously removed. In a very basic sense, it's a procedure of substitution. The egg now contains the patient's genetic material, or instructions. It is stimulated to divide and shortly thereafter forms a cluster of cells known as a blastocyst. This blastocyst has both an outer and inner layer of cells and it is the inner layer, called the inner cell mass that is rich in stem cells. The cells in the inner cell mass are isolated and then utilised to create embryonic stem cell lines, which are infused into the patient where they are ideally integrated into the tissues, imparting structure and function as needed.

> A major benefit of therapeutic cloning is that the cells removed are pluripotent. Pluripotent cells can give rise to all cells in the body with the exception of the embryo. This means that pluripotent cells can

potentially treat diseases in any body organ or tissue by replacing damaged and dysfunctional cells. Another distinct advantage to this type of therapy is that the risk of immunological rejection is alleviated because the patient's own genetic material is used. If a cell line were created with cells from another individual, the patient's body would be more likely to recognise the foreign proteins and then wage an attack on the transplanted cells. The ultimate consequence would be a rejected stem cell transplant. This is one of the major challenges of organ transplants, alongside the fact that there is a huge shortage of available organs for those who require the procedure. This means that therapeutic cloning has the potential to dramatically reduce the wait times for organ transplants as well as the immunological concerns associated with organ transplant therapy.

Therapeutic cloning is also important to enhancing our understanding of stem cells and how they and other cells develop. This understanding can hopefully lead to new treatments or cures for some of the common diseases affecting people today. In addition, the procedure would allow for scientists to create stem cell therapies that are patient specific and perfectly matched for the patient's medical condition.[1]

Sounds simple enough. The problem is that in the process of isolating the stem cells, the embryo from which the stem cells are taken is destroyed. The explanation above just happened to leave that part out. One wonders whether or not those kinds of omissions are intentional. Either way, we face the problem discussed in the chapter on embryonic stem cell research – the destruction of living embryos. Also, if the embryos being destroyed in the therapeutic cloning process are early stage human beings, then isn't destroying them immoral? It may be helpful to review the arguments in Chapter Seventeen on embryonic stem cell research.

"Therapeutic Cloning"

Reproductive cloning differs from therapeutic cloning in that reproductive cloning aims at producing a child. Cells from either a male or a female are used to generate an embryo that is a genetic copy, a clone, of the person who donated the cells. That embryo is then implanted in a woman's uterus (ideally the one who will be the clone's "mother") to develop the same way a naturally conceived baby would develop. In reproductive cloning, living embryos are not destroyed as they are in therapeutic cloning. Here is a brief but more scientific explanation of the process:

[1] Murnaghan, "Therapeutic Cloning," *Explore Stem Cells.*

In order to perform reproductive cloning, the nuclear DNA of a living organism in the form of an adult cell must be harvested. Also, the egg cell from a female of compatible species must be obtained. In a process known as somatic cell nuclear transfer (SCNT) the genetic information inherent in the egg cell is removed and replaced with the DNA of the harvested adult cell. By means of an electrical current, the egg is stimulated into cell division, the first portion of gestation. The dividing cells are then placed in the uterus of a surrogate mother, after which the cell becomes an embryo and gestates naturally, eventually resulting in a live organism that is genetically identical to the original adult cell.[2]

"Human Cloning"

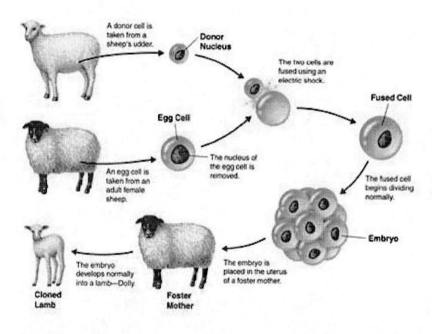

Suppose a couple, John and Mary, wanted a child but could not conceive naturally. They could agree that John would provide the genetic material for the baby – the baby that will be John Junior. A cell is taken from John and the genetic material is removed. Mary could provide an egg, or the egg from another woman could be used. The nucleus of the unfertilized egg would be removed and replaced with John's genetic material. The egg with John's genetic material in it would then be stimulated (electrically) to begin the process of cellular division and growth, creating an embryo. The embryo would then be implanted in Mary's uterus and in nine months John Junior would be born – an exact physical replica of John Senior. The process doesn't sound all that ominous, does it? In fact, it sounds a lot like in vitro fertilization, which is widely accepted as morally appropriate. The only difference is that the child is a genetic copy of one parent instead of being a genetic blend of two parents.

---

[2]   Albers, "How Does Reproductive Cloning Work", eHow.com.

"Discovery Channel Human Cloning"

What is the Issue?

What, exactly is the issue or problem with human cloning? If we are talking about *therapeutic cloning,* the issue is the destruction of living human embryos. What is the embryo's status? Is it a human being? If so, destroying it (killing it) would be wrong. If it is not a human being, but merely a clump of cells, then destroying it would not be wrong. The question has to do with the status of the embryo – is the human embryo a human or not? But if we are talking about *reproductive cloning,* no embryos are being destroyed. What, then, is the issue or question related to reproductive cloning? If no embryos are being killed, what's the problem? Many ethicists, some of whom are comfortable with a therapeutic cloning process that destroys embryos, are not comfortable with a reproductive cloning process where no embryos are destroyed. Their concerns lie in other areas. One such concern is that cloned children will not have what is called an open future, that is, he or she will be living out an identity that has already been lived. A second concern has to do with the clone's right to a unique genetic identity. A third concern is that cloning is playing God.[3] It involves humans overstepping their boundaries, interfering with things that ought to remain beyond their control. Are these concerns valid? Do they add up to cloning being immoral? The question of the morality of cloning must remain the focus. Some may have questions about human cloning and believe that it is best to ban cloning until the questions are answered and procedures and safeguards are put into place. All right. But that is not the same as saying that cloning is immoral. And what of those who advocate human cloning? Lots of discussions about cloning, for or against, fail to make it clear whether the practice is moral or immoral. Perhaps examining the arguments will allow us to determine the morality of the practice.

What are the Arguments?

There are arguments for cloning and against cloning. Let us assume that the arguments for cloning are advocating that the practice is moral and that those against it are advocating that it is immoral. Further, we must also restrict our inquiry to reproductive cloning. As noted above, since therapeutic cloning involves the destruction of living human embryos it is, according to the Principle of Essential Humanness and CEE, immoral – see Chapter Seventeen on embryonic stem cell research for the specific arguments. However, those arguments do not apply to reproductive cloning since reproductive cloning does not involve the destruction (killing) of living human embryos. What, then, are the arguments that human reproductive cloning is moral?

---

[3]   Manninen provides an overview of these three concerns (and a few others) in her article, "Cloning," *Internet Encyclopedia of Philosophy.*

As I see it, the best argument for the morality of reproductive cloning is that it is the only way for some people to have a genetically related child. Some couples, because of reproductive challenges, will not be able to produce a genetically related offspring. Reproductive cloning enables a couple of reproduce a clone of one of them, either the male or the female, thereby allowing them to have a genetically related child. Therefore, reproductive cloning is moral because it enables genetic reproduction where it would otherwise not be possible.[4]

"Cloning The First Human 1/5"
"Cloning The First Human 2/5"
"Cloning The First Human 3/5"
"Cloning The First Human 4/5"
"Cloning The First Human 5/5"

There does not appear to be anything here that devalues or diminishes humanness (the criteria I have provided in Chapters Twelve and Thirteen for determining whether an act is moral or immoral) in any way. If someone were to argue that cloning minimizes humanness because it minimizes the uniqueness of each individual, I would have to point out that identical twins are clones of each other. If one argues that cloning minimizes individual genetic uniqueness and is therefore immoral, then being an identical twin devalues humanness and is, therefore, immoral. But who would argue such a thing? Being genetically identical to another person does not devalue humanness.

What are the arguments that reproductive cloning is immoral? As noted above, one is that each person has a right to an open future and if one is a clone, the future related to the living of that specific genetic structure is not open because the life related to that genetic structure has already been lived. I'm not sure an awful lot of thought went into this argument. Again, identical twins have an identical genetic makeup. They are

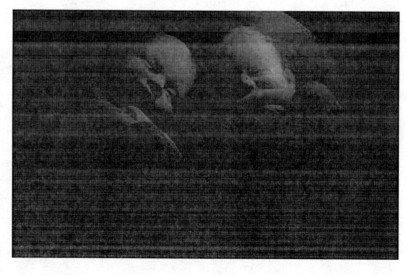

---

[4]   This is one of several arguments that Manninen provides in her material on Cloning.

physical clones of each other. Does that mean that what one twin does the other one must also do? Which one is the determining twin and which one is the determined twin? Is the older of the two (the one born first – if only by a few minutes) the one who determines the life of the specific genetic structure the twins share? Do these questions even make good sense? Just because clones share a single genetic identity, does not mean that they do not each have a single unique will and are not self-determined. Physically they may be identical, but psychically they are individuals who are self-determined. The open future argument is not a sound argument.

Another argument that reproductive cloning is immoral is that it involves humans playing God. The idea here is that God is somehow involved in the natural reproductive process and humans ought to be satisfied with it instead of trying to manipulate it to get what they want. Sandel makes this argument. His point is that the mystery involved in a genetic randomness of the natural process where humans do not know what they will get from the genetic pool requires a level of humility that is appropriate (morally right) for humans. Utilizing reproductive cloning amounts to humans trying to control that which ought not to be controlled.[5]

Sandel's argument is that when it comes to reproduction, randomness is moral and directedness is immoral. How is it that what amounts to a genetic crapshoot is morally superior to a guided process? Attempts to argue that human manipulation of the reproductive process is immoral have not resulted in a sound argument. If God has put the reproduction system in our reach, if he has made genetic engineering of different sorts possible, perhaps his goal is to allow us to become truly self-determined by allowing us to take a random process and guide it to specific ends. Perhaps there is a lesson for humankind to learn with the creative power God has put in our hands. Surely we're not going to argue that God is observing our tinkering and saying, *"Oops. I didn't mean for you to figure that out. I would prefer that you didn't mess with that."*

Another argument that is often put forward that cloning is immoral is that cloning is dangerous. Because of the possibilities of deformity and other disorders cloning is immoral. Deformity and disorders occur quite often. I'm not sure the possibility that something can go wrong makes a thing immoral. If that were the case, since any method of reproduction can result in a deformity or a disorder, reproduction itself, natural, old-fashioned reproduction, would have to be immoral. Whatever dangers exist must be taken seriously and additional research must attempt to eliminate or at least minimize the dangers involved. But to argue that the

5   Sandel, "The Ethical Implications of Human Cloning," in *Taking Sides: Clashing Views on Moral Issues*, 114-119.

dangers involved in reproductive cloning make it immoral is obviously false. Lots of things are dangerous – seriously dangerous: space exploration, scuba diving, parachuting, and numerous other activities – but the danger factor doesn't make them immoral.

These arguments are representative of the kinds of arguments presented to demonstrate the immorality of reproductive cloning. None of them appears to be sound. It might be that if it cannot be demonstrated that reproductive cloning is immoral, that it is, in fact, moral. Perhaps we need to think about the topic from the perspective of the Principle of Essential Humanness and CEE to see if we can make a determination.

The Morality or Immorality of Human Reproductive Cloning

If that which values and enhances humanness is moral, then we have to ask if reproductive cloning values or enhances humanness in any way. If it does, it would appear that it is moral. Consider the first argument we discussed in favor of reproductive cloning. Because of reproductive challenges, some couples cannot reproduce a child that is genetically related to them. But the desire to do so is part of our natural human desire. We want to reproduce, sending our genes into the future. This is a good desire and a moral process. Normally, when a child is reproduced 50% of its genes come from the father and 50% from the mother. This combination and recombination of genetic material generation after generation is healthy and benefits our species. While reproductive cloning, in contrast to natural reproduction, utilizes the genes of only one person in producing a child, it still involves a couple reproducing a child that is genetically related to at least one of them. It involves a normal and healthy desire that medical science has enabled people to satisfy. Why would a couple want to do this? Because they value their humanness and want to reproduce something of themselves, something of that which they value – the humanness of the genetic donor and their love for each other. How can this be anything other than valuing and enhancing their humanness? Therefore, how can it be anything other than moral? No embryos are destroyed; no life is lost. A new life is created. It was not created the old fashioned way, but the old fashioned way would not work. So, medical science assisted in the creation of life – a genetic duplicate of one of the parents. How can this be immoral? I think the answer, obviously, is that it is not immoral.

A number of ethicists are concerned with potential abuses related to reproductive cloning. Questions have been raised about: 1) the ownership of cloned individuals and the possibility of their becoming a mere commodity, 2) the lack of personal autonomy they might experience, 3) their lack of a unique personal identity – because

they are just a copy of one who already has the personal identity associated with their genetic structure, 4) the possibility of a *design your child* market.

These are interesting questions and it is right to bring them up. However, it is fairly obvious that none of these concerns has anything to do with the actual process of cloning. Each of these worries is a separate issue that is only tangentially related to reproductive cloning, and each is easily answered.

Concerning the *ownership* of a cloned person and that individual's personal autonomy, the process of creating a cloned embryo to be implanted in a woman's uterus is not that different from in vitro fertilization. Questions of ownership and personal autonomy are not a concern in that process. Why should they be a concern in reproductive cloning? Why would the fact that the cloned child is a copy of one parent's genetic structure instead of a blend of each parent's genetic structure reduce that child to an object without personhood? Why would the personhood of a child be contingent upon the sharing of the genetic material of two people instead of being a copy of just one? Do we really want to suggest that genetic differentiation is the basis of personhood? The question of ownership seems odd to me. It is as if it is being assumed that my genetic structure, for instance, belongs to me and a copy of it, then, would also belong to me. Since a clone is a copy of me, it belongs to me. But why would anyone assume that? Why do I own the rights (as it were) to my genetic structure? Is that the way we think when it comes to identical twins? Which twin owns the rights to the genetic structure that each of them shares? Or, are they joint-owners of that genetic structure? Should I copyright my genetic structure like I copyright the books I write, just to be sure I can prove my genetic structure is my own? The whole idea of ownership, whether of genetic structure or of a clone, is simply wrong-headed. A cloned person is no less a person than one who was conceived in vitro or anyone who is an identical twin.

"3D Animation of How IVF Works"

What about the *personal identity* question? This concern is more substantive because it has to do with what constitutes identity. What makes me, me? Is it my physical appearance, which is a result of my genetic structure? Few philosophers would espouse the idea that one's physical uniqueness is the basis for one's personal identity. Many would suggest that what makes me, me is my conscious awareness and my memories associated with it. I'm me because of who I have been and who I am. Maybe that's what personal identity is. But I think it is also the exercise of one's will. The *I* in Descartes' *I think, therefore I am*, is the person who is conscious to have experiences, to remember, and to act, react, and interact with others in the process of those experiences. The *I* who is aware and active is the person – a sentient, self-determined being. If that's what personal identity is, then the cloned child's personal identity will emerge as it develops just as the naturally conceived child's personal identity will emerge as it develops.

Someone may object, however, that the cloned child's genetic structure determines its identity – an identity that already exists in the person of the genetic donor. This assumes that we are biologically determined, that environment and experiences are not factors in the development of one's personality and identity. And that assumption, of course, is simply false. Psychological and sociological data make it abundantly clear that environment and experience shape our genetic predispositions. We become who we are because of the life we live and the choices we make, not because of our genetic structure. We are not biologically determined. The cloned child will have its own personal identity just as any other child will.

"Twins: Is It All in the Genes?"

What about the possibility of the emergence of a *design your child* market? You can go online to just about any car company and *build* or *design* your own vehicle by selecting from available features. You can select the base model you want and then begin to add features: color, the color and fabric of the interior, engine size, transmission, wheels, and gadgets and features of all sorts. Will parents be able to *design* or build their cloned child the way we design or build the car we want to drive? Maybe that sort of thing will be possible. Will everyone be rushing to the *design your child* clinic to get the exact physical model they want? Probably not. But what if some parents preferred to have children with blond hair and blue eyes who would be six foot tall and not susceptible to cancer? If genetic manipulation could assure parents of having exactly the physical specifications they wanted, why would that be problematic? Some would go so far as to call such behavior immoral. On what grounds? Again, is the randomness of the natural process (role the genetic dice and see what number comes up) morally superior to an intentional guided process? To demonstrate that it is will require more than assertion. It will require an argument. From the perspective of CEE, where morality is rooted in the valuing and enhancing of humanness, there is nothing morally reprehensible with doing what we can to enhance the possibility that our child will have the hair and eye color that we prefer and not be susceptible to certain diseases.

"Genetic Discrimination as Shown in Gattaca"

Having considered each of these concerns, it remains important to remember that none of them has anything to do with the process of reproductive cloning as a process. These questions, and others like them, are tangential to the subject. Reproductive cloning, as a process, does not, in any way that I can see, devalue or diminish humanness. It is not, therefore, immoral. If other problems arise after the fact, issues of ownership, autonomy and so forth, those issues must be dealt with individually. They ought not to be confused with the process of cloning. They are separate issues.

Another issue that has been raised has to do with the status of the cloned child. The question is, is the cloned "child" a child, a sibling, or something else? If it is something else, what is it? Some have argued that, technically, the cloned child is not a child. But neither is it a sibling. They suggest that it is a new category – a clone. This appears to be a case of extreme nitpicking. How is a cloned child any different from an in vitro child, other than the fact that it is a copy of one parent instead of a blend of each? Does that genetic difference make the child not a child? Is this not a case of taking a mole hill and making it into a mountain?

Summary

The idea of human cloning is intriguing for some and frightening for others. It's the stuff science fiction is made of. To assess the morality of human cloning requires that the facts be separated out from the fiction. There are two types of human cloning: therapeutic and reproductive. Therapeutic cloning involves the utilization of stem cells in the process of treating various diseases or disorders. It is problematic for many people because it involves the destruction of living human embryos.[6] Reproductive cloning, however, does not involve the destruction of embryos. Rather, an embryo is created using the genetic material of a donor. The embryo is implanted in a woman's uterus and the child develops normally. A number of questions have been raised about the morality of the process. However, none of the questions appear to be directly related to the actual process, but are only tangentially related. They, therefore, need to be dealt with separately.

As for the actual process of reproductive cloning, from a CEE perspective, the process does not appear to devalue or diminish humanness in any way. Far from it. It allows couples who could not otherwise produce genetically related offspring to do so – at least an offspring that is genetically related to one of them. It appears that the process is not immoral at all. It is different, it is new, for some it is confusing and for some frightening. But none of those things make it immoral.

---

[6] There may be ways, however, to generate stem cells (cells that are pluripotent) without destroying embryos. This would eliminate the problematic aspect of the process, making therapeutic cloning a very valuable tool.

Thought and Discussion Questions

1. Explain the processes of therapeutic and reproductive cloning.

2. Explain what, according to Rogers, makes therapeutic cloning problematic and reproductive cloning not problematic.

3. Explain your view on the personal identity concern for cloned persons. Include your explanation of what constitutes personhood.

4. Which of the objections or questions raised about reproductive cloning (even if the question is not directly related to the cloning process) do you feel is the most important question? Explain why.

5. Explain your view regarding reproductive cloning. Justify it with an argument.

Chapter 21
Sexual Morality

Introduction

Sex. The sex drive is one of the strongest drives humans experience. When the physical pleasure associated with sexual activity, especially orgasm, is combined with the drive to interact sexually, sex becomes a dominant theme of human existence. If anyone doubts the prominence of sex for human beings, a quick review of the facts will clarify the matter. There are 4.2 million pornographic websites. While these account for only about 12% of the total websites available for viewing, search engines report that each day there are 68 million searches for adult websites and 42.7% of people who use the internet visit adult websites. Internet porn is a 4.9 billion dollar a year business.[1] Regardless of your opinion regarding internet porn, one of the things this information reveals is how interested people are in sex.

Another set of statistics that reveal a great deal about sexual interest and attitudes are those related to the social phenomena known as Friends with Benefits – the practice of "friends" who satisfy each other's sexual needs without any commitment or emotional attachment ... *no strings attached* sex. 63.7% of males and 50.2% of females report engaging in a *friends with benefits* relationship (FWBR). Over 80% of the people involved in a FWBR said that they engaged in sex without any romantic attachments. For them, sex is simply sex for the pleasure it brings.[2]

The number of married individuals who engage in extra-marital affairs also reveals a great deal about American sexual attitudes. Data shows that approximately 50% of married women and 60% of married men will have an extra-marital affair at some point in their marriage. Statistically, that means that in about 80% of the marriages, someone is having an affair.[3]

What does all this information about sexual interest, attitudes, and practices tell us? That will depend, in part, on who is analyzing and commenting on the data. One of the things the data suggests is that sex is a huge part of our lives. Didn't we already know that? We are sexual creatures. We think about sex and have sex a lot. It might be surprising, then, to learn that for a long time now philosophers have not had much to

---

[1]   Ropelato, Internet Pornography Statistics, Internet Filter Software Review.
[2]   Grohol, "Friends with Benefits," at *Psych Central*.
[3]   Shugerman, "Percentage of Married Couples Who Cheat," at Catalogs.com

say about sex.[4] Ancient philosophers (Plato, for example, in *Symposium*) had some interesting things to say about sex. So did medieval philosophers (Augustine and Aquinas). But in modern times the subject has been largely (not entirely, but largely) ignored. Why is that?

"Plato, Symposium, Phaedrus and Pausa"

What is the Issue?

There are three basic issues involved when thinking about and discussing the ethics of sex. One has to do with whether or not sex itself, as a biological function, is a moral concern. Another has to do with our views regarding sex – what it really is and how we ought to think about it. A third concern is with the moral guidelines that regulate sexual activity.

Is sex itself, as a biological function, a moral concern? Goldman does not believe it is. "Any analysis of sex which imputes a moral character to sex acts in themselves is wrong. … There is no morality intrinsic to sex, although general moral rules apply to the treatment of others in sex acts as they apply to all human relations."[5] Goldman goes on to compare sex with business. Business itself, Goldman argues, is amoral. How we conduct business, however, is a moral issue. His point is that in our business dealings with others we may conduct business ethically or unethically, morally or immorally. But business itself, Goldman insistes, is amoral. It seems to me, however, that Goldman has missed an important point. Business only exists as an interaction or transaction with another party. If there is no interaction or transaction there is no business. Whenever and wherever business exists it involves interaction and transaction and therefore is either moral or immoral in the way it is conducted. It is not possible to think about or anticipate doing business without interaction with others and the potential morality or immorality of the interaction. In this respect, Goldman's analogy is flawed.

---

[4] Satris, "Must Sex Involve Commitment" in *Taking Sides: Clashing Views on Moral Issues*, 50.

[5] Goldman, "Plain Sex," in *Taking Sides: Clashing Views on Moral Issues*, 62.

I also think that comparing sex to business involves another flaw. While business cannot be conducted without interaction with others, sex can. An individual can pleasure him or herself, thus enjoying sexual pleasure without interacting with another. Goldman's analogy and his conclusion, then (based on the analogy), is not a good one.

So the question still stands: is sex itself, as a biological function, a moral concern? To answer this question we must decide what we mean by sex (what is sex?) and what kinds of things are moral concerns? What is sex? Is it a mere biological function? Is it simply a way to experience pleasure? Pleasure is certainly a part of sex, but since sexual intercourse is how the human species is propagated, how two people share their genetic material in the creation of a new life, it is obviously more than something that simply generates pleasure. It generates people too. Which part is more important: pleasure or propagation? Why would either be more important than the other? Over the centuries, due to the influence of Augustine and others who followed his lead, which unfortunately has meant the larger Christian community, sex has been seen as a means of reproduction only. Many people (following Augustine's lead) considered sex to be a necessary evil: we must have sex to reproduce, but we certainly should not think about it or enjoy it. This attitude is unfortunate.

Raymond Belliotti provides a concise overview of how many of our typical views regarding sex developed. Oddly enough, they begin about 2,500 years ago with Pythagoras and his teachings about body-soul dualism (the body was considered evil and bodily desires were evil desires that should not to be gratified). Pythagoras influenced Plato's thinking and Plato influenced Augustine, whose thinking became the foundation for much Christian thinking in general.[6] Augustine's view of sex as a necessary *evil* is what has led to sex in Western culture being thought of and described as something dirty or nasty.

If Augustine, however, had been as familiar with the Old Testament as he was with Plato he might not have made some of the mistakes he made.[7] I'm thinking specifically of the Old Testament book entitled Song of Solomon. It is a love poem that celebrates the joys of physical love. No one can read Song of Solomon in a simple straightforward manner and miss the point that God intends for humans to enjoy sex. It is good, healthy, and appropriate to enjoy sex. Those who miss that, allegorically interpreting the work as having to do with Christ's love for his church, have completely missed the point. The story in the book is not a spiritual allegory. It is an ancient Hebrew *Joy of Sex* poem.

---

[6] Belliotti, "Sex," in *A Companion to Ethics*, 315-326.

[7] I have a great deal of respect for both Plato and Augustine (more for Plato than for Augustine if I'm going to be entirely honest), but as mortal men and flawed human beings they were prone to mistakes, just as all of us are, and each of them made some pretty serious ones. Augustine's thinking about sex was one of his big ones.

God meant for his human offspring to enjoy sex. He even put an organ on the female's body (her clitoris) that has only one function – sexual pleasure. Why give her a clitoris if he did not intend for her to enjoy sex – to say nothing of her ability of achieve multiple orgasms spaced very closely together? Why would God create sex and sexual desire, making the desire for sex one of the strongest desires we have, and then make it wrong for us to act on it and enjoy it?[8] That doesn't make any sense. How is it that Augustine missed the obvious implications of all this?

Augustine carried a lot of guilt over what he considered promiscuous sexual activity during his youth. His guilt combined with ancient Pythagorean views of the body and bodily desires being evil led him to some very wrong conclusions about sex and sexuality – and these mistakes have been perpetuated in much of the "Christian" West for centuries. But the Pythagorean dualism of an evil body and evil bodily desires – especially the evil of sexual desires – that became the dominant Christian view regarding sex was not what the ancient Hebrews thought about sex. They understood it as one of God's gifts, to be enjoyed along with the responsibility of propagating the species. By all means, have children. But also have lots of sex and enjoy it. That was the ancient Hebrew view, and likely would have become the dominant Christian view (since Christianity was an outgrowth of ancient Judaism) had it not been for Augustine's guilt and the Pythagorean philosophy he embraced regarding the evil of the body and bodily desires.[9]

"Early Church Fathers: St. Augustine's Conversion"

Sex is for procreation. But sex is also for pleasure. So we should procreate and we should enjoy it. But *how* should we enjoy? Is sex merely a biological function (like breathing, walking, eating) that feels really good? Or is there a socio-emotive dynamic involved? Is sex just sex, or is it the deepest most intimate sharing that two individuals can enjoy? Both extremes are advocated in contemporary ethical literature. Goldman, referred to above, advocates that sex is just sex. Play tennis together, have sex together, each is just an activity that two people enjoy together.[10] Vincent Punzo takes the opposite position, that sex is the most intimate expression of love and sharing in which a couple can engage.[11] Who is right, Goldman or Punzo? Neither. It is difficult to see how something as important as sexual reproduction can be minimized to nothing of importance. Sex is just sex, Goldman and others argue. It is a biological activity that

---

8   That God wants us to enjoy sex does not imply that the enjoyment should not be moderated. We ought to enjoy food, too, but its intake must be moderated or we do damage to our body.

9   See also, Tuana and Shrage, "Sexuality," in *The Oxford Handbook of Practical Ethics*, 16.

10 Goldman, "Plain Sex," in *Taking Sides: Clashing Views on Moral Issues*, 58-64.

11 Punzo, "Morality and Human Sexuality," in *Taking Sides: Clashing Views on Moral Issues*, 52-57.

feels good. That's all it is. But it is the process for producing successive generations of humans. Sex is the process by which two human beings who are rational, self-aware, and self-determined create another rational, self-aware, self-determined human being. How can that process be nothing more than the physical pleasure it generates? Because of what sex has the potential to produce (another human being), it cannot be reduced to the pleasurable feelings it produces. Sex is much more than the pleasure it produces.

But is it the end-all of human interaction, the epitome of sharing oneself with another that Punzo and others advocate? If it were the end-all of human intimacy, there would not be such widespread disagreement about the nature of the sex act. If sex really is the epitome of human intimacy, why do so many people claim it is not? A huge percentage of Americans have abandoned that position, utilizing their own experience as a gauge, arguing that a physical coupling is not more intimate, for instance, than the mutual sharing of secrets, dreams, and fears with another person. In other words, in the view of many people, making oneself emotionally vulnerable is more intimate than the physical coupling of sex. Sex is intimate. But is it the *deepest* intimacy humans can enjoy? Many people are saying, no. Then why do some people think sex is the deepest intimacy that can be shared? Because that idea is part of our cultural sexual mythology. We pass that idea on from generation to generation, especially among females, linking sexuality to love, commitment and intimacy. But where does the idea come from? What arguments can one make to support the idea? Those who are Christians are going to want to refer to some passage in the Bible that says so. But they will not find one. There is no place in the Bible that describes sex as the epitome of intimacy. The discussion is simply not there. The idea is simply part of the rhetoric that has evolved in the effort to convince young people not to have sex until they are married and having sex with that one special person. The goal has merit, but the myth does not.

Sex is more than merely an avenue to physical pleasure. But it is less than the end-all of human intimacy. It ought to be enjoyed but it also ought to be reverenced as the vehicle for the creation of life – a life that can be nurtured best in the context of love, marriage, and family.[12] Sex is more than just sex. It is more than mere biological function. It is the physical process where we

[12] Sociological and psychological data suggest that children raised in a family where the parents are married and present fare better than children raised in other contexts. One such study is the *TANF Eighth Annual Report to Congress*—VII. Formation and Maintenance of Married Two-Parent Families.

replicate the essence of humanness. As such, it cannot be reduced to something no more important than sharing a cab or striking up a conversation with someone while standing in line to buy movie tickets.

Sex is important. Sex involves people interacting in an intimate way, even if not the most intimate way. It involves a level of intimacy that can lead to deep satisfaction or significant frustration and pain. Thus, there must be rules. Where people are interacting with other people and where the possibility for pain exists, there must be rules. The most challenging questions related to sexual morality are: what are the rules that govern sexual behavior and who makes them?

Some people (Goldman, for example) claim that there are no specific rules related to sexual activity. The only rules that apply are the general rules that would apply to any interpersonal interaction: be truthful, don't use people, don't hurt people, and so forth. Others (conservative Christians, for example) claim that God has given very specific rules regarding sexual activity: do not commit adultery, do not commit incest, do not participate in orgies, do not visit prostitutes, and do not engage in premarital sex. Which approach to sexual morality is correct?

What are the Arguments?

What we are doing here is moral philosophy, not theology. It is incumbent on us, therefore, to analyze arguments, not just make claims about God's expectations regarding sexual behavior.[131] So what are the arguments regarding sexual behavior – the arguments of those who claim that there are no rules and the arguments of those who claim that God has given us the rules? And are there any arguments that might be described as middle ground between the two extremes?

[13] For the Christians reading this text you must understand that I am a Christian and in complete sympathy with what the Bible says – *with what it actually says and the context it said it in*, not with what theologians say about it. As a philosopher who specializes in the Philosophy of Religion and Moral Philosophy, I am interested in helping people think clearly about important topics such as those discussed in this book. But we must think about them rationally and logically. We must understand that just because some theologian somewhere said such-and-such does not make it true. We must look for facts (not merely beliefs, but facts), analyze those facts, and reach conclusions based on sound reasoning. That is the logical process, the process of moral philosophy. When we do, we will arrive at the truth. When we utilize this process we can have an intelligent discussion with any rational person, Christian or not. But when we become lazy thinkers and our reason for what we believe is simply, "because God said so," not only have we failed to use the intellect God gave us, but we have closed the door for moral discussions with non-Christians. Why would we want to do that? So what I'm going to say in this section may not sound like traditional Christian teaching regarding sexual behavior. That is to be expected because what we are doing here is moral philosophy. It is rooted in logic and rationality. It is the process God expects us to engage in as we attempt to discover for ourselves how we ought to live. Children need rules – do this, don't so that – but grown people are expected to think for themselves and figure things out. So let's get beyond this "because God said so" foolishness and figure things out. That is what God wants us to do.

Goldman will serve as an example of those who claim that there are no rules that govern sexual behavior, other than the general rules of social interaction: be truthful, do not use people, do not hurt people, and so forth. When reading his presentation entitled *Plain Sex* (referenced above) one finds plenty of assertions, but no arguments. This appears to be typical of those who claim there are no rules that regulate sexual behavior. They make assertions; they don't offer much in the way of argument. I believe this is the case because there is really only one argument that can be made: cultural relativity – that each society makes up its own rules regarding sexual behavior in that society.

In Chapter Twelve, I argued that absolute cultural relativity is not a viable position. Moral absolutes exist. There are some things that are right every time and in every place, and some that are wrong every time in every place. Kindness, for example, is always good; so is helping the weak and the sick. Murder, rape, and child molestation, for example, are always wrong. Moral absolutes exist. But a list of moral absolutes is probably a short list, and what is on it is difficult to decide. For instance, are there any sexual behaviors on the list? This is one of the places where the discussion becomes challenging. Would incest, for instance, be on a list of moral absolutes that are always wrong? To answer that question one would have to ask, are there circumstances in which incest could be considered right and appropriate? If not, incest might be on the list of moral absolutes that are always wrong. Would rape be on the list? Would adultery be on the list? Would homosexuality be on the list? What about premarital sex? The only way to determine what is or is not on the list of behaviors that are always right or always wrong is to have an ongoing dialog about specific behaviors – in this case, sexual behaviors. The problem is that, at this time, the ethical community is not having that discussion.

For those that accept absolute cultural relativity, the matter appears to be settled. Each culture makes up its own rules regarding sexual behavior. If society accepts a sexual morality that includes a friends with benefits model of behavior, then that behavior is considered moral. A society of people determines what is and what is not sexually acceptable in their society. I suspect this is where theorists like Goldman would be most comfortable.

The problem with the position is that it is impossible to defend. Absolute cultural relativity just doesn't hold up under close scrutiny. Its weaknesses have been discussed and revealed in Chapter Twelve, and the reader should review that material before proceeding to be sure the flaws of absolute relativity are clear.[14]

---

[14] Societies of people do, to a degree, determine what is moral and immoral in their culture. For instance, I used to live and teach in Nigeria, West Africa. In Nigeria (and most African countries), it is not considered immoral if a woman's breasts are exposed. Yet, here in America we feel like women's breasts ought to be covered. It is a moral issue. Who is right regarding the covering of women's breasts, America or Nigeria? Neither. What parts of the

What about theorists such as Punzo and others who advocate a considerably more conservative approach, one rooted in the idea that for sexual activity to be moral it must involve a commitment – which is a subtle way of saying that sexual activity is only legitimate in the context of a marriage? What arguments do they make? Again, unfortunately, most of the advocates of the more traditional, conservative (religious?) approach make lots of assertions, but offer very few arguments. In fact, just about the only people who actually offer arguments to support their position are the most conservative Christian ethicists who, unfortunately, always seem to fall back on the Divine Command Theory – God said that this is wrong, so it is wrong. Period. End of discussion. Nothing about *why* God said a given behavior was wrong, nothing about the culture or circumstance of the time and place. The approach seems rather simple-minded and shortsighted. Why? Because there is too much cultural variation and there are too many unique circumstances to be considered.

To ignore the time and place in which a statement is made or a law is imposed is a foolish and irresponsible thing to do. For instance, Deuteronomy 22:28 describes the rape of a virgin and the penalty a man paid if he got caught in the act – 50 shekels of silver. Also, he had to marry the girl. Should we propose that today, in our society, the penalty for raping a woman should be a fine and marrying the woman? Also, under the Mosaic Covenant, there was no prohibition against a man visiting a prostitute. Should we make legalized prostitution part of our moral code today? Men can visit prostitutes if they want to. What about women? It would be hard to deny them the same opportunity, would it not?

Enacting the sexual code of the Old Testament in contemporary Western society would be extremely problematic. But what if we confine the application of the Divine Command Theory to the sexual code in the New Testament? In the New Testament adultery is forbidden. So is participating in orgies. Visiting a prostitute is considered immoral, as is homosexuality. But the idea of *sexual immorality* itself in the New Testament (from the Greek *porneia*) is not so thoroughly defined as to make it clear what is and is not included in the idea. It is not at all clear, for instance, if two consenting adults who are not married to other people are forbidden from engaging in sexual activity. There was no law against it in the Old Testament, and neither does the New Testament appear to forbid it. Lots of theologians and ministers lump premarital sex in with adultery, attempting to include it in the blanket term sexual immorality (sometimes referred to as fornication), but there is nothing in the New Testament to substantiate that

body must be covered and what parts can be exposed is for each society to decide. Decisions of these kinds involve a type or level of cultural relativity, but not absolute cultural relativity. *Absolute cultural relativity* is the idea that a culture makes up ALL of its moral rules, that there are no moral absolutes that it ought to recognize. *Relative cultural relativity* is the idea that a culture gets to make up most of its own rules while recognizing that moral absolutes exist and must be acknowledged.

claim. That the term sexual immorality includes premarital sex is merely an assumption. It may be a strongly held belief, but it is based on an unwarranted assumption.

These sorts of issues (the difficulty of applying the moral code of an ancient culture in a vastly different contemporary culture, for example) make using the Divine Command Theory problematic as a paradigm for contemporary moral philosophy. But the bigger issue with it is that only people who embrace Christian theism will even consider it. It is impossible to have a rational conversation about moral philosophy from a Divine Command Theory perspective with someone who does not embrace the Divine Command Theory. For instance, if the claim is made that homosexuality is immoral and someone asks, *why,* if the answer is, *because God says so*, unless the person who asked why is a Bible believing theist, the conversation is going nowhere. There's nothing left to talk about. If we want to have meaningful dialogs about morality, sexual or otherwise, we need better responses than, *because God said so*. And in the final analysis, this is all the Divine Command Theory has to offer. So it really doesn't provide anything to think about or work with.

Neither the liberal camp nor the conservative camp provides much in the way of argument. Each, however, is good at making assertions. Christian ethicists offer arguments rooted in the Divine Command Theory, but it proves ineffective as it has no broad appeal. Where does that leave us? Perhaps the Principle of Essential Humanness and Critical Ethical Eclecticism will provide a frame for meaningful dialog.

The Morality or Immorality of Sexual Behavior

The foundational idea for determining moral behavior is that *morality involves recognizing the intrinsic value of humanness (one's own and that of others), along with actions, reactions, and interactions that reflect an appreciation of human value. Immorality involves a failure to recognize the intrinsic value of humanness (one's own*

and that of others), along with a subsequent failure to act, react and interact in ways that reflect an appreciation of human value. Thus, an act is moral if it recognizes and or enhances human value, and is immoral if it fails to recognize or in some way diminishes the value of humanness.

How does this concept of morality help us in thinking about sexual morality? It provides us with a simple framework for determining the morality of different kinds of sexual behavior. Consider the act of adultery: does it value and enhance or devalue and diminish humanness? Since the act of adultery involves breaking one's marital vows it devalues one's own humanness. It is a dishonorable act. Acting in a way that brings less truth, less honor, less nobility to oneself devalues and diminishes one's humanness. Adultery also causes the spouse of the adulterer to feel betrayed, deceived, and devalued. There is a great deal of pain involved in having your spouse commit adultery. Because the act of adultery causes pain to one's spouse and involves the dishonorable act of breaking one's promise and betraying one's spouse, it devalues and diminishes humanness. Adultery, therefore, is immoral.

Consider the act of having sex with a child: does such an act value and enhance or devalue and diminish humanness? It devalues and diminishes the humanness of each of the individuals involved. The humanness of the adult is diminished because he or she is using a child to satisfy his or her own desire, thus violating the Kantian Categorical Imperative that we ought not to use people simply as a means to an end. The humanness of the child is diminished because the child is used without his or her informed consent – no one can give informed consent to that which they do not really understand. Additionally, the guilt and emotional pain that the victim normally experiences also diminishes the value of his or her humanness. Engaging in sex with children is immoral.

What about engaging in sexual activity with a close relative? In nearly every culture on the planet incest is taboo. One simply does not have sex with close relatives. Parents and children, siblings, grandparents, aunts and uncles, first cousins – sexual relations are forbidden between people that have these relationships with each other. Why? One reason is that long ago, even before adequate science existed to explain why, people figured out that where there is sex there can be pregnancy, and reproduction involving closely related people can result in unhealthy offspring – physical and mental abnormalities. But what if there is no pregnancy to result in unhealthy offspring? If the health issues are removed, is sex among close relatives immoral? Just about every group of people around the world thinks so. But does the act of having sex with a

close relative devalue or diminish humanness in some way? If one thinks in terms of what might be referred to as the natural order of things, it does. If *nature* intended, or if we say, *if the nature of things is such that*, sexual relations should not occur between close relatives, then when it does it is a violation of what appears to be the natural order. Is there such a thing as a natural order or a natural law? Certainly. The concept of natural law is simply a way of referring to the way nature works. If I hold a ball in my hand, holding it out over the floor, and then release it. What will happen? It will fall to the ground. Why? Gravity. Gravity is one of the "laws" of nature. It is part of how the world works. Many aspects of life work the way they do because of the natural laws associated with those things. Is sex with close relatives one of those areas of life where natural law comes into play?[15] Perhaps it is, since if pregnancy occurs, physical and/or mental problems are likely to occur. Perhaps those problems are nature's way of letting us know that sex ought not to occur between close relatives – whether or not pregnancy occurs.

But these issues, adultery and sex with children or close relatives, are not likely to generate much dispute. Most people in America would acknowledge the immorality of those behaviors. But what about sexual relations between unmarried consenting adults? In the past, most Americans embraced the idea that sexual relations ought to occur between people who are married and that people who are not married ought not to be having sex. To have sex without being married was considered immoral. But since the mid-1960s that point of view has been questioned and gradually discarded by large numbers of people (the Baby Boomer generation).

"SEX: The Revolution"

In 2008, USA TODAY reported: "The number of opposite-sex couples who live together, less than a million 30 years ago, hit 6.4 million in 2007, show federal data released Monday. Cohabiting couples now make up almost 10% of all opposite-sex U.S. couples, married and unmarried."[16] That was in 2007. The number today will be even higher. Additionally, these numbers have to do with couples living together. How many additional unmarried couples are having sex? Millions. Lots of them are high school and college students, or young adults no longer in school. Surprisingly, a large number of unmarried seniors (divorced, widowed, or never married) living in assisted living facilities are also sexually active.[17]

---

[15] I am aware that my dependence here on natural law theory will be questionable to some ethicists. I understand the normal objection but believe that in this case dependence on it is justified.

[16] Jayson, "Census Reports More Unmarried Couples Living Together," USA TODAY, July 28, 2008.

[17] There does not appear to be much statistical data on the subject, but a quick internet search on sex in senior facilities will produce a number of articles on the subject. Sex between unmarried seniors is a growing concern in facilities for seniors.

"Ethics – Sexuality in Long Term Care"

Is it immoral for unmarried consenting adults (including young people) to engage in sexual relations? If one asks, *do sexual relations between unmarried consenting adults devalue or diminish humanness in any way*, it is difficult to find a way to answer in the affirmative. The sex act itself is not immoral. And since unmarried consenting adults are not breaking marital vows or betraying anyone, it is difficult to see how the relationship can be immoral.[18]

To say that consensual sex between unmarried adults is not itself immoral is not to say that such relationships cannot be immoral or otherwise problematic. If one person is not honest with the other, if one person is simply being used, then the relationship is immoral. (Of course this would be true even if sex were not part of the relationship. Sex is not the only way a person can be "used.") Consensual sex means that both people understand exactly what is or is not happening and that each is clear on the nature of the relationship. No hidden agenda or deception can be involved if the activity is to be moral. Also, if the relationship results in pregnancy or health concerns (an STD), even if the act was not immoral it has resulted in a serious concern. The point here is that even if an act is not, in itself, immoral it may not be in one's best interest to engage in the act. What is moral and what is in one's best interest are not the same things. There may be things that are moral, but absolutely not in one's best interest to engage in.

It appears, then, that based on the Principle of Essential Humanness sexual acts such as adultery, and sexual relations with children and close relatives are immoral, but sexual relations between unmarried consenting adults may be moral, though they may not always be in one's best interests. There are other aspects of sexual behavior that have not been addressed in this section, but the reader who has grasped the idea behind the Principle of Essential Humanness and CEE can apply the method, asking and answering questions related to other sexual behaviors.

---

[18]   Conservative Christians, of course, will disagree with this assessment, insisting that the New Testament condemnation of "sexual immorality" includes premarital sex. Yet, as noted earlier in this chapter, there is nothing in the New Testament that specifically links premarital sex with sexual immorality. That premarital sex is included in behaviors identified as sexual immorality (or fornication) is nothing more than assumption, a case of eisegesis rather than exegesis.

Summary

We are sexual beings. Thinking about and engaging in sexual activity is a huge part of who and what we are. There are three basic issues involved when thinking about and discussing the ethics of sex. One has to do with whether or not sex itself, as a biological function, is a moral concern. Another has to do with our views regarding sex – what it really is and how we ought to think about it. A third concern is with the moral guidelines that regulate sexual activity.

Because sex is so pervasive, because it is how we propagate our species, and because it can involve such intense emotions, sex cannot be thought of as merely a biological function, like breathing or walking. Because of all that sex is and involves and because so much of sexual activity involves other people and has the potential not only for pleasure, but for emotional suffering, it is a moral concern.

A great deal of how Americans have thought about sex in the past was rooted in Augustine's mistaken conclusions regarding sex, mistakes that were rooted in ancient Pythagoreanism and that were uncritically accepted and incorporated into Christian theology. Christians were taught that sex, as a necessary evil, was dirty and nasty, not something to be celebrated and enjoyed as a gift from God. The ancient Hebrews had a more correct view of sex and expressed it in the Old Testament love poem entitled, Song of Solomon.

Since sex is a moral concern, how do we go about determining the morality of sexual behavior? Approaching it from the perspective of CEE will allow us to ask and answer questions about specific sexual behaviors, determining which are moral and which are immoral, depending on how that behavior impacts humanness, one's own and that of others.

Thought and Discussion Questions

1. Explain your thinking about whether sex is or is not a moral concern.

2. Why do you think attitudes towards sexual activity are so different today than they were 50 years ago? (Even though this was not discussed in the chapter it is worth thinking about.)

3. Explain your view regarding sex as the deepest expression of human intimacy. Your explanation should include a consideration of how men and women might think differently regarding this question.

4. Explain your view regarding emotional vulnerability (an intimate sharing of oneself – one's fears, dreams, hopes, aspirations, etc.) instead of sex as the deepest expression of intimacy.

5. Discuss whether or not approaching sexual morality from a CEE perspective is helpful. If it is not, how would you approach the issue?

Chapter 22
Social Justice

Introduction

What is social justice? To discover what social justice is we must first discover what justice is. The word Plato used most often that is translated by our English word *justice* is the Greek *dikaiosyne*, which referred to one's inner sense of righteousness, knowing when to do the fair and right thing. Plato is thinking about justice from the point of view of a person being a just person – knowing how to act in a just manner and then acting in that way. The Romans approached the subject of justice from a different perspective. Their idea of justice is found in the Latin phrase *suum cuique tribuere*, which means, *to allocate to each his own*. Here the idea is that each person ought to get that to which he or she is entitled. Getting what one deserves or is entitled to is just; not getting what one is entitled to is unjust.

If we use these ideas to help us define justice, we might say that on an individual basis, justice, or being a just person, involves doing the right thing in each situation. Plato believed that the just person was one who did his duty and did not interfere with others as they did their duty. This is sometimes called *non-comparative justice*. It has to do with each person doing the right thing, that which he or she ought to do. In contrast, *comparative justice* focuses on whether different individuals or groups of individuals are treated justly, fairly. This is what the Latin phrase, *to allocate to each his own*, is referring to. This is also called *distributive justice*. It is the idea that each person or group of people should receive that to which they are entitled. This idea is foundational in a contemporary discussion of *social justice* – the fair and equal distribution of those things to which people in a given society are entitled.

What is the Issue?

The issue is: *what are people entitled to?* How do we go about determining who is entitled to what? What does it mean that in America, all people are created equal and have, therefore, the right to life, liberty, and the pursuit of happiness? How do we work that out in a practical way so that all people, down to the very last person, gets that to which he or she is entitled?

If these are the issues involved in social justice, is social justice a moral issue? I suppose it depends on how one defines morality. Once again, the Principle of Essential Humanness suggests that *morality involves recognizing the intrinsic value of humanness (one's own and that of others), along with actions, reactions, and interactions that reflect an appreciation of human value. Immorality involves a failure to recognize the intrinsic value of humanness (one's own and that of others), along with a subsequent failure to act, react and interact in ways that reflect an appreciation of human value. Thus, an act is moral if it recognizes and or enhances human value, and is immoral if it fails to recognize or in some way diminishes the value of humanness.* If this is correct, then the kinds of issues involved in social justice most certainly are moral issues.

It is not uncommon to hear opponents of social justice to criticize the very idea of social justice. They argue that when one puts a word like *social* in front of a word like *justice*, creating a new focus, like *social justice*, instead of justice all by itself, that there is an agenda involved and one ought to be suspicious of that agenda. Of course there's an agenda involved. There's always an agenda, and there's nothing wrong with having an agenda. An agenda is simply a list of things to be done or accomplished. I have an agenda every day. Everyone does. The advocates of social justice have an agenda, and so do those who oppose the idea. There is an agenda in play when the opponents of social justice claim that there is no such thing as social justice, but only justice and injustice. All right, suppose we momentarily grant the argument and eliminate the term *social justice*. We will refer only to *justice* and *injustice*. The issue remains the same: what are all people entitled to and how do we see to it that justice is done and everyone gets what he or she is entitled to? The issue is the same, isn't it? Arguing about the word *social* being connected with the idea of justice is silly and a waste of time. So I'm going to retain the word. *Social justice* is a real and valid concern and it is a moral concern.

One of the concerns of social justice is *equality*. Our Declaration of Independence refers to it. We talk about equality quite often – we're all equal. But I wonder how many of us have thought deeply about what that means and what it does not mean.

We live in a society that recognizes that all people exist as equals. But how does that equality manifest itself? This is one of the concerns of social justice. As I teach philosophy and sociology classes, one of the things I notice is that students do not understand (have not thought about) the difference between *intrinsic equality* and what I refer to as

situational equality. Intrinsically, all people are absolute equals. Each person, simply by virtue of being a human being, has the same intrinsic value and worth. Equality. But each of us is also a unique individual with different strengths and weaknesses, different advantages and disadvantages, shaped by our contexts and experiences. We are different. Intrinsically we are equal, but situationally we are not equal, that is, not the same. Equality does not add up to sameness. I think people often (perhaps unconsciously) assume that being equal means being the same. It does not. Some people are smarter; some are better looking. Some are faster; some are stronger. Some are more charismatic; some are more influential. Some are more educated; some have more money. Do these differences mean that people are not equal? It depends on what you mean by equal. People can be intrinsically equal but situationally not equal. Students and professors, for instance, are intrinsically equal. By virtue of the fact that we are human beings we have the same intrinsic value and worth. But situationally students and professors are not equal. My students call me Doctor. I do not call any of them Doctor. I'm in charge of the class. They are not in charge of the class. In one sense we are equals; in another sense we are not at all equals. And this kind of *inequality*, if that is how we must describe it, is entirely appropriate and necessary – which brings us to another major concern in the social justice discussion – social stratification. Social stratification is the inevitable and appropriate consequence of living in a large, complex (and therefore, stratified) society. Why would social and economic stratification be both inevitable and appropriate in a large, complex society?

For about 123,000 years (give or take a few thousand years), humanoid social structure consisted of small egalitarian tribal bands of hunter-gatherers. They roamed about following flocks and herds that migrated between sources of water. The men would hunt; the women and children would gather seeds, grains, nuts, and vegetables. They were large, strong, well-fed people. Because they were small family or tribal groups (usually between 10 and 50 members) they were egalitarian, sharing everything in common and making decisions based on group consensus.

Then, about 12,000 years ago, in the Middle East, in a part of the world that became known as Mesopotamia, some of the tribal bands began living together, at least part of the time, in villages. The women probably discovered basic farming techniques and the men figured out they could capture, domesticate and keep flocks of goats and sheep. With those discoveries, they no longer needed to follow flocks and herds of animals for meat. They could settle down near water and stay in one place. Multiple tribal groups from nearby regions could live together. The transition took a couple thousand years to complete, but eventually people began living in horticultural-pastoral societies instead of hunter-gatherer societies. This transition from one social structure to another, from hunter-gatherer to horticultural-pastoral, was the single most significant social transition in human history. Why? Because it necessitated the development of new social components to make the new settled-living social structure viable.

"Mesopotamia: Crash Course World History"

As the tribal bands (often an extended family group) travelled about, they answered to no one. They made up their own rules, doing what made sense in their circumstances. But as multiple family groups began to live together, new components were necessary to facilitate living together in a more interdependent village context. For instance, they needed rules (laws) that applied to everyone in the village, not just family rules or traditions that differed from family to family. So, family heads met to discuss and make laws. In that process, the earliest forms of formal government developed. Eventually, there also needed to be some accepted medium of exchange. Early on they probably engaged in a trade or barter kind of exchange – a certain measure of grain for a goat, so many fish for milk and cheese. But eventually, as the village grew and more people were exchanging goods, especially if people came who were not from that village, an agreed upon medium of exchange (money) was needed. An economic

system developed. Religiously, each family had worshipped their gods in informal ways as they travelled about. But now, with multiple family groups living together, they needed some official form of religion and worship. Formal religious structures were established. Temples were built, priests were appointed, rituals developed. They also needed to protect themselves from rival villages. Military concepts and practices developed alongside diplomatic processes. In other words, as those small villages grew into larger complexes of people, the basic structures of modern interdependent society began to evolve.

The bigger a village became the more complex it became. The more complex it became the more specialized it became. There were people who specialized in building buildings, others in fishing, still others in working with leather. Some were farmers; some were shepherds. Some became religious leaders while others became politicians, or soldiers, or merchants. Some became influential, successful, and wealthy. Others did not. Often, whether or not one was successful, whether or not one became wealthy and influential, had to do with the choices one made about what one did or how one did it. The ingredients for success in life's endeavors were not so different 10,000 years ago than they are today: good choices, good timing, good skills, and good luck. After a generation or two, some people may have inherited their "success." Whether or not they kept it depended to a large degree on the same considerations: choices, timing, skills, and luck.[1]

---

[1] Without a doubt there was also some occasional ruthlessness involved.

In time, as a village grew, becoming a more complex society, it also became a stratified society. Some people, because of choices, timing, skills and luck, became people of influence and power. The people who performed the most important tasks for society (as they saw it, government and religious leaders first, then wealthy merchants) became the most influential people. A village of a few hundred could continue an egalitarian social structure, owning everything in common and making decisions based on a consensus of the population. However, as villages of a few hundred grew into cities of many thousands egalitarianism was no longer possible. Government could no longer operate on the basis of a group consensus, and private property became the only viable norm for ownership.

The more complex a city (society) became, the more stratified it became. It was inevitable. True egalitarianism was (is) only viable in a small group. Larger groups of people cannot be truly egalitarian – in the sense of anthropological egalitarianism, as practiced even today by small tribal bands of hunter-gatherers. As a society grows and becomes more complex, it will *inevitably* become a stratified society.[2] There is no way to stop it and no need. Social stratification is not only inevitable, it is appropriate. It provides incentives and rewards for effort, risk and accomplishment. It also identifies the people who provide, metaphorically speaking, oil for the machinery of society. While it is true that each person of a society is important, it is simply a fact that some people are more important to a smooth-running society than others. Those who make significant contributions to society (doctors, lawyers, educators, executives, investors, judges, politicians, researchers, inventors, and so forth) have, through hard work, earned their position in society. If justice is getting what one is entitled to, then stratification is just; it is the social position (high or low) one has *earned* and is entitled to. Stratification is not only inevitable it is appropriate. And it is just.

Given the tendencies of some in our contemporary society, this might sound pompous or even cruel. Many would respond that it is not. Because, they would argue, in addition to our society to being stratified, it is also meritocratic, allowing one to earn (or merit) his or her place in society, moving up or down the vertical stratification continuum. No one is stuck where he or she is. With effort and hard work anyone can move up from one strata to another. Our stratified society, some would argue, is eminently fair and appropriate. No one would argue that our

---

2   Those ancient societies that became stratified as they evolved did not intentionally decide to become stratified. There was no plan to become stratified. It was just the inevitable outcome of their growth and specialization.

society is perfect and doesn't need adjusting or tweaking. Of course it does. But, some would point out, we must know the difference between what needs to be fixed and what doesn't.

It is not possible to discuss social justice without discussing equality and social stratification. We need to discuss equality and we need to discuss social stratification, but we need to discuss them from a knowledgeable, informed perspective, understanding the difference between intrinsic and situational equality (that situational inequality is normal, natural, and appropriate) and that social stratification is both inevitable, appropriate, and just.

Another important aspect of the social justice discussion has to do with *terminology and the implications associated with it*. Specifically, I want to discuss the term *distributive justice*. If you look up the term in a dictionary of philosophy you will read something like the following: *the proportionate or equal distribution or allocation of things such as money property, privileges, opportunities, rights and so forth to members of a society*. The term is extremely misleading – at least in the context of American society. It implies that someone holds and distributes assets and resources. Those people who do the distributing must do so in a just manner. The problem is that in America (or any society characterized by private ownership and free enterprise) there is no agency or entity that holds and allocates assets and resources.[3] The American people own and hold their own assets and resources. To refer to assets and resources being "distributed" to people is simply inaccurate. It gives a false impression and skews the conversation. The term Distributive Justice needs to be replaced. *Acquisition Justice* would be a better, more accurate, term. In America, resources and assts are not distributed, they are acquired. The conversation will be more accurate and make more sense if we use terminology that is more accurate.

If we think in terms of acquisition rather than distribution, the focus of the conversation is shifted from those who distribute – a non-existent entity – to those who acquire – real people who earn and acquire. The responsibility for acquisition belongs to those who need to acquire. They need to do what is necessary in order to have the means to acquire. The social justice discussion needs to be reoriented from distribution concerns to acquisition concerns.

In shifting the focus of the discussion to acquisition, we need to stress the importance of access. All that people are entitled to, simply because they are human beings with the rights associated with humanness, must be accessible to everyone. These include the kinds of things the Founding Fathers of our society included in the documents they prepared: freedom of religion, of assembly, of speech, the right to vote,

---

[3] Nozick made this point in his material on distributive justice in his work, *Anarchy, State, and Utopia*.

the right to an education, and so forth; in short, the right to life, liberty, and the pursuit of happiness. A government of the people, by the people, and for the people acknowledges these rights and oversees the protection and accessibility of these basic rights, but it is still up to the individual of a free society to acquire that which is accessible. For instance, if education is accessible, it is up to the individual to acquire it. If having a voice in government is accessible by means of voting, it is up to the individual to exercise his or her right and vote. There is accessibility and there is acquisition. But there is no distribution.

A final point to be made under the *issues* heading has to do with what is referred to as the *inequality of wealth*. The widening gap in the income levels of rich and poor is pointed to as evidence that something unjust is occurring in our society. There is no doubt that some people in our society are making a lot of money while others are not. According to the 2010 U.S. Census data the median household income in the U.S. was $49,777. Half of the households made more than this, half made less. For a long time, income levels of the wealthy and the not wealthy went up and down proportionately. In other words, the gap between them remained more or less consistent. But beginning in the 1970s the gap began to widen and the wealthy became considerably wealthier without a corresponding increase in the income of average people. Basically, people who had money invested it and made a lot more money, or they used their talent to make money – sometimes inventing and marketing something, sometimes going into professional fields that paid very well. The point is that some people got very wealthy and the rest of us did not (and as a community college professor in Iowa I'm very much a part of the rest of us).

So what is the issue? It is this: in the social justice conversation, this economic fact of life (the wealthy getting wealthier) will occasionally be discussed in a way that suggests something unjust, something unfair and wrong, is going on when the rich get richer and the rest of us do not experience a similar increase in income. This is unfortunate. The reality is simply this: *if the wealth of the wealthy was generated legally, then they are entitled to it and nothing unjust or unfair has occurred.* If the wealthy got wealthy in a just manner, then their being wealthy is not and cannot in any way be unjust. They have that which they are entitled to because they earned it.

We often hear that salaries and bonuses of executives appear to be disproportionately large. An executive, an educated, experienced person running a company, who might have been in a position for several years leaves and gets a payout of 10 or 20, or 30 million dollars. Some people are outraged by that. I find that odd. Seldom do we hear outrage expressed at an actor who works for three or six months on a movie set pretending to be someone he is not and gets paid 20 or 30 million dollars. Between May of 2011 and May of 2012, Tom Cruise earned 75 million dollars – for pretending to be someone he isn't! But the fact is that Tom Cruise works hard and makes a lot of money for the studios who produce and distribute his movies. Why shouldn't he be paid a significant percentage of the profits that come from his labor? That's how a free market economy works. There is nothing unjust about Tom Cruise earning 75 million dollars in one year by pretending to be someone he isn't. And neither is there anything unjust about any other person (corporate executives, for examples) honestly earning a lot of money by doing what they do. There is nothing unjust about Bill Gatesbeing one of the richest men in America. He worked hard and smart and made lots of money. Good for him. The same is true for thousands of others who found (legal and just) ways to make lots of money. No one distributed it to them. They acquired it. They earned it.

These are some of the key issues that are part of the social justice conversation. To understand how the conversation is conducted, we need to examine arguments on each side of the concern.

What are the Arguments?

One of the most prominent social justice scholars was John Rawls. His 1971 book, *A Theory of Justice*, remains a foundational work in the field. Rawls insisted that for a society to be worthwhile it must be a just society. Who could possibly disagree with that? What does a society have to do to be a just society? Rawls utilized an interesting approach to make his point about how to establish and be a just society. Taking his lead from social contract philosophers such as Hobbes, Locke, and Rousseau, Rawls imagined a time (a completely fictitious time) when a group of people were determining how their society would be set up and run. He referred to this as the *original position*. Those people in that original position, in order to set up a just society, would have had to operate under a *veil of ignorance* regarding their own places in the society  so their decisions would not be biased toward benefits for themselves in that society. For instance, if I was one of those people, it would be necessary for me to be ignorant of the fact that my place in the society would be that of a professor, for if I knew I was a professor in that society, I might be tempted to provide additional benefits for professors. In Rawls' scenario, this group of people who do not know what their places and roles in the society under question will be, get together and determine how their society will be structured. What will they do? They will structure the society in such a way that all people have equal access and opportunity to what they need and to what is available. They will not necessarily require absolute egalitarianism, but will want to ensure that each person is assured a level of opportunity and access to resources that will offset any inequalities that might exist. But would they? Would people setting up a society do so in such a way so as to eliminate or at least minimize inequalities? I'm not convinced they would. Why am I not convinced? Because those who have established societies in the past, those who have been in an "original position," have not structured their societies so that inequalities were eliminated or minimized. Even in America, where "all people are created equal," the possibility for social and economic inequality was (and remains) possible because of America's capitalistic (build it as big as you can, earn as much as you can) free enterprise economic system. The Founding Fathers were in the original position but chose to allow social and economic inequalities to exist. Why? Because the only way for social and economic equality to exist is for government to create it artificially by limiting individual liberties or taking what the rich have earned to redistribute to those who have not earned it. The Founding Fathers opted for social and economic liberty rather than social and economic equality.

In his work, *A Theory of Justice*, in the section on "Justice as Fairness," Rawls explains it from the perspective of two principles:

> First: each person is to have an equal right to the most extensive basic liberty compatible with a similar liberty for others.

> Second, social and economic inequalities are to be arranged so that they are both (a) reasonably expected to be to everyone's advantage, and (b) attached to positions and offices open to all...[4]

Rawls goes on to explain, "All social values – liberty and opportunity, income and wealth, and the bases of self-respect – are to be distributed equally unless an unequal distribution of any, or all, of these values is to everyone's advantage."[5]

Rawls' creative and inventive explanation of how self-interested people would structure a society so that it was a just (fair) society is interesting. But it is rooted in the idea that assets and resources are held and distributed rather than owned and made accessible for acquisition. His conclusions, then, would have little to do with American society since, as noted already, we are not a society where an entity or agency holds and distributes assets and resources. Income and wealth are not distributed. They are

earned. Opportunity for earning must be equally available to everyone. But as soon as one begins to speak of wealth and income being distributed to members of society (at least American society) the conversation breaks down because it is not reflective of the way our (or any free market) economy and society works. Rawls' assertion that the people would require that wealth be "distributed" equally is an interesting assertion but is unwarranted, for as discussed already, the people who were in the

---

[4]   Rawls, A Theory of Justice, 33-46.
[5]   Ibid.

original position in structuring America did not structure America so that income was "distributed" equally.

As noted earlier, those using *distributive justice* language (Rawls and his followers) need to change their terminology to reflect the social and economic structure of America – a free enterprise *"earn your own way"* social structure, an acquisition structure. Social justice demands equal opportunity and access. Once equal opportunity and access is offered, including access to education and/or training that enable people to take advantage of the opportunities, the demands of social justice have been met. It is then up to individuals to participate and earn so they can acquire the assets and resources they need and desire. There is no distribution. There is earning and acquisition. The difference between terminology and perspective is enormous and crucial.

Rawls' conclusion and solution to what he considers the unequal, and therefore unjust, distribution of wealth and income is to *"redistribute wealth"* to the poor through taxation of the wealthy. In other words, Rawls' idea is that government ought to be the agency or entity that acquires wealth through taxation and redistributes it to the poor to ensure that fair and equal distribution occurs. Is this, as he suggests, fair? Is it just?

John Rawls was a Harvard professor. One of his colleagues, Robert Nozick, also a Harvard professor, disagreed with Rawls and offered an alternative position. Nozick embraced a libertarian perspective. Libertarianism is the idea that government should be limited and involved only in police and military protection, and in administering the legal system. All other functions often carried out by government ought to be done by charities, religious organizations, and businesses. Nozick, as noted already, also disagreed with the use of the term *distributive* justice. He believed it to be inaccurate and misleading. There is no entity that holds assets and resources so that they can be distributed. Nozick also questioned Rawls' idea concerning the *re*distribution of wealth that was not originally distributed in a just manner. First, how can something be redistributed when there was no distribution to begin with? Second, Nozick outlined a process that he referred to as *entitlement theory*. The idea is that people are entitled to hold that which they acquired in a just manner. Nozick identified three principles related to just acquisition and holding: *acquisition*, *transfer* and *rectification*.[6]

Acquisition refers to the original acquisition of property that no one owned previously. Borrowing from Locke, Nozick explained that if someone walking in the woods found a large branch on the ground and took it home and sharpened it so it could be used as a spear, the spear, by virtue of the person's initiative and effort, would belong to the person who made it. It would be his property. His ownership would be just.

[6]   Nozick, *Anarchy, State, and Utopia*, 149-275.

Transfer refers to property exchanging hands, the transfer of ownership. Transfer of ownership is just, Nozick argued, if, and only if, it is voluntary. The person must desire to transfer ownership of the property in question, through selling, trading, or giving it away. If the transfer is not voluntary, if it involves coercion or force the transfer is not just.

Rectification refers to the correcting, the rectification, of past injustices in the transfer of ownership. If, in the past, there had been unjust transfers due to coercion or force, those situations must be addressed and rectified so that present and future transfers can be just. The details of how a previous injustice would be rectified, Nozick left up to others. But once a previous injustice was rectified, just transfers could occur.

Nozick's argument is that *if these principles of entitlement have been met, if the property or wealth in question was acquired in a just and legitimate manner, then the individuals holding it are entitled to it*. There was no injustice involved in the original acquisition. If the original acquisition was just then it could not be just for the government to acquire the wealth by means of taxation (which would amount to a coerced and, therefore, an unjust transfer) in order to redistribute the wealth to others. Nozick was not arguing that taxation itself was wrong. He was arguing that if the government taxes the wealthy at a higher rate without their willing consent, the their legitimately acquired wealth against their will is immoral, just as taking anyone's rightful property against their will (stealing) is immoral.

Rawls or Nozick: who is right? Each individual must decide for him or herself. Personally, I think Nozick is right.

"Rawls and Nozick on Liberty & Equality"

Rawls and Nozick on Liberty & Equality

The Morality or Immorality of Social and Economic Inequality

Can the Principle of Essential Humanness and Critical Ethical Eclecticism shed any light on the morality or immorality of issues related to social justice? Certainly they can. If morality involves valuing humanness, then any activity that devalues or diminishes humanness is immoral. The key question is, *does social inequality amount to devaluing or diminishing humanness?* The answer is that it depends on how the inequality came about. Earlier we discussed the difference between *intrinsic equality* and *situational equality*. If the intrinsic equality of humanness is somehow diminished, then immorality has occurred. But situational inequality is an inherent part of human existence. Situational inequalities do not necessarily involve immorality. It is both natural and normal.

For instance, some inequalities are beyond anyone's control. Some people are faster than others, some are better looking, some are smarter. These kinds of situational inequalities reflect the random nature of the gene pool lottery involved in human reproduction. They do not involve any kind of social injustice. They do not involve any kind of immorality.

There are, however, other kinds of situational inequality. I am a college professor. There is a certain amount of prestige (not much but a little) associated with having a doctorate and being a professor, but not everyone enjoys that prestige because not everyone is a doctor and a professor. There is a certain inequality present: I enjoy a status that some people do not enjoy. But still there is no injustice or immorality involved because those who are not doctors and professors had the opportunity to get an education so that they could enjoy the prestige associated with being a doctor and a professor. The opportunity existed for them just as it did for me. They chose not to pursue it. Because they chose not to become a doctor and professor, there is no injustice in their not enjoying the prestige (small as it may be) associated with being a doctor and a professor.

What is the point? The point is that social justice or injustice and the morality or immorality associated with each hinges, not on situational equality or inequality, but on equality of opportunity and the choices people make. Most of the social inequality that exists in America today is the situational inequality that exists because of choices people make.[7] People are self-determined. They make choices. If people choose not to take advantage of the educational opportunities made available to them, if they choose not to follow a financially rewarding career path when such options are available to them, then no social injustice, and therefore no immorality, has occurred. Their humanness has not been devalued or diminished – at least not by others. If their choices result in a diminished humanness the immorality involved is their own.

As for the morality of a government acquisition and redistribution of wealth (via an unequal taxation[8] of the wealthy), as Nozick has pointed out, if the acquisition of wealth

[7]   We must remember that not making a choice to be or do something is making a choice. For instance, not making an intentional choice to learn to speak English correctly is making a choice that impacts how one presents oneself, which will impact opportunities for higher education and financially rewarding career options. Much of the economic inequality that exists in America today is the result of choices made or not made regarding education and career path.

[8]   There is nothing unjust about taxation itself. A society has expenses and it is right for the people of a society to fund the expenses of their society. However, it is unjust if one segment of society is required to pay a higher percentage of those expenses than another segment. Unequal taxation is unjust. My perspective here is not one of a wealthy person

was just, then taking it (in a non-voluntary transfer) to redistribute it is unjust and therefore immoral.

Summary

The issues associated with social justice are complicated. Just defining justice can be challenging. The Romans believed it meant to allocate to each his own. In other words, justice is people getting what they are entitled to. But social justice is not that simple. There are a lot of complex issues that have to be factored into people getting what they are entitled to. In this chapter we have discussed the difference between intrinsic equality and situational equality. Situational inequality is pervasive among humans. Some humans are better looking, stronger, smarter and so forth. Such inequalities are the result of the gene pool lottery of reproduction and do not involve any kind of injustice. Other kinds of situational inequality might involve choices people make, opportunities they choose or do not choose to take advantage of.[9] Situational inequalities that result from the choices people make regarding their lives do not result in social injustices. It is crucial, therefore, that in discussions concerning social justice we think clearly about what kind of equality we are considering.

We have also considered social stratification. We have seen that it is the inevitable result of social living and the growth of a small society into a big society. True egalitarianism (in the anthropological sense in which a tribal band has an egalitarian social structure) is simply not possible in a large complex society. In a large, complex

attempting to protect his own wealth. I'm a professor at a community college. I have no wealth. My analysis of the situation is strictly logical. In a free market meritocracy where one's place in society is determined by the choices one makes and the things one does, those who have more because of their initiative and energy cannot be penalized in the form of higher tax rates to subsidize those who have less because they did not exercise initiative and energy. And even if some have less, not because of choices they made but because of circumstances beyond their control, it is still unjust for the government to force a transfer of ownership (in the form of higher taxation) when the assets of the wealthy were acquired legitimately – as Nozick pointed out. A situational inequality that is no one's fault does not justify an unjust act toward those who are not to blame. If people are intrinsically equal and deserve equal opportunities to enjoy their humanness then they must bear equal responsibility (not unequal responsibility) as they live their lives. Unequal taxation is unequal treatment and is, therefore, unjust and immoral.

9   Some situational inequality may result from choices of others. If others make choices that impact me negatively there may be immorality involved. That kind of personal immorality, however, even if it results in a social situational inequality, is not the kind of social injustice normally under consideration in social justice discussions.

society, different social strata (classes) will exist. This is inevitable, natural, and appropriate.

We also discussed the challenges of social justice terminology. Specifically we analyzed the term *distributive justice*, focusing on the word distributive. It is an unfortunate word choice because it is both inaccurate and misleading. In America, there is no "distribution" of assets or resources. There is acquisition. The word and/or idea of distribution simply has no place in the social justice discussion.

Another major issue, perhaps *the* major concern, of the social justice discussion is the issue identified as the *inequality of wealth*. Without a doubt there is an inequality of income and wealth in America. The question is, does that inequality amount to a social injustice? Is it unfair, unjust, and immoral that some people make more and own more than others? Based on the fact that we live in a free market meritocracy, it appears that it is not.

We discussed the positions of Rawls and Nozick in relation to wealth and social justice. Rawls advocated *justice as fairness*; Nozick advocated *entitlement theory*. For me, Nozick's entitlement theory makes a lot more sense.

Finally, we considered social justice from the perspective of CEE, noting that as long as equal opportunity exists, situational inequality does not diminish humanness and is not, therefore, immoral.

Thought and Discussion Questions

1. Explain and discuss Rawls' theory: justice as fairness. Include a discussion of its strengths and weaknesses.

2. Explain and discuss Nozick's entitlement theory. Include a discussion of its strengths and weaknesses.

3. Explain and discuss Rogers' argument regarding intrinsic and situational equality.

4. Discuss the point made by both Rogers and Nozick regarding the term distributive justice. Be sure to discuss the ideas of the distribution and redistribution of wealth.

5. Discuss the role that CEE plays in determining the morality or immorality of different social justice issues.

Conclusion

We have covered lots of ground in this introductory study of moral philosophy. The study has been broken into three main sections: *Ethical Systems: A Historical Overview, Moral Challenges, Moral Solutions,* and *Contemporary Ethical Solutions.*

In the first section, *Ethical Systems: A Historical Overview*, we looked briefly at the different ethical systems that different peoples have utilized over the centuries to ask and answer important questions; questions such as: *what kind of a person ought one to be*, and *what is the right thing to do*? The section included material on ancient Hebrew moral philosophy, Jesus' moral philosophy and early Christian moral philosophy, ethical systems not normally covered in most moral philosophy texts. But given the influence of these systems on the development of Western culture, omitting them is inappropriate.

One of the goals of that first section is to allow readers to see how the focus of ethical systems shifted over the centuries, from asking, *what kind of a person ought one to be*, to asking, *what is the right thing to do*? The older of the two questions, *what kind*

of a person ought one to be, is the question asked by the ancient Hebrews and the ancient Greeks and was the central question of moral philosophy until the beginning of the modern era. The newer question, *what is the right thing to do*, arose as a result of new ideas, new discoveries, and new developments. Confronted with new and unfamiliar circumstances, or at least with new ideas about those circumstances, people asked, *what is the right thing to do*? The difference between the two questions is more important than one might think. The focus of each question is very different, and the answer to each produces different results. It's not that one question is better than the other. Each question is appropriate and helpful in the process of moral philosophy.

Some of the ethical systems we considered and evaluated proved to be helpful, and some proved to be problematic. The systems that appear to generate the greatest interest among contemporary ethicists are Utilitarianism and Kantian Deontological Ethics; however, since the middle of the 20th century, Virtue Ethics has generated a great deal of interest and many ethicists advocate a return to Virtue Ethics. This renewed interest in Virtue Ethics reorients the discussion, asking the older ethical question, *what kind of a person ought one to be*? The value of the approach is elegant in its simplicity: an excellent, virtuous person is likely to do the right thing most of the time. So if one works on becoming a virtuous person, he or she will likely do the right thing in whatever circumstance he or she is confronted with.

In the second section, *Moral Challenges, Moral Solutions*, the focus was on several key ethical concerns: 1) what morality is – the goal being to discover what makes an act moral or immoral, 2) the dead-end road of moral relativity, 3) whether or not moral absolutes exist, and 4) an explanation of the Principle of Essential Humanness and Critical Ethical Eclecticism (CEE) as a working model for moral thinking and acting.

I argued that *morality involves recognizing the intrinsic value of humanness (one's own and that of others), along with actions, reactions, and interactions that reflect an appreciation of human value. Immorality involves a failure to recognize the intrinsic value of humanness (one's own and that of others), along with a subsequent failure to act, react and interact in ways that reflect an appreciation of human value. Thus, an act is moral if it recognizes and or enhances human value, and is immoral if it fails to recognize or in some way diminishes the value of humanness.*[1]

I also argued that absolute moral (or cultural) relativity is not a viable paradigm for moral thinking and acting. Cultures are responsible for determining most of their moral standards, but must acknowledge the existence of a higher moral law and the reality of moral absolutes. Where moral absolutes are present, culture and circumstances are irrelevant. An act of kindness, for instance, can never be immoral; but torturing or molesting children can never be moral. Rape can never be moral. Moral absolutes exist. There may be cultures that say rape and child molestation are acceptable in their culture. The fact that those people say such acts are moral does not make those acts moral. Genocide, ethnocide, infanticide, Satee, and other such practices are simply not moral, ever, under any set of circumstances. Ethical systems that embrace and advocate absolute moral relativity are themselves immoral because they advocate immorality.

In this brief section, and in light of the Principle of Essential Humanness, I also proposed an ethical system that I refer to as Critical Ethical Eclecticism. The word *ethical* in the name is present for obvious reasons – it is an ethical theory. The word *eclectic* is also obvious – the theory borrows from and is composed of different aspects of other theories. But why include the word *critical* in the name? By *critical* I refer, not to criticizing other theories, although that is sometimes necessary, but rather to a critical, a careful and thoughtful, analysis of: 1) what contemporary society needs in a moral theory (what features must be included in a functional moral theory), and 2) what features of already existing moral theories can be borrowed to create a composite theory that will work well in contemporary society.

[1]   This is my own way of explaining morality, and other ethicists will have to evaluate and critique it for value and merit.

In the final section, *Contemporary Ethical Dilemmas*, we discussed nine different and very diverse kinds of issues and apply CEE in each case in an attempt to determine moral behavior in each of those different areas. Whether or not considering each of those moral issues from a CEE perspective was helpful will be up to the reader to decide.

The things I hope students and other readers will take away from this study are these:

1. That doing moral philosophy is absolutely essential for human beings because one of the things that makes us human is that we are moral beings, we make moral choices. To make good moral choices we need to think seriously about the kind of people we ought to be and about what the right thing to do is in any given situation.

2. That what is right and what is wrong does not depend on the whim of human desires and delights. Right and wrong, morality and immorality, grow out of what it is to be a human being. Since being a human being is a real, concrete reality, morality is also a real concrete reality. There is real objective right and wrong. Moral absolutes exist.

3. That moral courage is the courage to analyze one's own assumptions and beliefs and to evaluate the positions one has taken on ethical issues and to change one's mind where logic requires change.

Works Cited

Albers, John. "How Does Reproductive Work,"
  URL = http://www.ehow.com/how-does_4572562_reproductive-cloning-work.html

American Council on Science and Health. "Two Alternatives to Embryonic Stem Cell
  Research." October 2010.
  URL = http://www.acsh.org/factsfears/newsid.1912/news_detail.asp

Annas, Julia. *Plato: A Very Short Introduction*. Oxford: Oxford University Press, 2003.

Anscombe, G. E. M. "Modern Moral Philosophy," in *Journal of the Royal Institute of
  Philosophy*, Vol. 33. 124. January 1958, 1-19.

Aquinas, Thomas. *Summa of the Summa*. Peter Kreeft, Editor. San Francisco: Ignatius,
  1990.

Aristotle. "Nicomachean Ethics," in *The Basic Works of Aristotle*. Richard McKeon,
  Editor. New York: Modern Library Classics, 1941.

Austin, Michael W. "Divine Command Theory," in Internet Encyclopedia of Philosophy.
  James Fieser and Bradley Dowden, Editors. (2005)
  URL = http://www.iep.utm.edu/divine-c/

Baltzly, Dirk, "Stoicism", *The Stanford Encyclopedia of Philosophy (Winter 2010
  Edition)*, Edward N. Zalta (ed.),
  URL = http://plato.stanford.edu/archives/win2010/entries/stoicism/.

Barton, John. *Understanding Old Testament Ethics: Approaches and Explorations*.
  Westminister John Knox: Louisville, 2003.

Battin, Margaret. "Euthanasia and Physician-assisted Suicide," in *The Oxford Handbook
  of Practical Ethics*. Hugh LaFollette, Editor. Oxford: Oxford University Press, 2005.

Bedau, Hugo Adam. "Capital Punishment," in *The Oxford Handbook of Practical Ethics*.
  Hugh LaFollette, Editor. Oxford: Oxford University Press, 2005.

Belliotti, Raymond A. "Sex," in *A Companion to Ethics*. Peter Singer, Editor. Malden:
  Blackwell, 1993.

Bentham, Jeremy. *An Introduction to the Principles of Morals and Legislation*. Oxford:
  Clarendon, 1907. (A Bibliolife Network reprint).

Brennan, Andrew and Lo, Yeuk-Sze, "Environmental Ethics", *The Stanford
  Encyclopedia of Philosophy (Fall 2011 Edition)*, Edward N. Zalta (ed.),
  URL = http://plato.stanford.edu/archives/fall2011/entries/ethics-environmental/

Cochrane, Alasdair. "Environment Ethics," in *Internet Encyclopedia of Philosophy*. James Fieser and Bradley, Editors. (2006).
URL = http://www.iep.utm.edu/envi-eth/

Cohen, Carl. "The Case for the Use of Animals in Biomedical Research," in *Ethics: History, Theory, and Contemporary Issues*. Steven Cahn and Peter Markie, Editors. Oxford: Oxford University Press, 2006.

Copleston, Frederick, S. J. *A History of Philosophy: Volume II: Medieval Philosophy*. New York: Doubleday, 1993.

Cornford, F. M. *From Religion to Philosophy: A Study in the Origins of Western Speculation*. Princeton: Princeton University Press, 1991.

Crenshaw, James L. "Sipping From the Cup of Wisdom," in *Jesus and Philosophy*. Paul Moser, Editor. Cambridge: Cambridge University Press, 2009.

Darwall, Stephen. Utilitarianism: Act or Rule?" in *Conduct and Character: Readings in Moral Theory*. 6th Edition. Mark Timmons, Editor. Boston: Wadsworth, 2012.

Death Penalty Information Center.
URL: http://www.deathpenaltyinfo.org/number-executions-state-and-region-1976

Driver, Julia, "The History of Utilitarianism", *The Stanford Encyclopedia of Philosophy (Summer 2009 Edition)*, Edward N. Zalta (ed.),
URL = http://plato.stanford.edu/archives/sum2009/entries/utilitarianism-history/.

Environmental Protection Agency. "The National Water Quality Inventory Report to Congress (305(b) report)"
URL = http://water.epa.gov/lawsregs/guidance/cwa/305b/index.cfm

Floyd, Shawn. "Thomas Aquinas: Moral Philosophy," in *Internet Encyclopedia of Philosophy*. James Fieser and Bradley, Editors. (2006).
URL = http://www.iep.utm.edu/aq-moral/

Frey, R. G. "Animals," in *The Oxford Handbook of Practical Ethics*. Hugh LaFollette, Editor. Oxford: Oxford University Press, 2005.

Friend, Celeste. "Social Contract Theory," in *Internet Encyclopedia of Philosophy*. James Fieser and Bradley, Editors. (2004).
URL = http://www.iep.utm.edu/soc-cont/

George, R. P. and A. Gomez-Lobo. "Statement of Professor George (Joined by Dr. Gomez-Lobo)," in *Human Cloning and Human Dignity: An Ethical Inquiry*. The President's Council on Bioethics, Washington, D. C., 2002.
URL: http://bioethics.georgetown.edu/pcbe/reports/cloningreport/

Gilligan, Carol. *In a Different Voice: Psychological Theory and Women's Development*. Cambridge, Massachusetts: Harvard University Press, 1982.

---."Moral Orientation and Moral Development," in *Conduct and Character: Readings in Moral Theory*. 6th Edition. Mark Timmons, Editor. Boston: Wadsworth, 2012.

Glasgow, Joshua. "Kant's Principle of Universal Law," in *Conduct and Character: Readings in Moral Theory*. 6th Edition. Mark Timmons, Editor. Boston: Wadsworth, 2012.

Goldman, Alan H. "Plain Sex," in *Taking Sides: Clashing Views on Moral Issues*. 13th Edition. Stephen Satris, Editor. New York: McGraw Hill, 2012.

Gordon, John, Stewart. "Abortion," in *Internet Encyclopedia of Philosophy*. James Fieser and Bradley, Editors. (2004).
URL = http://www.iep.utm.edu/abortion/

Grohol, John. Friends with Benefits. *Psych Central*. 2008.
URL= http://psychcentral.com/blog/archives/2008/11/03/friends-with-benefits/

Gruen, Lori, "The Moral Status of Animals", *The Stanford Encyclopedia of Philosophy (Fall 2010 Edition)*, Edward N. Zalta (ed.),
URL = http://plato.stanford.edu/archives/fall2010/entries/moral-animal/.

Guthrie, W.K.C. *The Greek Philosophers from Thales to Aristotle*. New York: Harper & Row, 1975.

Haldane, John. Medieval and Renaissance Ethics," in *A Companion to Ethics*. Peter Singer, Editor. Malden: Blackwell, 1993.

Halwani, Raja. "Care Ethics and Virtue Ethics," in *Conduct and Character: Readings in Moral Theory*. 6th Edition. Mark Timmons, Editor. Boston: Wadsworth, 2012.

Harris, John and Soren Holm. "Abortion," in *The Oxford Handbook of Practical Ethics*. Hugh LaFollette, Editor. Oxford: Oxford University Press, 2005.

Hicks, Stephen, R. C. "Ayn Alissa Rand," in *Internet Encyclopedia of Philosophy*. James Fieser and Bradley, Editors. (2004).
URL = http://www.iep.utm.edu/rand/

Hobbes, Thomas. *Leviathan*. New York: Penguin, 1985.

Hooker, Brad. "Rule-Consequentialism," in *Conduct and Character: Readings in Moral Theory*. 6th Edition. Mark Timmons, Editor. Boston: Wadsworth, 2012.

Hursthouse, Rosalind, "Virtue Ethics", *The Stanford Encyclopedia of Philosophy (Summer 2012 Edition)*, Edward N. Zalta (ed.), forthcoming
URL = http://plato.stanford.edu/archives/sum2012/entries/ethics-virtue/.

Hutchinson, D. S. "Ethics," in *The Cambridge Companion to Aristotle*. Jonathan Barnes, Editor. Cambridge: Cambridge University Press, 1995.

Irwin, Terence. *Plato's Ethics*. Oxford: Oxford University Press, 1995.

Jayson, Sharon. "Census Reports More Couples Living Together," *USA TODAY*, July 28, 2008.
URL= http://www.usatoday.com/news/nation/census/2008-07-28-cohabitation-census_N.htm

Johnson, Robert, "Kant's Moral Philosophy", *The Stanford Encyclopedia of Philosophy (Summer 2010 Edition)*, Edward N. Zalta (ed.),
URL = http://plato.stanford.edu/archives/sum2010/entries/kant-moral/.

Jones, Garth. "The Authority of Scripture in Christian Ethics," in *The Cambridge Companion to Christian Ethics*. Robin Gill, Editor. Cambridge: Cambridge University Press, 2001.

Kaiser, Walter C. Jr. *Toward Old Testament Ethics*. Zondervan: Grand Rapids, 1983.

Kant, Immanuel. *Groundwork of the Metaphysics of Morals*. Translated and Analysed by H. J. Paton. New York: Harper Perennial Modern Thought edition, 2009.

Kidner, Derek. *Proverbs: An Introduction and Commentary*. Downers Grove InterVarsity: 1964.

Kohlberg, Lawrence. *The Philosophy of Moral Development: Moral Stages and the idea Of Justice*. New York: Harper and Row, 1981.

Kraut, Richard, "Aristotle's Ethics", *The Stanford Encyclopedia of Philosophy (Spring 2012 Edition)*, Edward N. Zalta (ed.),
URL = http://plato.stanford.edu/archives/spr2012/entries/aristotle-ethics/.

Kuhse, Helga. "Euthanasia," in *A Companion to Ethics*. Peter Singer, Editor. Malden: Blackwell, 1993.

Kymlicka, Will. "The Social Contract Tradition," in *A Companion to Ethics*. Peter Singer, Editor. Malden: Blackwell, 1993.

LaMarco, Nicky. "Diseases Caused by Air Pollution." Bright Hub.
URL = http://www.brighthub.com/environment/science-environmental/articles/17300.aspx

Little, Margaret Olivia. "The Moral Permissibility of Abortion," in *Taking Sides: Clashing Views on Moral Issues*. Thirteenth Edition. Stephen Satris, Editor. New York: McGraw Hill: 2012.

Long, D. Stephen. *Christian Ethics: A Very Short Introduction*. Oxford: Oxford University Press, 2010.

MacIntyre, Alasdair. *A Short History of Ethics: A History of Moral Philosophy from the Homeric Age to the Twentieth Century*. Second Edition. Notre Dame: University of Norte Dame, 1998.

Mackinnon, Barbara. *Ethics: Theory and Contemporary Issues*. 7th Edition. Boston: Wadsworth, 2012.

Manninen, Bertha A. "Cloning," in *Internet Encyclopedia of Philosophy*. James Fieser and Bradley, Editors. (2004). URL = http://www.iep.utm.edu/cloning/

Marquis, Don. "Why is Abortion Immoral," in *Taking Sides: Clashing Views on Moral Issues*. Thirteenth Edition. Stephen Satris, Editor. New York: McGrawHill: 2012.

Mendelson, Michael, "Saint Augustine", *The Stanford Encyclopedia of Philosophy (Winter 2010 Edition)*, Edward N. Zalta (ed.),
URL = http://plato.stanford.edu/archives/win2010/entries/augustine/.

Mill, John Stuart. *Utilitarianism.* 1863.

Moseley, Alexander. "Egoism," in *Internet Encyclopedia of Philosophy*. (2005) James Fieser and Bradley Dowden, Editors.
URL = http://www.iep.utm.edu/egoism/

Moser, Paul. "Introduction: Jesus and Philosophy," in *Jesus and Philosophy: New Essays*. Paul Moser, Editor. Cambridge: Cambridge University Press, 2009.

Murnaghan, Ian. "Therapeutic Cloning," at *Explore Stem Cells*.
URL = http://www.explorestemcells.co.uk/therapeuticcloning.html

Murphy, Mark C. "Hobbes's Social Contract Theory," in *Conduct and Character: Readings in Moral Theory*. 6th Edition. Mark Timmons, Editor. Boston: Wadsworth, 2012.

Murtagh, Kevin. "Punishment," in *Internet Encyclopedia of Philosophy*. (2005) James Fieser and Bradley Dowden, Editors.
URL = http://www.iep.utm.edu/punishme/

Noddings, Nell. *Caring: A Feminist Approach to Ethics and Moral Education*. 2nd Edition. Berkeley: University of California Press, 2003.

Nozick, Robert. *Anarchy, State, and Utopia*. New York: Basic Books, 1974.

O'Keefe, Tim. "Epicurus," in *Internet Encyclopedia of Philosophy*. (2005) James Fieser and Bradley Dowden, Editors.
URL = http://www.iep.utm.edu/epicur/

---. "Cyrenaics," in *Internet Encyclopedia of Philosophy*. (2005) James Fieser and Bradley Dowden, Editors.
URL = http://www.iep.utm.edu/cyren/

O'Neill, Onora, "Kantian Ethics," in *A Companion to Ethics*. Peter Singer, Editor. Malden: Blackwell, 1993.

Parry, Richard, "Ancient Ethical Theory", *The Stanford Encyclopedia of Philosophy (Fall 2009 Edition)*, Edward N. Zalta (ed.),
URL = http://plato.stanford.edu/archives/fall2009/entries/ethics-ancient/.

Penner, Terry. "Socrates and the Early Dialogs," in *The Cambridge Companion to Plato*. Richard Kraut, Editor. Cambridge: Cambridge University Press, 1992.

Pettit, Philip. "Can Contract Theory Ground Morality," in *Conduct and Character: Readings in Moral Theory*. 6th Edition. Mark Timmons, Editor. Boston: Wadsworth, 2012.

---. "Socratic Ethics and the Socratic Psychology of Action," in *The Cambridge Companion to Socrates*. Donald R. Morrison, Editor. Cambridge: Cambridge University Press, 2011.

Plato. "Republic," in *Plato: Complete Works*. John Cooper, Editor. Indianapolis: Hackett, 1997.

Preston, Ronald. "Christian Ethics," in *A Companion to Ethics*. Peter Singer, Editor. Malden: Blackwell, 1993.

Punzo, Vincent C. "Morality and Human Sexuality," in *Taking Sides: Clashing Views on Moral Issues*. 13th Edition. Stephen Satris, Editor. New York: McGraw Hill, 2012.

Rachels, James and Stuart Rachels. *The Elements of Moral Philosophy*. 6th Edition. New York: McGraw Hill, 2010.

Rachels, James. "The Ethics of Virtue," in *Ethics: History, Theory, and Contemporary Issues*. Steven Cahn and Peter Markie, Editors. Oxford: Oxford University Press, 2006.

Rawls, John. *A Theory of Justice*. Cambridge, MA: Belknap Press, 1971.

Regan, Tom. "The Case for Animal Rights," in *Ethics: History, Theory, and Contemporary Issues*. Steven Cahn and Peter Markie, Editors. Oxford: Oxford University Press, 2006.

Rogers, Glenn. *Understanding American Culture: The Theological and Philosophical Shaping of the American Worldview*. Mission and Ministry Resources: Bedford, 2006.

---. *Becoming: A Philosophical Treatise on Human Potential*. Bedford: Simpson and Brook, 2010.

---. *Proof of God? Inquiries into the Philosophy of Religion, A Concise Introduction*. Estherville, Simpson and Brook, 2012.

Rogerson, John. "The Old Testament and Christian Ethics," in *The Cambridge Companion of Christian Ethics*. Robin Gill, Editor. Cambridge: Cambridge University Press, 2001.

Ropelate, Jerry. "Internet Pornography Statistics," at Internet Filter Software Review. URL= http://internet-filter-review.toptenreviews.com/internet-pornography-statistics-pg4.html

Rosenthal, Elizabeth, "As the Climate Changes, Bits of England's Coast Crumble," *New York Times*, May 4, 2007. URL = http://www.nytimes.com/2007/05/04/world/europe/04erode.html?_r=1

Rowe, Christopher. "Ethics in Ancient Greece," in *A Companion to Ethics*. Peter Singer, Editor. Malden: Blackwell, 1993.

Rubenstein, Richard. *Aristotle's Children: How Christians, Muslims, and Jews Rediscovered Ancient Wisdom and Illuminated the Dark Ages*. Orlando: Harcourt, 2003.

Sandel, Michael J. "The Ethical Issues of Human Cloning," in *Taking Sides: Clashing Views on Moral Issues*. Thirteenth Edition. Stephen Satris, Editor. New York: McGrawHill:2012.

Sanders-Saudt, Maureen. "Care Ethics," in *Internet Encyclopedia of Philosophy*. (2005) James Fieser and Bradley Dowden, Editors. URL = http://www.iep.utm.edu/care-eth/

Satris, Stephen. "Must Sex Involve Commitment," in *Taking Sides: Clashing Views on Moral Issues*. 13th Edition. Stephen Satris, Editor. New York: McGraw Hill: 2012.

Schneewind, J. B. "Autonomy, obligation, and virtue: An overview of Kant's moral philosophy," in *The Cambridge Companion to Kant*. Paul Guyer, Editor. Cambridge: Cambridge, 1992.

Sharples, R. W. *Stoics, Epicureans and Sceptics: An Introduction to Hellenistic Philosophy*. London: Routledge, 1996.

Shaver, Robert, "Egoism", *The Stanford Encyclopedia of Philosophy (Winter 2010 Edition)*, Edward N. Zalta (ed.),
URL = http://plato.stanford.edu/archives/win2010/entries/egoism/.

Shepard, Jon M. *Sociology*. 10th Edition. Belmont: Wadsworth, 2010.

Shoemaker, David W. "Egoisms," in *Conduct and Character: Readings in Moral Theory*. 6th Edition. Mark Timmons, Editor. Boston: Wadsworth, 2012.

Shrader-Frechette, Kristin. "Environmental Ethics," in *The Oxford Handbook of Practical Ethics*. Hugh LaFollette, Editor. Oxford: Oxford University Press, 2005.

Shugerman, Lindsey. "Percentage of Married Couples Who Cheat," at *Catalogs.com*. 2012.
URL= http://www.catalogs.com/info/relationships/percentage-of-married-couples-who-cheat-on-each-ot.html

Siegel, Andrew, "Ethics of Stem Cell Research", *The Stanford Encyclopedia of Philosophy (Fall 2008 Edition)*, Edward N. Zalta (ed.),
URL = http://plato.stanford.edu/archives/fall2008/entries/stem-cells/

Simpson, Peter. "Contemporary Virtue Ethics and Aristotle," in *The Review of Metaphysics*. Vol. 45, No. 3 (Mar., 1992), pp. 503-524.

Stephens, William. "Stoic Ethics," in *Internet Encyclopedia of Philosophy*. (2005) James Fieser and Bradley Dowden, Editors.
URL = http://www.iep.utm.edu/stoiceth/

Sullivan, Roger J. *An Introduction to Kant's Ethics*. Cambridge: Cambridge, 1994.

Sweet, William. "Jeremy Bentham," in *Internet Encyclopedia of Philosophy*. (2005) James Fieser and Bradley Dowden, Editors.
URL = http://www.iep.utm.edu/bentham/

TANF Eighth Annual Report to Congress. "VII. Formation and Maintenance of Married Two-parent Families."
URL= http://www.acf.hhs.gov/programs/ofa/datareports/annualreport7/chapter07/chap07.pdf

Thomson, Judith Jarvis. "A Defense of Abortion," in *Ethics: History, Theory, and Contemporary Issues*. Steven Cahn and Peter Markie, Editors. Oxford: Oxford University Press, 2006.

Timmons, Mark. "Consequentialism," in *Conduct and Character: Readings in Moral Theory*. 6th Edition. MarkTimmons, Editor. Boston: Wadsworth, 2012.

Tong, Rosemarie and Williams, Nancy, "Feminist Ethics", *The Stanford Encyclopedia of Philosophy (Summer 2011 Edition)*, Edward N. Zalta (ed.), URL = http://plato.stanford.edu/archives/sum2011/entries/feminism-ethics/.

Trull, Joe E. *Walking in the Way: An Introduction to Christian Ethics*. Nashville: Broadman, 1997.

Tuana, Nancy and Laurie Shrage. "Sexuality," in *The Oxford Handbook of Practical Ethics*. Hugh LaFollette, Editor. Oxford: Oxford University Press, 2005.

Van Den Haag, Ernest. "In defense of the Death Penalty." in, *Ethics: History, Theory, and Contemory Issues*. Steven Chan and Peter Markie, Editors. Oxford: Oxford University Press, 2006.

Van Inwagen, Peter. *An Essay on Free Will*. Oxford: Oxford University Press, 1986.

Witherspoon Council on Ethics and the Integrity of Science, "Appendix A: The Science of Embryonic Stem Cell Research," *The New Atlantis*, Number 34, Winter 2012, pp. 61-81.

World Health Organization. "Air Quality and Health." Fact Sheet N313 September 2011. URL = http://www.who.int/mediacentre//factsheets/fs313/en/index.html